BEGINNERS'
HEBREW GRAMMAR

BY

Rev. HAROLD L. CREAGER, B. D.

FORMER INSTRUCTOR IN HEBREW,
GETTYSBURG THEOLOGICAL SEMINARY

WITH THE COLLABORATION OF

Rev. HERBERT C. ALLEMAN, D. D.

PROFESSOR OF OLD TESTAMENT LANGUAGE AND LITERATURE,
GETTYSBURG THEOLOGICAL SEMINARY

D. C. HEATH AND COMPANY

BOSTON	NEW YORK	CHICAGO
ATLANTA	DALLAS	SAN FRANCISCO
	LONDON	

COPYRIGHT, 1927,
BY D. C. HEATH AND COMPANY

3 B 6

PRINTED IN U.S.A.

492.45
c866
24432

PJ
4567
C7

PREFACE

Opinions have differed widely concerning the amount of grammatical discipline which should precede the reading of a foreign literature. The position taken in this book is that the Western student of Hebrew, with its characteristically Semitic peculiarities, should acquire a fairly thoro knowledge of its grammatical forms and syntactic principles before attempting any serious reading; for it is almost impossible, from the heterogeneous examples met in various selections, to pick up a sufficiently systematic knowledge to develop facility in general reading. This aims, therefore, to be a fairly comprehensive treatment, rather than a mere introductory sketch.

However, with a view to making the language a living reality to the student, two periods of elementary reading in the Hebrew Bible are arranged. The extract printed in Ch. VI with interlinear translation both provides the practice needed to familiarize the appearance and pronunciation of Hebrew words, and gives some introduction to the general structure of the language. And the section annotated in Ch. XXXVIII proves advantageous in fixing the forms and usages of nouns and regular verbs before undertaking the weak verbs.

iii

Other features which, it is hoped, will commend the book, are the following:

1. The carefully arranged vocabularies and exercises, in which *all* the more common words are used, and thoro practice is afforded on both the forms and principles as explained.

2. A unique method of treating irregular verbs, which has proved in practice to facilitate the mastery of these difficult and confusing forms.

3. The constant effort to give reasons for seeming peculiarities, and to explain principles thoroly; the arrangement of the material in analytic, and frequently in tabular, form; and the generally logical order of the chapters.

4. The inclusion of material of secondary importance in subordinated form. The paragraphs and notes marked with an asterisk deal with matters that are specially irregular, rare, complicated, or theoretical, and are not intended for the beginner's study, but for later reference. And the printing of numerous other sections in small type is designed to facilitate the proportionate handling of subsidiary points, or the abbreviation of the course, if desired.

The author is greatly indebted, as is every student of Hebrew, to the standard works of Gesenius, Davidson, and Harper; and he wishes gratefully to acknowledge the invaluable aid derived from them in the preparation of this grammar.   H. L. C.

TABLE OF CONTENTS

PART ONE. ORTHOGRAPHY

PART TWO. PARTICLES. ADJECTIVES. PRONOUNS

PART THREE. NOUNS

v

PART FOUR. REGULAR VERBS. VERB AND SENTENCE SYNTAX

PART FIVE. IRREGULAR VERBS

PART SIX. APPENDIX

SUPPLEMENTARY INDEX

PART ONE
ORTHOGRAPHY

CHAPTER I

THE ALPHABET

A. The Hebrew Language

1. Hebrew belongs to the Semitic group of languages, which includes the Arabic, Phoenician, Syriac, Babylonian, Ethiopic, etc. These languages have broad similarities among themselves, and many decided contrasts with those of the Indo-European family.

Fundamental differences appear in such matters as tense, mood, voice, case, etc., in which the underlying conceptions and grammatical usages are very dissimilar to ours; also in the word roots, which in general show little kinship with those of Western languages.

2. *The primitive alphabet contained only consonants,* no vowels; originally only consonants were written, and it was not until about the sixth century A.D. that a complete system of auxiliary symbols to represent the vowels was devised, by Jewish scholars known as the Massoretes.

3. The direction of writing is *from right to left;* e. g., רמה is "Ramah," and נ מ ר ד is "Nimrod."
h m r   d r m n

B. The Letters

1. There are 22 consonants[1]. In their names as given below the long vowels have their Latin value—*a* as in *father, e* as in *prey,* and *i* as in *machine; aw* equals *ow* in *now;* and *dh* equals *th* in *rather.*

---

[1] In memorizing these it will be found convenient to divide them into groups of 4, 4, 6, 4, 4.

3

	Common Form	Final Form	Name	Sound and Symbol
1	א		'Āleph	'
2	ב		Bēth	b[1]
3	ג		Gimel	g
4	ד		Dāleth	d[1]
5	ה		Hē	h
6	ו		Waw	w[2]
7	ז		Zayin	z
8	ח		Hēth	ḥ
9	ט		Tēth	ṭ
10	י		Yōdh	y
11	כ	ך	Kaph	k[1]
12	ל		Lāmedh	l
13	מ	ם	Mēm	m
14	נ	ן	Nūn	n
15	ס		Sāmekh	ṣ
16	ע		'Ayin	'
17	פ	ף	Pē	p[1]
18	צ	ץ	Tsādhe	t͡s[3]
19	ק		Qōph	q
20	ר		Rēsh	r
21a	שׂ		Sīn	s
21b	שׁ		Shīn	s͡h[3]
22	ת		Taw	t[1]

[1] These letters sometimes have a slightly different sound; see further in Ch. IV, B.

[2] Sometimes pronounced and transliterated "v".

[3] When two English letters are used as the equivalent of a Hebrew consonant, we *tie* them; together they represent a single sound.

a. Note the five letters which have a special *final* form; this is used when the letter occurs at the left end of a word[1].

b. The symbol שׁ (21) stood for the two sounds *s* and *sh*[2]; they have been distinguished by the auxiliary dots—making, practically, 23 consonants.

2. Many letters are quite similar in appearance. Study carefully the following groups[3]:

בּ (2) and כּ (11)	ו (6), י (10), and ר (20)
ג (3) and נ (14)	ט (9), מ (13), and פ (17)
ד (4), ך (11f), and ר (20)	כ, ך (11) and ב, ן (14)
ה (5), ח (8) and ת (22)	ם (13f) and ס (15)
ו (6), ז (7), and ן (14f)	ע (16) and צ, ץ (18)

3. The letters are of uniform height, except that,— ל (12) extends above the line; י (10) does not reach to the bottom of the line; and ק (19) and four of the final forms extend below the line.

The beginner should practice writing between parallel lines in order to get the letters uniform; e.g., וַיִּקְטֹל.

C. Notes on Pronunciation

1. The Hebrew alphabet has many sounds just like those of English. It lacks several of our sounds (e.g., *j* and *x*); and it includes some which

---

[1] When a word ends in "ka" the final form of Kaph is used, for it is the final *consonant;* e.g., "baneyka" is בָּנֶיךָ.

[2] Probably the sounds were not differentiated in the early language; cf. the *Shibboleth* incident, Jg.12:6.

[3] The small projecting "horn" characteristic of some letters is the "tittle" to which Jesus referred (Mt. 5:18); and the "jot" there mentioned is *Yodh*, the smallest letter of the alphabet.

have no exact equivalent in English. The spelling is nearly phonetic.

2. א (1) practically has no sound[1]; it merely represents a catch in the breath, or a very slight aspiration. In transliteration it is represented by the *smooth breathing* of Greek; e.g., אָדָם, 'dm ("'Adam" *or* "'Edom").

3. ח (8) is a difficult sound. It is a very strongly aspirated *h*—a harder sound than ה (5)—which becomes practically equal to *ch* in the Scotch *loch* or German *ich*[2].

4. ט (9) and ס (15) were probably firmer sounds than ת (22) and שׂ (21a), but are now pronounced just like them. Dotted *t* and *s* (ṭ, ṣ) indicate ט and ס; plain *t* and *s*, ת and שׂ.

5. ע (16) is an aspiration midway in strength between א (1) and ה (5). We transliterate it by a *rough breathing*, and practically neglect it in pronunciation[3]; e.g., בַעַז, b'z ("Bo'az"); שִׁנְעָר, shn'r ("Shin'ar").

6. צ (18) is a very sharp sibilant—not strictly including a *t* sound, but probably best indicated in English by the digraph t͡s[4].

7. ק (19) is practically equal to *k*, being a slightly harder sound. Unlike the English *q*, it is never followed by the *w* sound.

---

[1] It serves the practical purpose of giving something to which to attach a vowel sound. The consonants serve a double purpose—indicating by their own sound a root idea, and carrying such vowels as will give a particular meaning to it.

[2] The symbol "ḥ" has been chosen as less confusing than the "ch" or "hh" sometimes used.

[3] The LXX sometimes transliterated it by a rough breathing (e.g., Ἐλι for עֵלִי); sometimes, where it apparently had a secondary and harder sound, by a Gamma (e.g., Γαζα for עַזָּה); and sometimes, on the contrary, by a smooth breathing (e.g., Ὀζιας for עֻזִּיָּה).

[4] The transliterations "c̦" or "ṣ" are sometimes used.

D. Classification

1. Labials: ב, ו, מ, פ.
2. Sibilants: ז, ס, צ, שׂ, שׁ.
3. Linguals: ד, ט, ל, נ, ת.
4. Palatals: ג, י, כ, ק, ר.
5. Gutturals: א, ה, ח, ע.

EXERCISES

1. Name the following letters:

נ, ך, ת, א, שׁ, ץ, ל, מ, ח, ג, ד, ע, ט, פ, כ, ס, ר, ם,
י, ק, ה, ז, פ, ו, שׂ, ב, ן, צ, כ, ו, שׁ, ה, ץ, ק, ך, נ, ת, א,
ן, ז, ף, מ, ט, פ, ב, ר, ד, ע, צ, שׁ, ג, ס, י, ח, ל, ם.

2. Identify the following proper names[1]:

שֵׁם – כַּרְמֶל – גּשֶׁן – כָּלֵב – שֶׁדֶרֶךְ – פֶּלֶג – שָׂרָה – גִּלְגָּל –
מִכְמָשׁ – בִּלְדַּד – רִבְקָה – מַלְאָכִי – תַּרְשִׁישׁ – חֶבְרוֹן –
בֶּן הֲדַד – מוֹאָב – נָתָן – מִדְיָן – בִּנְיָמִן – עָמוֹס – גְּרִזִים –
אֶשְׁכֹּל – גִּבְעָה – מִצְפָּה – דַּמֶּשֶׂק – חֲזָאֵל – בְּאֵר שֶׁבַע –
אָסָף – צִידֹן – בֵּית לֶחֶם – זְכַרְיָה – קְטוּרָה – שִׁטִּים –
יָרָבְעָם – עֵין גֶּדִי.

3. Name the Hebrew equivalents for the consonants in
the following words (the vowels are marked for later use):

---

[1] In some of these words פ=*ph*, ת=*th*, י=*j*. In some, ו indicates
the vowel *o* or *u;* and י, *i* or *e.*

sārēk, pᵊnōt, timalnāh, gulgōlet, yeḥᵊzeh, t͡sedeq, 'ayil, sh̭ᵊlāḥām, yūkal, pārasnū, yim'aṣū, mᵊ'aṭ, mizbaḥ, t͡si-wītīkā, qādōsh̭, hēṣīr, ṭohᵒrāh, bᵊnēy.

4. Transliterate:

Dan, nilḥamah, sh̭alom, Serug, keyoṣep, yirbem, zibḥek, toqep, tiqṭol, weyaqat͡s, parasta, weḥezeh, nakah, hit͡sdiyq, pag, hit͡sliḥaka, 'eret͡s, nish̭ba', wesagab, ṣuṣat, male', ya'aber, 'Edom, sh̭opeṭ, 'Ezra', he'emantem, Par'oh, Yisra'el, nimlaṭ, sh̭om'akem, 'Eglon.

CHAPTER II

THE VOWEL SYSTEM

A. Vowel Symbols

1. In primitive writing, long vowels were often indicated by certain consonants, called *vowel letters*, which suggested their sounds—*o* and *u* by ו, *i* and *e* by י, *a* by א or ה.

2. Supplementing these now is the Massoretic system of dots and lines, called *vowel points; these are written below the consonants which they follow*—except long *o* and *u*.

B. The Ordinary, or Full, Vowels

Symbol	Name	Sound	As in
—	Pathah	short *a*	fat, bad
—ָ	Qamets	long *a*	far, calm
—ֶ	Segol[1]	short *e*	fed, let
—ֵ	Tsere	long *e*	fete, they
—ִ	Hireq	short *i*	fit, bill
י—ִ	Long Hireq	long *i*	field, police
—ָ	Qamets Hatuph[2]	short *o*	fog, soft
ֹו—	Holem	long *o*	fold, go
—ֻ	Qibbuts	short *u*	full, put
וּ—	Shureq[3]	long *u*	flute, rude

[1] This simpler spelling is adopted in preference to the usual (and technically proper) *Seghol* (סֶגוֹל); see Ch. IV, B, 1, b. (So also *Dagesh* for *Daghesh*).

[2] *Hatuph* means "swift"; long *a*, pronounced quickly, becomes practically identical with short *o*.

[3] Shureq is always a plain *ōō* sound, and never includes the *y* sound which is so often associated with *u* in English; it is never *u* as in *muse*, but as in *ruse*.

1. Note that the *sound* of each vowel occurs in its *name*.

2. The symbol —, unfortunately used for two sounds, is *usually Qamets*. It is Qamets Hatuph in the following cases:

    a. When it stands in an unaccented, closed syllable (see below in E); e.g., הָשְׁבַּר, hosh-bar.

    b. When it precedes a Hateph Qamets (see below in C); e.g., יַעֲלָה, yo-'o-leh.

    *c. When it stands in an inflectional form derived from a form which has Holem (or other *o* sound); e.g., רָמְחָי (ro-mᵊ-ḥēy) from רֹמַח; שָׁמְרִי (sho-mᵊ-rī) from שֹׁמֵר; and הָחָרְמוּ (ho-ḥo-rᵊ-mū) from הָחָרֵם.

C. The Half Vowels

1. The name *half-vowel* is applied to several very short, obscure sounds—somewhat like those occurring in the English words "habil*i*tate" and "gutt*u*ral," French "*je* donn*e*rai," etc. These half-vowels are four in number:

—̣	Shewa (ᵊ)	—̤	Hateph Segol (ᵉ)
—̱	Hateph Pathah (ᵃ)	—̰	Hateph Qamets (ᵒ)

    a. *Shewa* (—̣) indicates the slightest possible vocalization—resembling the first vowel in *derive* or the second in *coroner*, pronounced just as quickly as can be done without reducing the words to *drive* and *corner*. The sound is neutral in quality, and is best transliterated by the phonetic symbol ᵊ; e. g., כְּמוֹשְׁלִי, kᵊ-mō-shᵊ-lī[1].

---

[1] In translating proper names, various letters have been used. The first vowel in each of the names *Samuel, Methusaleh, Philistine,*

b. The other three sounds are slightly fuller, each having a distinguishable touch of the full vowel indicated in the symbol and name[1]; e. g., הַיְחֱזַק, hᵃ-ye-ḥe-zaq.

3. The three *Hateph vowels* are often called *Compound Shewas*, and the — *Simple Shewa*. *The Compound Shewas are used with gutturals, the simple Shewa with other consonants.*

The simple Shewa is too short to secure the proper pronunciation of the peculiar guttural sounds (cf. the sounds in "bᵊlieve" and "hᵃbitual"), and is *never* used with them; very seldom a compound Shewa occurs with an ordinary consonant—especially ק or ר—when a fuller or more distinct sound is desired.

D. Diagrams

1. This table shows the two-fold classification of the vowels—as to *quality* (into three groups, according to the three basic sounds), and as to *quantity*.

---

and *Sodom* represents a Shewa. In semi-technical literature it is often represented by an apostrophe; small *e* is also used.

[1] The word *Hateph*, like *Hatuph*, means "swift"; these three half-vowels are simply shorter, quicker pronunciations of the corresponding full vowels. All the half-vowels arose in the evolution of the parts of speech and inflectional forms of the language, and represent primitive full vowels which have been thinned down and partly lost in those processes; e.g., corresponding to the verb stem חָלַם is the noun חֲלוֹם, and the plural of מוֹקֵשׁ is מוֹקְשִׁים.

Class	Sound	Full Vowels		Half Vowels	
		Long	Short	Extra Short (Compound form)	Extra Short (Simple form)
a	a	ָ	ַ	ֲ	
i	e	ֵ	ֶ	ֱ	ִ
	i	ִי	ִ		
u	o	וֹ	ָ	ֳ	
	u	וּ	ֻ		

2. This diagram represents physical relations between the vowels — that the *o* sounds are intermediate between the *a* and *u*, and the *e* sounds between the *a* and *i*; also the relation of the half-vowels.

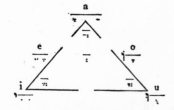

E. Syllabification and Accent

1. *Every syllable must begin with a consonant;* with the single exception that sometimes the first syllable of a word consists of a Shureq only (e. g., וּמָה, ū-māh). Every syllable must, of course, have a vowel; and it may, or may not, have another consonant after the vowel. Therefore—

a. If two consonants stand together without an intervening vowel, the syllable division occurs between them; but if there is just one consonant between two vowels, it goes with the *following* vowel; e. g., the words מִשְׁפָּטֵנוּ, הִרְחַקְתָּ, and מְקוֹמִים are syllabified mish-pā-ṭē-nū, hir-ḥaq-tā, and mᵃ-qō-mīm.

b. Each word has exactly as many syllables as vowels[1].

c. A syllable ending in a vowel sound is called an *open* syllable; one ending in a consonant is said to be *closed*[2].

2. Hebrew words are most frequently accented on the last syllable. When the accent on a word in these exercises falls on the penult, it is indicated by placing the mark ⎯⎯ over the first consonant of the syllable. The main accent on a word can never fall farther from the end than that[3].

a. A closed syllable having a long vowel is always accented. An open syllable having a full short vowel is accented, except when a half-vowel immediately follows. The accent can never fall on a consonant with a half-vowel. Examples: תִּקְטֹלְנָה, taq-ṭēl'nāh; יָמִים, yā-mīm'; רֶגֶל, re'gel; קְטָלוּ, qi-ṭəlū'; מַרְאֶנּוּ, mar-'ē'nū; קָמְתֶּם, qam-tem'.

---

*[1] Except that Pathah Furtive, or a final Shewa, is not considered as making an extra syllable. Also, on theoretical grounds, grammarians commonly regard a consonant and half-vowel as insufficient for an independent syllable, and count them in with the next consonant-vowel group as making only one syllable together; then, e.g., נִקְדְּשׁוּ (niq-dəshū) is counted a dissyllable, and הֲלֹא (hălō') a monosyllable. And this system is convenient in some cases; but it is so unnecessarily confusing to the beginner that it is not followed here.

*[2] Only a syllable with a full vowel can be closed. A silent letter at the end of a syllable does not close it; e.g., all the syllables of וֵאלֹהֵינוּ (wē'-lō-hēy-nū) are open. But a diphthongal sound closes a syllable.

*[3] Except that, in a very few cases in which the penult has a half-vowel, the accent is on the ante-penult; e.g., לַיְלָה.

b. The secondary accent on a preceding syllable is indicated by the mark ⎯⎯, called *Metheg*; e. g., הֹורַשְׁתֶּם (hō''rash̄-tem'), יֵעָשֶׂה (ya'''ᵃ-seh').

EXERCISES

1. Name the vowels and pronounce:

(a) הָאָרֶץ – נֹוסַר – חַיִל – יַזְכִּיר – קָטוּל – הִגַּשׁ – הָלַךְ –

נִשְׁפַּךְ – הִגְדִּילוֹ – הָעֶצֶם – תָּגְלֶה – רֵעֵהוּ – חֶמְטָה –

זִכְרֹן – תַּשְׁכֶּמְנָה – מָקֹום.

(b) הֶחֱרִישׁ – לְאִשְׁתֹּו – חֲלִי – אֲשֶׁר – יֵלְכוּ – בַּעֲשָׂנְךָ –

יִקְטְלוּ – צָהֳרַיִם – יִשְׁאֲלוּ – וְיִיקַץ – אֲנַחְנוּ – שְׁנַיִם –

חָלָיְנוּ – וַחֲצִי – וּמְעִיל – יַעֲשֶׂה – וּלְזַרְעֲךָ – פָּעֳלוֹ – יֵחֲזַק –

מַחֲלֻקְתְּכֶם.

2. Transliterate:

a. haskēl, sh̄orāsh̄īm, 'Ōbadyāhū, 'Īzebel, Ḥuldāh, qārā'-tī, yārūts̄, 'Ēden, yiṣpōr, hish̄mīdū, ḥokmāh, yīṭab, tiglūhā, ṣēṭīm, ūmōqēsh̄.

b. qirbᵊkā, ho'ᵒzarten, ḥᵃnū, ūmeḥᵉzāh, bᵊtōk, sh̄ā'ᵃlāh, 'ᵒnī, hᵉyōt, naḥᵃlātᵊkā, ḥᵒdāsh̄īm, ta'ᵃbōr, Yirmᵊyāhū, ṣᵊbībōtayik, mo'ᵒmad, wᵊlaḥᵃts̄ar, heḥᵉzīqām.

3. Name the vowels in Exercise 3, Ch. I.

CHAPTER III

THE VOWEL SYSTEM (CONTINUED)

A. Consonants in the Vowel System

1. Combinations of certain vowels with the consonants ו and י indicate sounds similar to our *diphthongs*.

a. Pathah (or Qamets) with a following Yodh is pronounced as *ai* in *aisle*; e. g., סוּסַי, ṣūṣay.

b. וֹי— is pronounced as *oi* in *oil;* e. g., הוֹי, hōy.

c. יָו— is pronounced as *au* in *Faust*[1], the Yodh not being sounded at all; e. g., אֵלָיו, 'ēlāyw.

2. Several consonants are, in certain cases, entirely *silent;* they are then called *Quiescents*[2].

a. A י after an *e* sound is silent; e.g., חֵיל (ḥēyl), סוּסֶיהָ (ṣūṣeyhā).

b. An א not at the beginning of a syllable is silent after *any* vowel; e. g., קָרָאנוּ (qārā'nū), רֵאשׁ (rē's̄h)[3].

---

1 So also are the rarer וֶ— and וְ—.

*2 The letters א, ה, ו, and י are also called *weak;* not only are they thus sometimes silent (especially as vowel letters), but also they sometimes disappear entirely in inflection—even when they originally had true consonantal value. The י in Long Hireq is silent, being merely the sign of the length of the vowel; so also is the ו in Holem and Shureq, the dot being the real vowel.

3 The silent א is usually an original consonant which, altho it has lost its sound, is retained on etymological grounds—as, e.g., *gh* remains

c. A ה at the end of a word is almost always silent (for exceptions see Ch. V, B); e. g., נָטָה (nāṭāh)[1].

3. Vowel letters are sometimes omitted, especially when a word would otherwise have several Yodhs or Waws; the vowels are then said to be *written defectively.*

a. Holem may be designated simply by a dot written *above the preceding consonant;* e. g., חֹלִי, ḥōlī. Note as special cases that—

(1) If the preceding letter is שׁ, or the following one is שׁ, the dot used as a diacritical mark on the consonant indicates the vowel also; e. g., שֹׂחֵק, sōḥēq; מֹשֶׁה, Mōsheh.

(2) The dot is written *after* a ל; e.g., לֹט, lōṭ.

*(3) A Holem is occasionally written defectively with a consonantal Waw; e.g., לֹוֶה (lōweh—for לוֹוֶה); עָוֹן ('āwōn—for עָווֹן).

*(4) If the following consonant is a silent א, the dot may be placed *over it;* e.g., יֹּאמַר, yō'mar.

b. The י may be omitted from Long Hireq[2]; e. g., דָּוִד (Dāwīd—for דָּוִיד).

---

in the English *might* and *though.* (*Occasionally at the end of a syllable it retains consonantal value; e.g., נֶאְדָּר, Ex. 15:11).

[1] But at the end of a syllable within a word a ה is always pronounced; e. g., in יִהְיוּ (yihyū).

[2] Also sometimes from ◌ֶ or ◌ֵ; e.g., סוּסֵהֶם for סוּסֵיהֶם.

c. In place of Shureq, Qibbuts may sometimes be written; e.g.,
יִקְטְלֻהוּ (yiqtᵊlūhū—for יִקְטְלוּהוּ).

d. In some words this defective writing is regularly used, in others
it is optional. A final vowel, or a vowel used in a diphthong, is *never*
written defectively.

B. Changes of Vowels

1. Sometimes in inflecting words or making up compounds, two
half-vowels are thrown together, making an unpronounceable form
(e.g., בְּנְאֹם, כֹּהֲנֵךְ). *The first one is then heightened to a full short vowel*—
which is just the natural tendency in trying to pronounce such combinations.

a. A simple Shewa before another simple Shewa commonly becomes Hireq (e.g., בִּנְאֹם for בְּנְאֹם); or, the vowel from which it was
originally shortened may be restored (e.g., מוֹקְשֵׁךְ for מֹקְשֵׁךְ).

b. A compound Shewa before a simple Shewa regularly heightens
to its corresponding full vowel; e.g., אַדְמַת for אֲדְמַת.

c. A simple Shewa before a compound Shewa becomes the cognate
full short vowel; e.g., זַעֲקַת for זְעֲקַת, and בָּעֳנִי for בְּעֳנִי.

2. Of the present long vowels, some were originally long and always
remain so; they are called *fixed* or *unchangeable* vowels[1]. Others were
heightened from short vowels when they stood under or immediately
before the accent, and may be shortened again if the accent is moved;
they are called *tone-long* vowels, for their length is due to *tone position*[2].

---

*[1] The same is true of vowels long by *coalescence* or in compensation
for the omission of D.F. Also, a full short vowel in a closed syllable is
usually unchangeable.

*[2] Occasionally in verbs, but never in nouns, a tone-long vowel is
two full syllables from the accent; e.g., הַפְּקֵדְךָ, וְקָטַלְתָּ.

a. Long Hireq and Shureq are always fixed. Tsere and Holem (the secondary vowels of their classes), and Qamets, are usually tone-long, occasionally fixed.[1]

'**b.** A tone-long vowel may come from either short vowel of its class; and may shorten to either, or to the corresponding Hateph vowel or simple Shewa.

3. Various other changes which occurred in the evolution of the language help to explain present forms; e.g., sometimes an' *a* was, in the technical terminology, *deflected* to an *e*, or *attenuated* to an *i*[2], or *obscured* to an *o*, etc.

EXERCISES

1. Name the vowels and pronounce:

$$ תֹּהַם - עָשָׂהוּ - גּוֹי - שְׂמָחִים - יַעֲצִיךָ - אֲדֹנִי - $$

$$ תִּטְמָאנָה - דְּרָשָׁיו - מְשָׁלִים - אָמַר - אֵילֶךְ - מֶחֱזֶה - $$

$$ בֹּקֶר - שָׁנֵאָנוּ - תֹּאַר - אֱלֹהַי - הָעָשׂוּי - שֹׁחַט - שָׁלַשׁ - $$

$$ תֹּאחֲזוּ. $$

2. Transliterate (write defectively as many vowels as possible):

'ozneyhā, tēbōs͟hū, 'ᵃbōy, malᵊkēy, rī's͟hōn, sōrēp, 'ᵃnās͟hay, S͟hᵊlōmōh, 'ehᵉpōk, rō's͟h, timt͟se'nāh, tō'ᵃbōtāyw, wa'dōnāy, s͟hōpēṭ, lᵊha'ᵃlōtō, yᵊdēykem, gō'ēl.

---

[1] Tsere followed by Yodh is always fixed; e.g., in הֵיכָל.

*[2] Rather unusual cases of this occur in מִשְׁחַת, cst. of מָשְׁחַת, in גִּלְגִּלִים, plu. of גַּלְגַּל, in וִירִשְׁתֶּם from יָרַשׁ, etc.

CHAPTER IV

DAGESH

Dagesh is the name given to a dot placed in the middle of a letter[1]. It serves two distinct purposes, in which it is called *Dagesh Forte* and *Dagesh Lene.*

A. Dagesh Forte

1. In the use known as Dagesh Forte, this dot indicates the *doubling* of a consonant[2]; e. g., חִנָּם is ḥin-nām.

a. Note that a letter with D.F. both closes one syllable[3] and is the initial letter of the next; i.e., the syllable division occurs in it.

b. D.F. can be used only when the two consonant sounds are not separated by a vowel. When the letter is repeated after an intervening vowel, it must be written twice; e.g., "bāzᵊzū" is written בָּזְזוּ, not בָּזוּ.

c. A special use of D.F. occurs in such words as אֵלִיָּה ('Ēlīyāh), in which, of the two Yodhs indicated by י, the first simply makes the preceding Hireq long, and only the second is a true consonant. Similarly, in words like וַיַּט (way-yaṭ), the first Yodh combines with the Pathah in a diphthongal sound, the second has its ordinary consonantal value.

---

1 Note its position in ן, צ, and שׁ.

*2 It is sometimes said that it really only makes the pronunciation of the letter very firm, being just a stronger degree of the same hardening as is shown by D.L. But at any rate the practical effect is to double the letter.

*3 A syllable closed thus is said to be *sharpened.*

19

2. Any letter can take D. F., *except the gutturals and* ר; their sounds are such that they cannot be doubled. Also—

a. D.F. very seldom occurs in the last letter of a word which has lost a primitive final vowel; e.g., אַתְּ, 'att, formerly אַתְּי, 'attī[1]. *Usually such doubling is not indicated;* e.g., קַל for קַלְּ, (cf. Ch. LI, B, 1).

*b. Several letters, especially י and ק, do not usually take D.F. when they have Shewa[2]; e.g., וַתְּהִי and וַיְהִי are parallel forms; less frequently a D.F. is thus omitted from ו, ל, מ, or a sibilant before a guttural.

*3. D.F. is commonly used—(a) as a distinctive mark of certain grammatical forms (e.g., קִטֵּל, qiṭ·ṭēl, is a special form of the verb קָטַל); and (b) to represent a letter partly lost or assimilated into another (e.g., יִמָּלֵט for יִנְמָלֵט; cf., in English, "im-moral" for "in-moral")[3].

B. Dagesh Lene. Aspirated Letters

1. The use of this dot as Dagesh Lene is confined to the letters בּ, גּ, דּ, כּ, פּ, and תּ. Each of these had

---

[1] Note that a final Shewa is written (an orthographic remnant of the early vowel), but it is not sounded nor transliterated; this pointing, however, secures a very firm pronunciation of the consonant.

*[2] The letter sometimes has *Raphe* (note 3, page 21) to mark the omission of the Dagesh; e.g., וּלְמִקְצֵה (Dt. 4:32).

*[3] D.F. is sometimes used where there is no particular need for it: either to strengthen the pronunciation of a word (in which case it is called *Dagesh Euphonic* or *Dagesh Firmative*—e.g., נִצְּרָה for נִצְרָה); or to connect short words in special phrases (being then called *Dagesh Conjunctive*; e.g., וֹהִ־לְּךָ).

two sounds, distinguished by means of it, as follows:

a. The *hard* or sharp sound, as given in Ch. I (the original simple *b, g*, etc.) is used *when the letter does not immediately follow a vowel sound; a D. L. is then placed in the letter*, as an indication of the hard sound; e. g., תַזְכִּיר, tazkîr[1]. The hard sound is also used when the letter is doubled, for the D. F. includes the effect of the D. L.; e. g., כַּפּוֹ, kap-pō.

b. A softer or *aspirated* sound is used *when the letter immediately follows any vowel sound and is not doubled[2]; the letter is then written plain, without a Dagesh[3]*. The sounds are:

---

[1] D.L. is used in any of these letters when it stands after a vowel-less consonant, or is the initial letter of a word that stands alone or at the beginning of a sentence or phrase; e.g., אִם תִּסָּתֵר פֹּה תִּמָּצֵא, "If you hide here, you will be found."

[2] E.g., thruout the sentence עָמְדוּ לִפְנֵי בְנוֹתָיִךְ, "They stood before thy daughters." The aspirated sound is used not only when one of these letters stands at the end of a syllable, or at the beginning of a syllable following an open syllable; but also when it is the initial letter of a word closely connected grammatically with an immediately preceding word ending in a vowel sound (but if there is a break in sense, and a consequent pause in speech, the hard sound and D.L. is used).

[3] The Massoretes, in their MS. copies of the O. T., placed a stroke (called *Raphe*) above each of these letters when it was aspirated; e.g., בַיִث, bayith. In printed text, however, the special aspiration mark is not used—altho it would seem more reasonable to mark specially the departure from the original sound.

	Transliterated	Pronounced as	E. g.
בּ	b̄h (or β)	v in live	עֲבְדִי 'ab̄h-dī
גּ	ḡh (or γ)	simple g	הָגוּ hā-ḡhū
דּ	d̄h (or δ)	th, soft, as in this, bathe	אֵיד 'ēyd̄h
כּ	k̄h (or χ)	simple k; or as German ch in ich	תוֹך tōk̄h
פּ	p̄h (or φ)	ph in phonograph	בְּפִי bᵊp̄hī
תּ	t̄h (or θ)	th, sharp, as in think, bath	זֹאת zō'tᴴ

c. As an aid to remembering these letters, and as a convenient designation for them, they have been combined into a mnemonic word, *Beghadhkephath* (בְּגַדְכְּפַת).

2. There is no difficulty in distinguishing D. F. from D. L. The latter never occurs after a vowel sound; but it is evident that a doubled letter can be pronounced only after a vowel[1].

EXERCISES

1. Name the vowels and Dagesh, and pronounce:

כָּבְדוּ – יְכָלְתֶּם – כַּפִּים – הַמִּשְׁפָּט – הַדָּבָר –

הֶעֱמַדְתֶּם – שַׁבָּת – וְאַרְבַּע – גְּדֹל – לְחֶיֵי – הָעֶבֶד –

וַנִּסָּתֵר – אֲדֹנָיְהוּ – בִּבְנֹתוֹ – עֲזַרְתִּים – חַטָּאת – חָרְבָּה –

עֲמַדְתִּים – תִּכָּבֵד – מָחֳרָת – נִפְתַּח – אִתִּיוֹת – דָּנִי.

---

[1] A similar consideration will distinguish a doubled Waw from a Shureq; e.g., צַוָּה must be t̄siw-wāh.

2. Transliterate: (In the first six words *h* is attached to each aspirated letter; thereafter it is left to the student to judge the use of D. L.)

tikhrᵊt͡hū, kammazkīr, haggᵊd͡hōlīm, tip͡htaḥ, dibh͡ᵊ-reyk͡hā, ṭᵊmē' p͡hānīm, 'ᵃbāday, lammalkāh, mizzō't, bᵊqaṭṭēl, ye'ᵉbal, kamma'ᵃseh, miṣgᵊrōt, bᵊnēy Dāwīd, ṣappᵊrū, wᵊhammᵊzūzōt, ṣōbᵊbīm, hat͡st͡sedeq, pitḥō· 'ᵃmallē', kāmūṣ, wayyis͡hpal, malkᵊkem, lō' bāttēy, nātatt, bas͡hs͡hāmayim, Lᵊwīyīm.

CHAPTER V

OTHER MARKS AND PRINCIPLES

A. Maqqeph

Maqqeph is a short horizontal stroke sometimes written at the top of the line to connect two (or more) words which are closely united grammatically[1]; e. g., בֶּן־דָּוִד, "Son of David." The two words are joined by a hyphen in English transliteration (ben-Dāwīdh)[2].

B. Mappiq

When a final ה is not silent (Ch. III, *A*, 2, c), but is pronounced as a consonant, the fact is indicated by placing in it a dot called *Mappiq;* e. g., דָּמָה (dāmāh).

C. Silent Shewa

1. The mark —, already familiar as the sign of a half-vowel, has another use: *whenever a single consonant closes a syllable within a word, a Shewa is placed under it;* e. g., יִכְבַּד, yikh-badh. It serves here merely as a *syllable divider, an indication of the absence of any vowel sound*

---

[1] Words so joined form a compact phrase—practically one word—and only the last one receives a full accent. As a result of this a vowel in the first word is frequently shortened; e.g., בֶּן־ is for בֵּן .

[2] Remember, however, that Maqqeph is *not* a hyphen; it dare not be used to divide a Hebrew word into syllables.

after the consonant. In this use it has no sound whatever, and is called *Silent Shewa* or *Quiescent Shewa;* in
the use previously studied, it is called *Vocal Shewa* (or,
Shewa Mobile).

a. It is never used at the end of a word[1]; except that
in final Kaph it is used whenever the ך does not have a
vowel; e. g., סוּסֵךְ (ṣūṣēkh), סוּסָיִךְ (ṣūṣeykhā).

b. Note that silent Shewa is not used when a syllable ends in a
silent letter—for then the syllable is *open;* e.g., we write סוּסֵיכֶם
(ṣū-ṣēy-khem), not סוּסֶיכֶם; and קָרָאתִי (qā-rā'-thī), not קָרְאתִי.
Neither is it used when a syllable is closed by a letter doubled by D.F.;
e.g., "lib-bō" is לִבּוֹ, not לִבְּוֹ.

c. When a word ends in two full consonants, both have [Shewa;
the first is silent; the second, strictly speaking, is vocal—analogous
to that in אַתְּ (Ch.IV,A, 2, a and note); e. g., קָטַלְתְּ, qā-ṭalt. When a
word ends in a full consonant followed by a silent letter, the first has
silent 'Shewa, the second nothing; e.g., שָׁוְא, shāw'.

2. Silent and vocal Shewa can usually be differentiated by observing
the following principles:

a. When two Shewas occur together, the first is silent, the second
vocal; for it is never possible for two of either kind to occur together;
e.g., יִכְבְּדוּ, yikh-bᵊ-dhū.

b. A Shewa before a letter with Dagesh must be silent; and a
Shewa before a Beghadhkephath letter without D.L. is thereby shown
to be vocal; e.g., יִכְבַּד, yikh-badh; יַלְדִי, ya-lᵊ-dhēy.

c. Any Shewa representing a vowel thinned down in inflection
is vocal; e.g., כָּבְדוּ, from כָּבֵד.

---

[1] A special exception is indicated in Ch. XLII, B, 5.

d. A Shewa after a long vowel is almost always vocal; a Shewa after a short vowel is usually silent.

D. Summary of Peculiarities of the Gutturals

1. *The gutturals and* ר *never take Dagesh*[1]. When one of these letters should have a D. F. in a grammatical form, the preceding vowel is often lengthened to compensate for its absence; e. g., while a certain form of קָטַל is קַטֵּל, the corresponding form of בָּרַךְ is בֵּרֵךְ.

a. This lengthening is always required before א and ר, and usually before ע; but in the case of ה and ח, whose sounds are almost as strong naturally as that of a doubled letter, it is seldom required[2].

b. Pathah becomes Qamets, Hireq or Segol becomes Tsere, and Qamets Hatuph or Qibbuts becomes Holem.

2. Not only do the gutturals never take simple vocal Shewa, requiring instead a compound Shewa, but also they often prefer a compound Shewa to a silent Shewa; e. g., יַחֲזִיק is a parallel form to יַקְטִיל.

3. They have a preference for *a* vowels, either under or preceding them; e. g., יַחְגֹּר is a parallel form to יִקְטֹל. In the case of א, however, the preference is usually for Segol or Hateph Segol.

4. When a guttural at the end of a word is preceded

---

[1] Do not confuse Mappiq with Dagesh. It is similar in form but not in function.

[2] In such cases the guttural is commonly said to have a *Dagesh Implicit*.

by any long vowel except Qamets, it is very difficult to pronounce. In such cases the pronunciation is facilitated by slipping in before the guttural a Pathah, called *Pathah Furtive*[1]; e. g., the word רוּחַ is pronounced "rūah," and written רוּחַ[2]. Note that this Pathah, altho pronounced before the guttural, is written under it. Of course a final א or ה, being silent, does not require this Pathah (but חַ does); ר never takes it.

E. Accent Marks

The Massoretes invented a variety of accent marks, which not only indicate the tone syllable of a word, but also serve as punctuation marks. Three of these are used in the following chapter:

1. Under the word before the principal logical and grammatical pause in a sentence (which in English might be shown by a semi-colon or colon) is placed the mark——, called *Athnāḥ*.

2. At secondary pauses (such as might require a comma in English) the mark —— (called *Zāqēph*) is used.

3. The last word of a sentence has the mark —— (called *Sillūq*, identical in form with Metheg); and is followed by the Hebrew period, which is ׃ .

---

1 The use of this furtive Pathah may be compared with our custom in English of slipping in an *e* sound before a final *r—our*, e.g., being pronounced like *flower*. (See note 1, page 13).

*2 But when an ending is added to such a word, so that the guttural becomes the initial letter of another syllable, the Pathah is of course not needed and is dropped; e.g., רוּחוֹ.

EXERCISES

1. Name the Shewas and pronounce:

נִבְקְעוּ – כָּמֶה – וְעַל־כֵּן – הַצְלִיחַ – בְּשִׂמְחַתְכֶם – תַּחְתִּי – הַמְּנַצֵּחַ – וַיַּרְא – יֵשְׁבִי – יְהוֹשׁוּעַ – מַעְיָנֹת – כָּתַבְתְּ – אֶת־שֶׁם־מַלְכָּה – לִזְבֹּחַ – נַבְרִיאֵל – חָקַתְךָ – עֲבָדֶיךָ – גְּבֹהַּ – וְעָבִיו – מִתְדַּפְּקִים – בָּרִיחַ – הָשָּׁבַר – שְׁכֹלְתִּי.

2. Transliterate:

kaṣpēk, nērd, lē'mōr, yaldēnū, wayyashq, sāmēaḥ, mal'āk, hitgallēytā, biqqēa', ḥēt', 'art͡sāh, liqra't, t͡s°lōaḥ, t͡siddaqt.

3. Pick out all words in exercises 1 and 2 of Ch. II which should have silent Shewa or D. L., and write correctly.

4. Write the following sentences in Hebrew:

(1) Bō' ben-Yishay l°hēykal 'elōah, wayyābē' 'et-zib°ḥēy hat͡st͡s°dāqāh; wayyizbaḥ 'ōtām 'al-hammizbēaḥ.

(2) Hibṭiaḥ hannābī' 'et-melek Y°hūdāh ba'dōnāy, w°lō' b°ba'al; 'al-kēn bōrak way°kubbad.

5. Read the following sentences:

1) וַהֲלַכְתֶּם מִתְּקוֹעַ וִישַׁבְתֶּם בַּמִּגְדָּל בְּשָׂדֶהוּ וְשָׂמוֹחַ יִשְׂמַח בָּרוּחַ לִרְאֹת אֶתְכֶם: 2) יָרְחַק שִׁבְטְךָ אֶל־אַרְצֵנוּ וְיָשַׁבְתִּ עִם מִשְׁפַּחְתִּי וְדָרְשׁוּךְ כָּל־בְּנֵי מַטִּי: 3) כִּי יִרְבּוּ עַבְדֵי בְנוֹתֶיךָ תִּבְנֶינָה קִיר גָּדֹל:

CHAPTER VI

FIRST HEBREW READINGS   (Exodus 3:1–4:9)

יִתְרוֹ	אֶת־צֹאן²	רֹעֶה	הָיָה	מֹשֶׁה
Jethro	of the-flock	shepherding	was	Moses

נָהַג	וְהוּא⁴	מִדְיָן	כֹּהֵן	חֹתְנוֹ³
led	and-he	; Midian	of the-priest	, his-father-in-law

הַר	אֶל־	הַמִּדְבָּר	אַחַר	אֶת־הַצֹּאן⁴
of the-mountain	unto	the-desert	behind	the-flock

---

¹ אֵת (אֶת־) is the sign of the direct object.

² In indicating the genitive relation, the two nouns are placed side-by-side, without a preposition; sometimes the first noun is modified in form. The first noun is said to be in the *Construct State;* the definite article is usually to be supplied with it in translation.

³ A pronoun used as a possessive, or as the object of a preposition, is written as a *suffix* to the noun or preposition.

    a. The following suffixes occur in this chapter:

‏ִי– *or* ‏ִי–	—my *or* me	‏ָה–	— her, it
‏ְךָ– *or* ‏ִיךָ–	—thy *or* thee	‏ֵנוּ–	— our *or* us
‏וֹ– *or* ‏ִיו–	—his, its,	‏ְכֶם– *or* ‏ִיכֶם–	— your *or* you
	or him, it	‏ָם– *or* ‏ֶהֶם–	— their *or* them

    b. The vowels of the noun or preposition itself are usually somewhat changed; e.g., the simple noun here is חֹתֵן, and אֵלָיו in vs. 2 is אֶל plus ‏ִיו–.

⁴ The conjunction ו, the prepositions בּ and לְ, and the article ה, are written as *prefixes*.

29

יְהוָֹה⁵   מַלְאַךְ   וְשָׁם   חֹרֵבָה: הָאֱלֹהִים 2
Jehovah   of the-angel   And-there   . to-Horeb   , God

מִקֶּרֶב⁸   אֵשׁ   בְּלַבַּת⁷־   אֵלָיו³¹   נִרְאָה⁶
from-the-midst   fire of   in-a-flame   unto-him   appeared

בֹּעֵר   הַסְּנֶה   וְהִנֵּה   רָאָה   הַסְּנֶה
was-burning   the-bush   and-behold   , he-looked   ; a-bush of

אָמַר⁹   אֻכָּל: אֵינֶנּוּ⁹³   וְהַסְּנֶה   בָּאֵשׁ 3
Said   . was-consumed   not   and-the-bush   , in-the-fire

אֶת־   וְאֶרְאֶה   נָּא   אָסֻרָה־¹⁰   מֹשֶׁה
that-I-may-see   now   I-will-turn-aside"   , Moses

יִבְעַר⁹   לֹא־   מַדּוּעַ   הַזֶּה   הַגָּדֹל   הַמַּרְאֶה⁹
does-burn-up   not   why   , this   great   sight

---

⁵ The Jews never pronounced the name of Deity indicated by the consonants יהוה—at least, not in later times—and the true pronunciation has been lost. The vowels printed with it are the vowels of אֲדֹנָי, "Lord," which was regularly pronounced instead of it. Whenever this word occurs, אֲדֹנָי is to be read. (The real word may have been יַהְוֶה, "Yahweh,"— certainly not "Jehovah").

⁶ From the verb רָאָה. In the inflection of verbs, several preformative letters are used, such as א, ה, י, ל, נ, ת. (This particular form has the significance of a "Middle voice").

⁷ Construct state of לַבָּה, plus בְּ (notes 2 and 4).

⁸ The noun קֶרֶב with the preposition מִן prefixed; the נ of the מִן has been assimilated into the ק and is represented by the D.F. (cf. Ch. IV, A, 3, b).

⁹ Note the word order in these phrases.

¹⁰ From סוּר; cf. note 6.

לִרְאֹות⁶	סָר¹⁰	כִּי	יְהֹוָה	רָאָה⁹	4 הַסְּנֶה:
, to-look	he-turned	that	Jehovah	Saw .	"the-bush

הַסְּנֶה	מִתּוֹךְ	אֱלֹהִים	אֵלָיו	וַיִּקְרָא⁹
the-bush	of from-the-midst	God	to-him	and-called

הִנֵּנִי¹¹:	וַיֹּאמֶר	מֹשֶׁה	מֹשֶׁה	וַיֹּאמֶר
. "Here-am-I"	, and-he-said	; "Moses	Moses"	, and-said

נְעָלֶיךָ	שַׁל¹²	הֲלֹם	אַל־תִּקְרַב	5 וַיֹּאמֶר
thy-shoes	put-off	;hither	Do-not-draw-nigh"	,And-he-said

אַתָּה	אֲשֶׁר	הַמָּקוֹם	כִּי	רַגְלֶיךָ	מֵעַל
thou	which	the-place	for	; thy-feet	from-upon

הוּא¹⁵:	אַדְמַת־קֹדֶשׁ¹⁴		עָלָיו	עֹמֵד
	. "holy-ground	13is	on-it	art-standing

אֱלֹהֵי	אָבִיךָ		אֱלֹהֵי	6 וַיֹּאמֶר אָנֹכִי
the-God	, thy-father	of	the-God	13am I" , And-he-said

וֵאלֹהֵי	יִצְחָק		אֱלֹהֵי	אַבְרָהָם
of and-the-God	, Isaac	of	the-God	, Abraham of

יָרֵא	כִּי	פָּנָיו	מֹשֶׁה	וַיַּסְתֵּר	יַעֲקֹב
he-was-afraid	for	, his-face	Moses	and-hid	;"Jacob

---

11 *Lit.*, "Behold me."

12 From נָשַׁל. One of the three consonants of a verb root is frequently lost in inflectional forms.

13 Hebrew has no real equivalent for the verb "to be"; the proper form must be supplied in translation.

14 *Lit.*, "Ground of holiness."

15 Not translated.

7 וְלֹא הִבִּיט[16] אֶל- הָאֱלֹהִים: וַיֹּאמֶר יְהוָֹה,

and-not did-look upon . God And-said ,Jehovah

רָאִיתִי אֶת-עֳנִי עַמִּי אֲשֶׁר

"I-have-seen the-affliction of ,my-people who

בְּמִצְרָיִם וְאֶת- צַעֲקָתָם שָׁמַעְתִּי

are in-Egypt ; and their-cry have-I-heard

מִפְּנֵי נֹגְשָׂיו כִּי יָדַעְתִּי אֶת-

from-before their-taskmasters ; for I-know

8 מַכְאֹבָיו: וָאֵרֵד[17] לְהַצִּילוֹ[18]

. their-sorrows And-I-have-come-down to-deliver-them

מִיַּד מִצְרַיִם וּלְהַעֲלֹתוֹ[19]

from-the-hand of ,the–Egyptians and-to-bring-them-up

מִן הָאָרֶץ הַהִיא אֶל- אֶרֶץ טוֹבָה וּרְחָבָה,

from land that unto a-land good ,and-broad

אֶל- אֶרֶץ זָבַת[20] חָלָב וּדְבָשׁ אֶל-

unto a-land flowing milk , and-honey unto

---

[16] From נָבַט; cf. notes 6 and 12.

[17] From יָרַד.

[18] From נָצַל.

[19] From עָלָה. A certain form of the verb indicates a causative influence on action; here, e.g., this form of the verb "to go up" means "to cause to go up, to bring up." The form is marked either by a preformative ה (as here), or by a Long Hireq (as in אוֹצִיא, vs. 11), or by both (as in הַשְׁלִיכֻהוּ in 4:3).

[20] From זוּב.

מְקוֹם	הַכְּנַעֲנִי	וְהַחִתִּי
the-place of	the-Canaanite	and-the-Hittite

וְהָאֱמֹרִי	וְהַפְּרִזִּי	וְהַחִוִּי
and-the-Amorite	and-the-Perizzite	and-the-Hivite

9 וְהַיְבוּסִי: וְעַתָּה הִנֵּה צַעֲקַת

and-the-Jebusite .   And-now   behold   the-cry   of

בְּנֵי־ יִשְׂרָאֵל בָּאָה[21] אֵלָי וְגַם־

the-children   of   Israel   has-come   unto-me ;   and-also

רָאִיתִי אֶת־הַלַּחַץ אֲשֶׁר מִצְרַיִם

I-have-seen   the-oppression   with   which   the-Egyptians

10 לֹחֲצִים אֹתָם: וְעַתָּה לְכָה[22] וְאֶשְׁלָחֲךָ

are-oppressing   them.   And-now   go,   and-I-will-send-thee

אֶל־ פַּרְעֹה וְהוֹצֵא[23] אֶת־עַמִּי בְּנֵי־

unto   Pharaoh;   and-bring-forth   my-people   the-children

11 יִשְׂרָאֵל מִמִּצְרָיִם: וַיֹּאמֶר מֹשֶׁה אֶל־

of   Israel   from-Egypt."   And-said   Moses   unto

הָאֱלֹהִים מִי אָנֹכִי כִּי אֵלֵךְ[22] אֶל־

God,   "Who   am   I,   that   I-should-go   unto

פַּרְעֹה וְכִי אוֹצִיא[23] אֶת־בְּנֵי

Pharaoh,   and-that   I-should-bring-forth   the-children

---

[21] From בּוֹא.

[22] From הָלַךְ.

[23] From יָצָא; cf. notes 12 and 19.

12 יִשְׂרָאֵל   מִמִּצְרָיִם: וַיֹּאמֶר   כִּי¹⁵   אֶהְיֶה
of   Israel   "? from-Egypt   , And-he-said   that   I-will-be"

עִמָּךְ   וְזֶה־   לְךָ   הָאוֹת   כִּי
; with-thee   and-this   shall-be   to-thee   the-sign   that

אָנֹכִי   שְׁלַחְתִּיךָ   בְּהוֹצִיאֲךָ²⁴   אֶת־
I   : have-sent-thee   when-thou-bringest-out   אֶת־

הָעָם   מִמִּצְרַיִם   תַּעַבְדוּן   אֶת־הָאֱלֹהִים
the-people   ,from-Egypt   ye-shall-serve   God

13 עַל   הָהָר   הַזֶּה: וַיֹּאמֶר   מֹשֶׁה   אֶל־   הָאֱלֹהִים
upon   mountain   "this.   And-said   Moses   unto   God ,

הִנֵּה   כִּי   בָא²¹   אָנֹכִי   אֶל־   בְּנֵי
"Behold,   when   I   come   unto   the-children   of

יִשְׂרָאֵל   וְאָמַרְתִּי   לָהֶם   אֱלֹהֵי   אֲבוֹתֵיכֶם
Israel   and-I-say   ,to-them   The-God'   of   your-fathers

שְׁלָחַנִי   אֲלֵיכֶם   וְאָמְרוּ   לִי   מַה־
has-sent-me   ;'unto-you   and-they-say   ,to-me   What'   is

14 שְׁמוֹ   מָה   אֹמַר   אֲלֵהֶם: וַיֹּאמֶר
; '? his-name   what   shall-I-say   "? unto-them   And-said

אֱלֹהִים   אֶל־   מֹשֶׁה   אֶהְיֶה   אֲשֶׁר   אֶהְיֶה   וַיֹּאמֶר
God   unto   Moses   , "I-am"   what   I-am"   ;   , and-he-said

כֹּה   תֹאמַר   לִבְנֵי   יִשְׂרָאֵל
Thus"   shalt-thou-say   to-the-children   of   ,Israel

---

²⁴ *Lit.*, "In thy bringing out."

15 אֶהְיֶה | שְׁלָחַנִי | אֲלֵיכֶם: | וַיֹּאמֶר | עוֹד
"I-am" ' | has-sent-me | ".'unto-you | And-said | again

אֱלֹהִים | אֶל־ | מֹשֶׁה | כֹּה | תֹּאמַר | אֶל־
God | unto | , Moses | Thus" | shalt-thou-say | unto

בְּנֵי | יִשְׂרָאֵל | יְהֹוָה | אֱלֹהֵי
the-children | of | , Israel | , Jehovah' | the-God | of

אֲבוֹתֵיכֶם | אֱלֹהֵי | אַבְרָהָם | אֱלֹהֵי
,your-fathers | the-God | of | , Abraham | the-God | of

יִצְחָק | וֵאלֹהֵי | יַעֲקֹב | שְׁלָחַנִי | אֲלֵיכֶם
,Isaac | and-the-God | of | , Jacob | has-sent-me | ; 'unto-you

זֶה. | שְׁמִי | לְעוֹלָם | וְזֶה | זִכְרִי
this | is | my-name | , forever | and-this | is | my-memorial

16 לְדֹר דֹּר: | לֵךְ22 | וְאָסַפְתָּ | אֶת־זִקְנֵי
.to-all-generations | ,Go | and-gather | the-elders | of

יִשְׂרָאֵל | וְאָמַרְתָּ | אֲלֵהֶם | יְהֹוָה | אֱלֹהֵי
,Israel | and-say | , unto-them | ,Jehovah' | the-God | of

אֲבוֹתֵיכֶם | נִרְאָה | אֵלַי | אֱלֹהֵי | אַבְרָהָם
, your-fathers | has-appeared | unto-me — the-God | of | , Abraham

יִצְחָק | וְיַעֲקֹב | לֵאמֹר | פָּקֹד25 | פָּקַדְתִּי | אֶתְכֶם
,Isaac | and-Jacob — ,saying | Surely" | I-have-looked-upon | you

17 וְאֶת־ | הֶעָשׂוּי26 | לָכֶם | בְּמִצְרָיִם: | וָאֹמַר
and | what-is-done | to-you | .in-Egypt | And-I-say | that

---

25 *Lit.*, "Looking I have looked."

26 From עָשָׂה.

מִצְרָיִם		מֵעֳנִי	אֶתְכֶם	אַעֲלֶה
Egypt	of	from-the-affliction	you	I-will-bring-up

וְהַחִתִּי	הַכְּנַעֲנִי		אֶל־	אֶ֫רֶץ
and-the-Hittite	the-Canaanite	of	the-land	unto

וְהַחִוִּי	וְהַפְּרִזִּי	וְהָאֱמֹרִי
and-the-Hivite	and-the-Perizzite	and-the-Amorite

חָלָב		²⁰זָבַת	אֶ֫רֶץ	אֶל־	וְהַיְבוּסִי
milk	with	flowing	a-land	unto	,and-the-Jebusite

לְקֹלֶ֑ךָ	וְשָׁמְעוּ	18 וּדְבָשׁ׃
;to-thy-voice	And-they-will-hearken	'."and-honey

יִשְׂרָאֵל	וְזִקְנֵי	אַתָּה	²¹וּבָאתָ
, Israel	of and-the-elders	thou	, and-thou-shalt-come

אֵלָיו	וַאֲמַרְתֶּם	מִצְרַ֫יִם	מֶ֫לֶךְ	אֶל־
, unto-him	and-ye-shall-say	; Egypt	of the-king	unto

עָלֵ֫ינוּ	נִקְרָה	הָעִבְרִיִּים	אֱלֹהֵי	יְהֹוָה
; with-us	has-met	,the-Hebrews of	the-God	, Jehovah'

שְׁלֹ֫שֶׁת	דֶּ֫רֶךְ	נָא	²²נֵלְכָה־	וְעַתָּה
three	of a-journey	, we-pray-thee	, let-us-go	and-now

לַיהוָה	וְנִזְבְּחָה	בַּמִּדְבָּר	יָמִים
to-Jehovah	that-we-may-sacrifice	,in-the-desert	days

אֶתְכֶם	²⁷יִתֵּן	לֹא־	כִּי	יָדַ֫עְתִּי	וַאֲנִי	19 אֱלֹהֵ֫ינוּ׃
you	will-permit	not	that	know	And-I	׃our-God

---

²⁷ From נָתַן.

מֶּ֫לֶךְ	of	מִצְרַ֫יִם	לַהֲלֹךְ	וְלֹא	בְּיָד
the-king		Egypt	to-go	not —	by-a-hand

20 חֲזָקָה:	וְשָׁלַחְתִּי	אֶת־יָדִי	וְהִכֵּיתִי²⁸
.mighty	And-I-will-stretch-forth	my-hand	and-smite

אֶת־מִצְרַ֫יִם	בְּכֹל	נִפְלְאֹתַי	אֲשֶׁר	אֶעֱשֶׂה
Egypt	with-all	my-wonders	which	I-will-do

בְּקִרְבּוֹ	וְאַחֲרֵי־כֵן	יְשַׁלַּח	אֶתְכֶם:
; in-its-midst	and-afterwards	he-will-send-away	. you

21 וְנָתַתִּי²⁷	אֶת־חֵן	הָעָם־	הַזֶּה	בְּעֵינֵי
And-I-will-give	favor	to-people	this	in-the-eyes

מִצְרָ֑יִם	וְהָיָה	כִּי	תֵלֵכוּן²²
; the-Egyptians of	and-it-shall-come-to-pass	when	ye-go

22 לֹא	תֵלְכוּ	רֵיקָם:	וְשָׁאֲלָה	אִשָּׁה
that	not	ye-shall-go	.empty	And-shall-ask	a-woman

מִשְּׁכֶנְתָּהּ	וּמִגָּרַת²⁹	בֵּיתָהּ
from-her-neighbor	and-from-the-sojourner	in-her-house

כְּלֵי־	of	כֶּ֫סֶף	וּכְלֵי	זָהָב	of	וּשְׂמָלֹת
vessels		silver	and-vessels	gold		;and-garments

וְשַׂמְתֶּם³⁰	עַל־	בְּנֵיכֶם	וְעַל־
and-ye-shall-put-them	upon	your-sons	and-upon

---

²⁸ From נָכָה.

²⁹ From גּוּר.

³⁰ From שִׂים.

בְּנְתֵיכֶם , וְנִצַּלְתֶּם אֶת־מִצְרָיִם:
your-daughters , and-ye-shall-despoil ".the-Egyptians

Chap. 4

31 וַיַּעַן מֹשֶׁה וַיֹּאמֶר וְהִנֵּה לֹא־
And-answered Moses , and-said But-behold" not

יַאֲמִינוּ לִי , וְלֹא יִשְׁמְעוּ בְּקֹלִי
they-will-believe me , and-not will-hearken ; to-my-voice

כִּי יֹאמְרוּ , לֹא־ נִרְאָה אֵלֶיךָ
for , they-will-say Not' has-appeared unto-thee

2 יְהֹוָה: וַיֹּאמֶר אֵלָיו יְהֹוָה , מַה־ זֶּה
". 'Jehovah And-said unto-him , Jehovah What" this is

3 בְּיָדֶךָ וַיֹּאמֶר , מַטֶּה: וַיֹּאמֶר,
in-thy-hand "? , And-he-said . "A-rod" ,And-he-said

הַשְׁלִיכֵהוּ אַרְצָה ; וַיַּשְׁלִכֵהוּ אָרְצָה
Cast-it" to-the-ground ; and-he-cast-it ,to-the-ground

32 וַיְהִי לְנָחָשׁ ; 33 וַיָּנָס מֹשֶׁה מִפָּנָיו:
and-it-became a-serpent ; and-fled Moses .from-before-it

4 וַיֹּאמֶר יְהֹוָה אֶל־ מֹשֶׁה , שְׁלַח יָדְךָ
And-said Jehovah unto Moses , Stretch-forth" thy-hand

וֶאֱחֹז בִּזְנָבוֹ ; וַיִּשְׁלַח יָדוֹ
and-seize-it "by-its-tail; and-he-stretched-forth his-hand

---

31 From עָנָה.

32 From הָיָה.

33 From נוּס.

וַיַּחֲזֶק	בֹּו	וַיְהִי	לְמַטֶּה	בְּכַפֹּו:
and-laid-hold	on-it,	and-it-became	a-rod	in-his-hand.

5 לְמַ֫עַן יַאֲמִ֫ינוּ כִּי־ נִרְאָה אֵלֶ֫יךָ
So-that" | they-may-believe | that | has-appeared | unto-thee

יְהֹוָה אֱלֹהֵי אֲבֹתָם אֱלֹהֵי
Jehovah | the-God | of | their-fathers, | the-God | of

אַבְרָהָם אֱלֹהֵי יִצְחָק וֵאלֹהֵי יַעֲקֹב:
Abraham, | the-God | of | Isaac, | and-the-God | of | Jacob".

6 וַיֹּ֫אמֶר יְהֹוָה לֹו עֹוד הָבֵא־[21] נָא יָדְךָ
And-said | Jehovah | to-him | again, | Put" | now | thy-hand

בְּחֵיקֶ֫ךָ וַיָּבֵא יָדֹו בְּחֵיקֹו
in-thy-bosom" ; | and-he-put | his-hand | in-his-bosom;

וַיֹּוצִאָהּ[23] וְהִנֵּה יָדֹו מְצֹרַ֫עַת
and-he-took-it-out, | and-behold | his-hand | was | leprous,

7 כַּשָּׁ֫לֶג: וַיֹּ֫אמֶר הָשֵׁב[34] יָדְךָ אֶל־
like-snow. | And-he-said, | Return" | thy-hand | into

חֵיקֶ֫ךָ וַיָּ֫שֶׁב יָדֹו אֶל־ חֵיקֹו
thy-bosom" ; | and-he-returned | his-hand | into | his-bosom;

וַיֹּוצִאָהּ מֵחֵיקֹו וְהִנֵּה־
and-he-took-it-out | from-his-bosom, | and-behold

8 שָׁבָה[34] כִּבְשָׂרֹו: וְהָיָה
it-had-returned | like-his-flesh. | And-it-shall-come-to-pass"

---

[34] From שׁוּב.

יִשְׁמְעוּ וְלֹא לָךְ יַאֲמִינוּ לֹא אִם־
will-hearken and-not , thee they-will-believe not if

וְהֶאֱמִינוּ הָרִאשׁוֹן הָאֹת לְקֹל
that-they-will-believe , first the-sign of to-the-voice

וְהָיָה הָאַחֲרוֹן: הָאֹת לְקֹל
,And-it-shall-come-to-pass . latter the-sign of the-voice

הָאֹתוֹת לִשְׁנֵי גַּם יַאֲמִינוּ לֹא אִם־
signs both even they-will-believe not if

לְקֹלֶךָ יִשְׁמְעוּן וְלֹא הָאֵלֶּה
,to-thy-voice will-hearken and-not ,these

הַיְאֹר מִמֵּימֵי וְלָקַחְתָּ
the-river of from-the-water that-thou-shalt-take

הַמַּיִם וְהָיוּ³² הַיַּבָּשָׁה וְשָׁפַכְתָּ
the-water and-shall-become ; on-the-dry-ground and-pour-it

לְדָם הַיְאֹר מִן תִּקַּח³⁵ אֲשֶׁר
blood the-river from thou-takest which

בַּיַּבָּשֶׁת:
".on-the-dry-ground

---

³⁵ From לָקַח.

PART TWO
PARTICLES. ADJECTIVES. PRONOUNS.

CHAPTER VII

THE ARTICLE. SENTENCE STRUCTURE

A. The Article

1. The definite article is not a separate word, but is written as a *prefix*. It consists properly of a הַ, *pointed with Pathah and followed by D.F. in the first letter of the word*[1]; e. g., הַצֹּאן, "the flock." Before the gutturals and ר, however, which cannot take the Dageš, this pointing is modified as follows (cf. Ch. V, D, 1):

a. Before א or ר the הַ always has Qamets (the Pathah being lengthened to compensate for the omission of Dagesh); e. g., הָרֹאשׁ.

b. Before ע, also, Qamets is used; except that, when the ע itself has Qamets and is unaccented, the article takes Segol; e. g., הֶעָיֵף, הָעֹבֵד.

c. Before ה or ח, the article retains the simple Pathah; e. g., הַחֹדֶשׁ, הַהוּא; except that—

(1) When the ה has Qamets, or the ח has either Qamets or Hateph Qamets, the article regularly takes Segol; e. g., הֶחָמָרִים, הֶחָג, הֶהָדָר.

---

*1 Originally it was probably הַל; but if so, the ל was assimilated into the following consonant (which is the probable origin of the D.F.).

(2) With a few special words, the article takes Qamets; e. g., הָהָר (see below in 2), הָהֵמָה (see Ch. X, C, 1, a).

d. Summary of the rules:

Before	the article is pointed
(1) Ordinary consonants	הַ·
(2) ה or ח—except as in (5)	הַ
(3) ע—except as in (5)	הָ
(4) א or ר	הָ
(5) עָ (unaccented), הָ, חָ, or חֶ	הֶ

2. In three common nouns, אֶרֶץ, הַר, and עַם, a vowel is lengthened when the article is prefixed; the forms then are הָאָרֶץ, הָהָר, and הָעָם[1]. In the plural these words follow regular rules.

3. The definite article is used in Hebrew whenever it is in English—except as stated in Ch. XV. Also, —

a. When a noun is used in the "vocative," the article is usually prefixed to it as a sign of this use; e.g., לֹא שָׁמַע הָאִישׁ אֵלֶיךָ הַמֶּלֶךְ, "The man did not hearken unto thee, O King."

*b. It is frequently used in a *generic* sense, where the English might use an indefinite article (for which Hebrew has no real equivalent)[2], or none at all; especially so with an individual thing taken as a

---

*[1] Similarly also in the case of הַצַּר, צָר, and a few other words.

*[2] The numeral אֶחָד, "one," is sometimes used for "a, an."

type and name of the class to which it belongs, or with a whole category of objects taken collectively, or with an abstract noun.

* c. It is also used with certain proper names, to indicate the individual as the supreme member of the class; thus אֱלֹהִים often takes the article;   so does לְבָנוֹן ("the white").

B. Elements of Sentence Structure

1. The name *verbal sentence* is commonly used for a sentence in which the predominant feature is a finite verb — i.e., one which can make some assertion of action (or, less commonly, of condition) about a subject.

a. *The predicate usually precedes the subject*, for the vivid nature of Hebrew gives to the action the place of prominence and emphasis[1]. If the subject is a personal pronoun, it is not usually expressed, but is contained in the verb.

b. A direct object usually follows the subject[1]. If it is a *definite* noun, the particle אֵת, called the *sign of the accusative*, is regularly used before it[2]. This is usually joined to the noun by Maqqeph, and then the Tsere is

---

[1] To secure varied emphasis, and under other special conditions, the order is often varied.

[2] If a verb has two coördinate (definite) direct objects, *both* take אֵת. This particle is never used with an indefinite noun, or with the indirect object of a verb, or with the object of a preposition; and it is frequently omitted in poetry. A noun is made definite by the definite article, a demonstrative, a possessive pronoun, or a genitival modifier.

shortened to Segol (cf. note 1, page 24); e.g., רָאָה הָאִישׁ
אֶת־הַמֶּלֶךְ, "The man saw the king."

2. The term *nominal sentence* is commonly applied to sentences in which a noun, pronoun, adjective, adverb, participle, or prepositional phrase gives a description of the subject, without any verbal action[1].

a. The essential parts of such a sentence are the two nouns (or other equivalent words); and in Hebrew they are commonly written *without any copula*—a word such as "to be" not being a necessity[2]; e.g., הָאִישׁ הַמֶּלֶךְ, "The man is the king." Time must be inferred from the context.

b. *The subject regularly comes first, the predicate nominative second,* when both are nouns.

---

[1] Hebrew grammarians also apply this term to sentences which have a finite verb *following* the subject; for, in such, the attention is focused on the noun, and it has assumed greater importance than the verbal action (cf. Ch. XXXII, B).

[2] The verb הָיָה, which properly means "to become," is sometimes used as is our *to be*; and a few other special methods of coupling are sometimes used. The predicate nominative is often referred to as *the predicate*, for it fulfills almost the same assertive function with reference to the subject as does the verb in a verbal sentence.

VOCABULARY

אִישׁ	man, husband (plu. אֲנָשִׁים).	נָבִיא	prophet
		עַל	upon; near; concerning
בַּת	(f) daughter (plu. בָּנוֹת)	עִם	with
הֵיכָל	temple, palace	זָכַר	to remember
הַר	mountain	רָאָה	to see, look
מֶלֶךְ	king	שָׁמַע	to hear, hearken

Note: All nouns are masculine, except those marked (f). The verbs are in the 3ms Perfect; e.g., the form זָכַר means "He remembered."

EXERCISES

1) רָאָה הַנָּבִיא אֶת־הָהָר: 2) זָכַר אֶת־הָאֲנָשִׁים:
3) הָאִישׁ עִם הַבַּת עַל־הַהֵיכָל: 4) שָׁמַע הַנָּבִיא אִתְּךָ (thee)
הַמֶּלֶךְ (See A, 3, a): 5) רָאָה הַמֶּלֶךְ אֲנָשִׁים עַל־הָהָר:
6) הָאִישׁ נָבִיא: 7) שָׁמַע הַמֶּלֶךְ עַל הַבָּנוֹת: 8) הַבָּנוֹת
עַל הַהֵיכָל: 9) הַנָּבִיא עִם הַמֶּלֶךְ: 10) זָכַר אֶת־הַהֵיכָל:
11) הַבַּת עַל־הָהָר:

1. The king remembered the temple. 2. The daughters are near the mountain. 3. The prophet saw men. 4. The king is with the man. 5. He heard concerning the prophet. 6. Ye (אַתֶּם) are near the temple, O men. 7. He saw a mountain. 8. The king is near the

palace.   9. The men are near the temple.   10. The king
heard a prophet.   11. The husband remembered the
daughter.

Prefix the article to the following words:

רֶגֶל, דָּבָר, אֶרֶץ, חֲלִי, קָנֶה, עֵץ, חַטָּאת, עַם, הַזֶּה,

נַעַר, רִיב, הָמוֹן, בְּרִית, עָב, חָנוּת, סֵפֶר, עָוֹן, מָגֵן, עִיר,

חֳדָשִׁים.

CHAPTER VIII

PREPOSITIONS

A. The Inseparable Prepositions

1. There are three prepositions which are always written as prefixes to their objects:

a. בְּ, meaning "in, on (of place or time); among; with (indicating means, instrument, or manner—not accompaniment)."

b. כְּ, meaning "like; according to."

c. לְ, meaning "to, for." It includes various "dative" uses, such as—

> (1) Indirect object; e.g., נָתַן אִישׁ לַבַּת, "He gave the daughter a husband."
>
> (2) Dative of advantage or disadvantage; e.g., הַהֵיכָל לַמֶּלֶךְ "The palace is for the king."
>
> (3) Dative of possession; e.g., בַּת לָאִישׁ (*lit.*, A daughter is to the man), "The man has a daughter."
>
> (4) It may also indicate direction towards, altho אֶל is more common in this meaning.

2. The standard pointing of these prepositions is Shewa; e.g., לְהַר, "to a mountain". There are the following variations (cf. Ch. III, B, 1):

a. Before a simple Shewa, it becomes Hireq; e.g., "for a blessing" is לִבְרָכָה, in place of the impossible לְבְרָכָה.

> (1) An initial י carrying Shewa drops its Shewa and

49

coalesces with the Hireq, forming Long Hireq;

e.g., בִּירִיחוֹ becomes בִּירִיחוֹ, "in Jericho."

b. Before a compound Shewa, the preposition takes the corresponding full short vowel; e.g., "like men" is כַּאֲנָשִׁים, in place of the impossible כְּאֲנָשִׁים.

(1) With the divine names, this short vowel and the Hateph vowel coalesce into one vowel under the preposition, the א becoming silent ; כֵּאלֹהִים becomes כֵּאלֹהִים; and לַאֲדֹנָי becomes לַאדֹנָי; and, as the vowel points of אֲדֹנָי are used with יְהוָֹה (note 5, page 30), "to Jehovah" is לַיהוָֹה.

c. When prefixed to a noun which has the article, the ה of the article (which is a very weak letter) is *elided*, and the preposition takes the vowel which the article had in place of its own Shewa; e.g., לְהַמֶּלֶךְ becomes לַמֶּלֶךְ, "for the king." This is a peculiarity of these three prepositions only.

*d. Qamets is used in some cases: under ל with the infinitives of several weak verbs, before a strong disjunctive accent, and with a few special words; under בּ and כּ only with the demonstratives[1].

B. Other Prepositions

1. The preposition מִן, meaning "from,"[2] is *usually*

---

*[1] Likewise, the conjunction ו has Qamets with words stated in pairs, and before a strong disjunctive accent.

*[2] It is also sometimes used *partitively;* e.g., יָצְאוּ מִן־הָעָם (Ex. 16:27), "Some of the people went out."

prefixed to its object.   The וּ is a very weak letter, and is readily assimilated into the following consonant—which, being thus doubled, takes D.F. (Ch. IV, A, 3, b); e.g., "from a king" is מִמֶּלֶךְ instead of מִנְמֶלֶךְ (*mimmelek* for *minmelek*).

a. But before a guttural or ר, which cannot take the D.F., the Hireq is lengthened to Tsere in compensation for the omitted Dagesh (Ch. V, D, 1); e.g., מִן plus הַר gives מֵהַר, in place of the impossible מִהַר[1].

b. When the word begins with a י carrying Shewa, the Dagesh is omitted (Ch. IV, A, 2, b); the י then drops the Shewa and coalesces with the Hireq to make Long Hireq, just as with the Inseparables; e.g., "from Jericho" is מִירִיחוֹ, in place of מִירְיחוֹ.

c. If the noun has the article, מִן may be, and frequently is, written separately in full; e.g., מִן־הָהָר, "from the mountain."

2. All other prepositions are written as separate words before noun objects; but it is not uncommon to join them with Maqqeph.

3. Prepositions are not infrequently compounded; e.g., מֵעַל (for מִן־עַל), "from upon, from."

VOCABULARY

אֱלֹהִים God; gods	בְּרָכָה (f) blessing; gift
אֶרֶץ (f) earth, land, country (*see* 7, A, 2)	יְהוָֹה Jehovah (*instead of this pronounce* אֲדֹנָי)
בֵּן son (plu. בָּנִים)	יְרוּשָׁלֵם Jerusalem

---

*[1] In a very few cases Hireq is retained, the guttural having Dagesh Implicit; e.g., מְהִיוֹת, מְחוּץ.

עַם people (*see* 7, A, 2)   הָלַךְ to go, walk

אֶל unto   יָשַׁב to sit; dwell, inhabit

אֶת with   נָתַן to give

EXERCISES

1) הָעָם בָּאָרֶץ: 2) הַנָּבִיא כַּמֶּלֶךְ: 3) רָאָה הַבֵּן הֵיכָל
בִּירוּשָׁלֵם: 4) בַּת לַנָּבִיא: 5) שָׁמַע הָאִישׁ לַיהוָֹה: 6) הָלַךְ
הַמֶּלֶךְ מֵהָהָר: 7) נָתַן בְּרָכָה לֵאלֹהִים: 8) רָאָה אֶת־
הָאָרֶץ מֵעַל הָהָר: 9) הָאָרֶץ לָעָם: 10) הַבָּנִים בַּהֵיכָל:
11) יָשַׁב הָעָם אֶת־הָאָרֶץ: 12) הָלַךְ הַבֵּן אֶת הָאִישׁ אֶל־
יְרוּשָׁלֵם:

1. He went unto the country for a prophet. 2. The
king had sons. 3. The husband heard from a prophet.
4. He gave the temple to the people with a blessing.
5. The people went from God. 6. The earth is Jehovah's·
7. The son dwelt in Jerusalem with the daughter. 8. He
dwelt like a prophet among men. 9. He looked from the
palace to the country. 10. God gave the country a prophet. 11. The sons are like the king.

CHAPTER IX

MISCELLANEOUS PARTICLES

A. Interrogatives

1. There is no question mark in Hebrew. Simple questions, not introduced by an interrogative pronoun or adverb, are indicated by prefixing to the first word of the sentence the so-called *He Interrogative*—הַ pointed, ordinarily, with Hateph Pathah; e.g., הֲרָאָה אֶת־הָאִישׁ, "Did he see the man?"[1]   There are the following variations in the pointing:

a. If the first vowel of the word is Shewa, the Hateph Pathah must heighten to full Pathah; e.g., הַבְּרָכָה.

b. Before any guttural, unless it have Qamets, the הַ has Pathah; e.g., הָאִישׁ.

c. Before any guttural with Qamets, the הַ has Segol; e.g., הֶאָמַר.

2. There are two interrogative pronouns: מִי, "Who?" (invariable in form), and מַה, "What?" The usual position for either is first in a sentence.

---

[1] The interrogative particle is sometimes omitted—to inject an element of sarcasm into the question, or for metric or euphonic reasons ; e.g., Ex. 8:22; 1 Sam. 11:12.

a. מָה is usually joined by Maqqeph to the following word; and it is ordinarily followed by D.F. in the first letter of that word; e.g., מַה־נָּתַן, "What did he give?" Before gutturals it is pointed as follows:

(1) מָה before א, ר, or ע; except as in (3).

(2) מַה before ה or ח; except as in (3).

(3) מֶה before ה, ח, or ע with Qamets[1].

b. "Why?" is expressed by the phrase "For what?"— written לְמָה before ordinary consonants (no D.F. being used after it), לָמָה before gutturals.

c. When used as direct object, מִי takes אֶת; מַה does not.

d. מַה is frequently used in an exclamatory way with a noun, adjective, or verb; e.g., מַה־נּוֹרָא הַמָּקוֹם הַזֶּה (Gen. 28:17), "How dreadful is this place!" (see also Gen. 27:20; Num. 24:5; Ps.8:2).

*3. An *indirect question* is introduced by אִם; so, usually, is the second member of a compound question (e.g., הַהַמֶּלֶךְ בַּהֵיכָל אִם בָּהָר, "Is the king in the palace or on the mountain?"); so also a question to which a negative answer is expected (e.g., אִם זָכַר אֶת־הַנָּבִיא, "He did not remember the prophet, did he?"; אִם שָׁפַטְתִּי אִישׁ אֶחָד בַּשֶּׁקֶר, "Have I judged any man falsely?").

---

*1 The pointing מֶה sometimes occurs before ordinary consonants, especially when Maqqeph is not used; and מָה sometimes precedes a ה.

B. The Conjunction וֹ

ı. The coördinate conjunction is the letter וֹ, written as a prefix to the following word[1]. Its usual pointing is simple Shewa; e.g., הַבֵּן וְהַבַּת, "the son and the daughter." But—

a. Before a *labial* (בּ, מ, or פּ) it becomes Shureq; e.g., וּבֵן, "and a son".

b. Before a word whose first vowel is Shewa, it becomes Shureq (e.g., וּלְאִישׁ, "and for a man"); except that, if a word begins with י carrying Shewa, the וֹ takes Hireq, just as the prepositions do (e.g., וִירִיחוֹ, "and Jericho").

c. Before a compound Shewa (including those in the divine names) it follows the same principles as do the inseparable prepositions.

2. It is frequently used adversatively; the context must decide whether it means *and* or *but* (cf. the Greek δέ).

C. Adverbs

ı. Hebrew has very few adverbs. An ordinary adverb is usually written after the verb or adjective it modifies; sometimes at the beginning of the sentence.

---

[1] When phrases or sentences are joined, it is attached to the first word in the second and succeeding phrases. וֹ...וֹ means "both...and." וֹ is sometimes called the *copula;* when this name is used, it must be carefully distinguished from the other use of the same word—as a name for the connective "to be".

2. The common adverb of negation is לֹא. In a verbal sentence it usually comes first (or, after an interrogative); in a nominal sentence it precedes the word negatived.

D. The Particle כִּי

1. This particle commonly means either "that" (introducing an indirect statement or a result clause—but not a purpose clause), or "for, because".

2. Less frequently it is a conjunction, "when; if". And sometimes it introduces a direct quotation, being equal to our quotation marks or the ὅτι of N.T. Greek.

3. The combination כִּי אִם, by a special idiom, is used after a negative statement to mean "but" (וְ is the regular adversative after a positive statement).

E. Inflection of Nouns

1. The plural of a masculine noun is formed by adding ־ִים to the singular; e. g., הֵיכָל, "palace," הֵיכָלִים, "palaces."

a. Several words with irregular plurals have been given; the feminine אִשָּׁה below has an irregular plural which looks like a masculine; the plural of הַר, which is הָרִים, will also be used.

b. The word אֱלֹהִים is in form a plural. Nevertheless, when used in reference to the true God, it is construed and read as a singular.

2. Hebrew nouns have no case forms. Fuller details are given in Part Three.

VOCABULARY

אָדוֹן master, lord

אִשָּׁה (f) woman; wife (plu. נָשִׁים)

בַּיִת house

מַלְאָךְ messenger; angel

עֳנִי poverty, misery, affliction

קוֹל voice, sound

אִם if; whether

אָמַר to say

בָּנָה to build

רָצָה to delight in, be gracious to(*with Accus.*); receive graciously

שָׁאַל to ask (about, לְ)

EXERCISES[1]

1) לְמִי הָלַךְ לִבְרָכָה: 2) מַה־שָּׁאַל הַבֵּן לַמַּלְאָךְ וְלַמֶּלֶךְ: 3) הַבְנֵה הֵיכָל וּבֵית עַל־הָהָר: 4) שְׁאַל אִם הַבֵּן כָּאָדוֹן: 5) מַה־הֵיכָל לַיהוָֹה: 6) וֵאלֹהִים עִם הַנָּבִיא בָּאָרֶץ:

7) לֹא הָלַךְ לַבַּיִת כִּי אִם שָׁאַל לַבַּת: 8) מִי אָמַר כִּי לֹא אֶת הָעָם יְהוָֹה: 9) אִם הַמַּלְאָךְ פֹּה לָמָה לֹא שָׁמַע

---

1 In several of the longer chapters two sets of exercises are furnished—so arranged that the chapter may easily be divided if desired. The first half of each set covers the first half of the grammatical material of the chapter; and, in so far as practicable, only the words of the first vocabulary are used in the whole first set and the first half of the second set—the second vocabulary containing less important words.

אֶת־הַקּוֹל: 10) מִי הָלַךְ אֶל־הַנָּבִיא כִּי הַמֶּלֶךְ בָּעֳנִי:
11) הָאִישׁ פֹּה בַּבַּיִת: 12) רָאָה הָאָדוֹן אֶת־הָאִשָּׁה וְלֹא
רָצָה אֹתָהּ (her):

1. Whom did the messenger remember? 2. He asked whether he delighted in the temple and the house (*note 2, page 45*). 3. Both men and gods were on the mountain. 4. Did he build the house and not inhabit (it)? 5. And what did the master say in affliction? 6. Why did he not hear a sound from the son?

7. The son inhabited the house because the master said (so). 8. Who asked about the palaces? 9. He did not see the messengers here, but he heard the women. 10. Why did he say that the voice was from the prophet, if he did not hear (it)? 11. The messenger went unto the mountains, but the king did not go.

SUPPLEMENTARY VOCABULARY

אֶבֶן	(f) stone	כֶּרֶם	vineyard
גָּמָל	camel	אוֹ	or
חֲלוֹם	dream		
יְרִיחוֹ	Jericho	אַחֲרֵי	behind; after
יִשְׂרָאֵל	Israel	עַד	as far as; until
כֶּלֶב	dog	פֹּה	here

SUPPLEMENTARY EXERCISES

1) לָמָּה בָנָה הָאִישׁ אֶת־הַבַּיִת וְאֶת־הַהֵיכָל: 2) הֲנָתַן
הָאָדוֹן אֶת־הַבְּרָכָה אוֹ הַבֵּן: 3) וַאֲנָשִׁים כֵּאלֹהִים בָּאָרֶץ:
4) לָמָּה רָצָה הַמַּלְאָךְ אֶת־הַקּוֹל: 5) הַבָּנִים בָּעֳנִי:
6) הֲהָלַךְ הַנָּבִיא לָאִשָּׁה:

7) בַּחֲלוֹם רָאָה כִּי הַנָּשִׁים בֶּהָרִים: 8) לֹא יָשַׁב
בַּכֶּרֶם כִּי אִם הָלַךְ אֶל־הַבַּיִת: 9) לֹא הָלַךְ לִירוּשָׁלַם
אוֹ עַד יְרִיחוֹ: 10) זָכַר כִּי שָׁמַע אֶת־הַקּוֹל פֹּה: 11) הַכֶּלֶב
לֹא לָאִשָּׁה כִּי נָתַן אֹתוֹ (it) לַבֵּן: 12) הַגָּמָל בַּכֶּרֶם וְהָאָדוֹן
עַל הָאָבֶן:

1. What a house the son built! 2. And poverty is in
the land. 3. The prophet had a wife and a son and a
daughter. 4. Who asked for a gift? 5. Why did the
master delight in the angel?

6. The camel and the vineyard are the master's.
7. The stone is not in Jericho. 8. When he saw the dog
he remembered the dream. 9. The king did not hear the
son or the wife. 10. Did he graciously receive the messengers from Israel? 11. The master did not dwell here,
but he built a house.

CHAPTER X

ADJECTIVES AND DEMONSTRATIVES

A. Inflection of Adjectives

There are no case forms. Gender and number are indicated by adding the following afformatives:

Fem. Sing., הָ—; e.g., טוֹבָה, fem. of טוֹב

Masc. Plu., יִם—; e.g., טוֹבִים, plu. of טוֹב

Fem. Plu., וֹת—; e.g., טוֹבוֹת, plu. of טוֹבָה

B. Position and Agreement

1. An *attributive* adjective—i.e., one which directly modifies and simply describes a noun—is written immediately after it, and always agrees with it in gender and number. *If the noun is definite, the adjective also takes the definite article;* e.g., הַבַּת הַטוֹבָה, "the good daughter."

2. A *predicate* adjective—i.e., one which makes some assertion about the noun — usually *stands first in the sentence, and does not take the article* (even tho its noun be definite); e.g., "The woman is good" is written טוֹבָה הָאִשָּׁה—the Hebrew order of thought being "Good (is) the woman." If there is one subject, the adjective agrees with it in gender and number; but if there are two or more (noun) subjects, it agrees with the nearer[1].

---

*[1] But if there are two pronoun subjects, it is plural, taking the

C. The Demonstratives

	Masc.	Fem.		Masc.	Fem.
this	זֶה	זֹאת	that	הוּא	הִיא
these	אֵלֶּה		those	הֵן or הֵנָּה הֵם or הֵמָּה	

1. When used *attributively*, a demonstrative is exactly like an adjective. It follows the noun; and, since it makes the noun definite, both take the article; e.g., הָאִישׁ הַזֶּה, "this man."

a. With the words הֵמָּה, הֵם, and הֵנָּה, the article is irregularly pointed with Qamets (Ch. VII, A, 1, c, [2]).

b. The demonstrative is placed after an ordinary adjective; e.g., הַנָּשִׁים הַטּוֹבוֹת הָהֵנָּה, "those good women."

2. When a demonstrative is used *pronominally*, it regularly *stands first in the sentence, without the article;* e.g., הוּא הָאִישׁ, "That is the man." This is called the *predicate position,* altho in English the demonstrative stands as subject; the noun is really the logical subject.

D. Adjectives Used as Substantives

1. As in other languages, an adjective can be used with the article as the equivalent of a noun; e.g., הַטּוֹבִים מֵתוּ

---

gender of the nearer. Also, a pronoun subject often precedes the predicate adjective, especially if it be second person.

קְטַנִּים, "The good die young"[1]. Of course, in this usage, it can have the article even when predicate.

2. The *feminine*, singular or plural, is used without the article as an indefinite neuter; e. g., שָׁמַע גְּדוֹלוֹת, "He heard great things." The same is true of the demonstrative; e. g., זָכַר זֹאת, "He remembered this."

E. Comparison

There are no special inflectional forms for the comparative and superlative; rather clumsy circumlocutions are used to express these ideas.

1. To express the comparative, the preposition מִן is used (indicating *separation from* in a qualitative sense); e.g., חָזָק אֲנִי מִן־הָאִישׁ (*lit.*, Strong am I from the man), "I am stronger than the man"[2].

2. There are two methods of expressing the superlative:

a. Emphasizing the comparative idea by means of the word כֹּל, "all"; e.g., רָם הוּא מִכֹּל הֶהָרִים, (*lit.*, High is that one from all the mountains), "That is the highest mountain."

This word כֹּל is not an adjective, but a noun, and therefore is not

---

[1] So especially when the English would use an indefinite "men" with a partitive genitive (Ch. XXV, 1, c).

[2] This form of expression has extended uses; e.g., עָיֵף מִקּוּם הוּא, (*lit.*, He is weak from to arise), "He is too weak to arise"; אָהַב אֶת־יוֹסֵף מֵאֶחָיו, "He loved Joseph from his brothers—i.e., more than his brothers."

inflected to agree with the following noun. It is usually, however, joined by Maqqeph, and then its vowel is shortened to Qamets Hatuph; e. g., כָּל־הַמַּלְאָכִים, "all (of) the messengers."

b. Emphasizing the adjectival idea itself; either—

(1) By the addition of a qualifying phrase with בְּ; e.g., הָאִישׁ הָרָם בְּיִשְׂרָאֵל, (lit., the tall man in Israel), "the tallest Israelite"[1]; or,

(2) Simply with the definite article; e.g., הַכֶּרֶם הַגָּדוֹל לַמֶּלֶךְ, (lit., The vineyard, the large one, is to the king), "The king has the largest vineyard."

VOCABULARY

בְּרִית (f) covenant		חָכָם wise	
סוּס horse		טוֹב good	
עֶבֶד servant		צַדִּיק just, righteous	
רֹאשׁ head;top(plu. רָאשִׁים)			
שַׁעַר gate		רָם high, tall	
גָּדוֹל great, large		מְאֹד very	

EXERCISES

1) זָכַר הָעֶבֶד הַזֶּה אֶת־הַבְּרִית הַטּוֹבָה הַהִיא: 2) הוּא הַר רָם וְלֹא רָמִים הֶהָרִים הָאֵלֶּה: 3) רָאָה סוּס גָּדוֹל

---

[1] Another form, the equivalent of this, is the use of the adjective in the Cst.; e.g., רָם בָּנַי, (lit., the tall one of my sons), "my tallest son."

עַל־הַשַּׁעַר הַהוּא: 4) טוֹבוֹת מְאֹד הַבָּנוֹת הָהֵנָּה: 5) מַה־
צַדִּיק הַמֶּלֶךְ הֶחָכָם הַהוּא: 6) הֲלֹא רָם מְאֹד הָרֹאשׁ:
7) חָכָם מִן־הָעֶבֶד הָאָדוֹן: 8) הֲזָכַר הַנָּבִיא הַצַּדִּיק
זֹאת: 9) שָׁאַל לְעֶבֶד הֶחָכָם בַּהֵיכָל: 10) טוֹבָה מִכָּל־
הַנָּשִׁים הָהֵן הַבַּת הַהִיא: 11) וְגָדוֹל אֱלֹהִים מֵאִישׁ:
12) הֲזֶה הַמַּלְאָךְ הַטּוֹב:

1. Those women are very good, but this is not a good woman. 2. Who was not gracious to that wise servant when he built these high palaces? 3. This master and those messengers are great. 4. He did not go from the house with the messengers, but he said, "These are righteous men." 5. That woman on the horse near that gate is from this good country.

6. That king was the wisest in Israel when he said this.* 7. These women are not better than those men. 8. This righteous prophet is the greatest of these sons. 9. He said good things here about the righteous. 10. He went to the highest mountain, but did not dwell upon the top.

SUPPLEMENTARY VOCABULARY

יְאֹר river (*especially the Nile*)   חִיצוֹן outer

שֻׁלְחָן table   קָרוֹב near

שָׁמַיִם heaven (*a plural*)   רִאשׁוֹן first

אַחֵר other, another   תָּמִים upright, perfect

חָזָק strong   אַחֲרֵי־כֵן afterwards

1) הֲלֹא רָמִים הֶהָרִים הָהֵמָּה: 2) חָכָם הָאִישׁ וְהָאִשָּׁה:
3) הָלַךְ הַמֶּלֶךְ הַגָּדוֹל הַזֶּה אֶת הָעֶבֶד הַהוּא אֶל הָאִשָּׁה
הַזֹּאת: 4) הַנָּשִׁים הַטּוֹבוֹת הָאֵלֶּה בְּעֵינָי: 5) הִיא אֶבֶן
רָמָה: 6) טוֹבָה הָאָרֶץ וְהָעָם:
7) הַמַּלְאָךְ הַתָּמִים הַזֶּה לֹא קָרוֹב לָאָדוֹן מִן־הָעֶבֶד
הָאַחֵר הַהוּא: 8) אַחֲרֵי־כֵן נָתַן לַבֵּן אֶת־הַשֻּׁלְחָן הֶחָזָק
בִּירוּשָׁלֵם: 9) רָמִים הַשָּׁמַיִם מֵהֶהָרִים: 10) גָּדֹל מִכָּל־
הַהֵיכָלִים הַבַּיִת עַל־הַיְאֹר: 11) חָזָק הַשַּׁעַר הַחִיצוֹן מִזֶּה:
12) אָמַר כִּי זֹאת הַבְּרִית הָרִאשׁוֹנָה אֶת הָעָם בָּאָרֶץ
הַזֹּאת:

1. Isn't that covenant good?   2. How high those mountains are!   3. This man went unto that high gate, for he
heard a very great sound.   4. Did the prophet give a
blessing to those good daughters?   5. Has the wise messenger a large head?

6. Is this high gate the greatest in the outer temple?
7. Is another man stronger than the king?   8. God is
near unto the just, for He delights in a perfect people.
9. Afterwards he said that that was the first good table
in this house.   10. Are not the heavens much higher than
the earth (*say*, very high from)?

CHAPTER XI

PERSONAL PRONOUNS. PERFECT TENSE

A. The Nominative Forms of the Pronouns

1. In this table are shown the simple forms of the pronouns, which are used as "Nominatives." The forms used in the "oblique cases" are given in the following chapters.

אָנֹכִי, אֲנִי I	אֲנַ֫חְנוּ we
אַתָּה thou (m)	אַתֶּם ye (m)
אַתְּ thou (f)	אַתֵּ֫נָה, אַתֶּן ye (f)
הוּא he, it	הֵ֫מָּה, הֵם they (m)
הִיא she, it	הֵ֫נָּה they (f)

a. When two forms are given, the first is more common[1].

b. Note that the third person forms are the same as the demonstratives.

*c. Several primitive forms are of some importance:

(1) אַתְּ is for אַתִּי (see Ch. IV, A, 2, a and note).

(2) אַתֶּם and אַתֶּן were originally אַתּוּם and אַתִּן.

(3) הוּא was originally of common gender, and is so used thruout the Pentateuch; elsewhere the separate form for the feminine is used.

2. Of course these pronouns find their most common

---

*1 A few other forms occur rarely: אַתָּ, נַ֫חְנוּ.

66

use as subjects of nominal sentences; usually a first or second person pronoun stands first in the sentence, a third person last. Also, to emphasize the subject of a verb, the proper pronoun is sometimes used with it (usually preceding the verb).

*3. A third person pronoun is frequently used in a nominal sentence as the practical equivalent of the copula; e.g., שְׁלֹשֶׁת הַסַּלִּים שְׁלֹשֶׁת יָמִים הֵם (Gen. 40:18), "The three baskets are three days"[1]. The phrase יְהֹוָה הוּא הָאֱלֹהִים is translated "Jehovah, He is God," for emphasis; but ordinarily no special emphasis is intended, and the pronoun is entirely neglected in translation.

B. Inflection of the Perfect Tense

The *Perfect*, or ordinary past tense, is inflected by adding to the stem the personal endings, which are chiefly fragments of the personal pronouns[2]. In the paradigm, note not only the endings, but also the accent and the changes in the stem itself (i.e., the four forms in which a full vowel is thinned down to vocal Shewa); also the

---

[1] According to strict syntax, the first noun simply states the subject of thought and stands as an absolute, and the real grammatical subject is the pronoun. This usage is common in colloquial English; cf. also Longfellow's line, "The smith, a mighty man is he."

[2] The forms in the first and second persons are undoubtedly the result of the amalgamation of the simple form of the verb with the pronoun subjects originally spoken in full after it; hence it is true in a very real sense that a verb now contains in itself a pronoun subject.

order of conjugation—the 3ms being the simplest or basic form.

3ms	קָטַל	he killed		3cp	קָטְלוּ	they killed
3fs	קָטְלָה	she killed				
2ms	קָטַלְתָּ	thou killedst		2mp	קְטַלְתֶּם	ye killed
2fs	קָטַלְתְּ	thou killedst		2fp	קְטַלְתֶּן	ye killed
1cs	קָטַלְתִּי	I killed		1cp	קָטַלְנוּ	we killed

VOCABULARY

גְּבוּל	boundary, territory		כֹּה	thus (*refers ahead*)
גּוֹי	nation		כֵּן	thus (*refers back*)
דָּבָר	word; thing		לָקַח	to take
זָהָב	gold		מָלַךְ	to rule (over, עַל)
חוֹמָה	(f) wall		שָׁכַח	to forget

EXERCISES

1) וְלֹא אַתְּ אִשָּׁה טוֹבָה: 2) שָׁכְחוּ אֶת־הַחֲלוֹם וְלֹא

לָקְחוּ אֶת־הַזָּהָב: 3) שָׁמְעָה הַבַּת לַנָּבִיא הַזֶּה כִּי חָכָם

הוּא מְאֹד: 4) יָשַׁבְנוּ עַל הַגְּבוּל הַחִיצוֹן: 5) הַשְׁמַעְתֶּם

אֶת־הַדָּבָר הַזֶּה: 6) שָׁאַלְתִּי אִם בַּהֵיכָל הִיא וְאִם בַּחוֹמָה:

7) הָאַתֶּנָה בָעֳנִי הַנָּשִׁים: 8) מָלַכְתָּ עַל־גּוֹי גָּדוֹל: 9) הֲכֵן

אָמְרוּ לַמֶּלֶךְ: 10) אַתֶּם הָאֲנָשִׁים הַצַּדִּיקִים בְּיִשְׂרָאֵל:

‏(11 הֶאָמַרְתָּ הָאָדוֹן כִּי אֲנַחְנוּ טוֹבִים מְאֹד: (12 הֲלֹא
לָקַחְתָּ אֶת־הַגְּבוּל הַהוּא כִּי גָדֹל מְאֹד הוּא:

1. Am I not stronger than these horses? 2. We remembered this wall, for it is high. 3. Thou art great, O God. 4. I did not hear that he is a just man. 5. How good they (f) are! 6. Thus shall the word be from the great king to those nations. 7. Thus ye took that gold. 8. They ruled over those territories. 9. And we are the people from that nation. 10. This woman forgot that blessing. 11. Hast thou said a good word?

CHAPTER XII

THE PRONOUNS AS POSSESSIVES

A. Possessive Pronoun Suffixes

1. Possession by a pronoun is indicated by attaching to the noun a fragmentary, modified form of the pronoun as a suffix[1]; e.g., "my horse" is סוּסִי—i.e., סוּס plus the final ־ִי of אֲנִי (*lit.*, the horse of me).

2. These affixed pronouns have two different forms, according to the number of the noun with which they are used. These we call *singular-noun suffixes* and *plural-noun suffixes;* and the terms *singular suffix* and *plural suffix* indicate the number of the pronoun.

B. Suffixes to Singular Nouns

1. Table of singular-noun suffixes, attached to סוּס:

Singular Suffixes		Plural Suffixes	
סוּסִי	my horse	סוּסֵנוּ	our horse
סוּסְךָ	thy (m) horse	סוּסְכֶם	your (m) horse
סוּסֵךְ	thy (f) horse	סוּסְכֶן	your (f) horse
סוּסוֹ	his horse	סוּסָם	their (m) horse
סוּסָהּ	her horse	סוּסָן	their (f) horse

---

[1] This is the result of a coalescence of the pronoun with the noun; cf. note 2, page 67. The second person suffixes, having כ where the

70

2. Between the noun and the *characteristic* or consonantal part of most of the suffixes, some vowel, full or half, is used. For practical purposes in learning the forms, these may be considered as part of the suffixes—altho most probably they are remnants of primitive case endings on the noun itself, which serve now in a *connective* capacity.

C. Suffixes to Plural Nouns

1. When suffixes are attached to masculine plural nouns, the plural ending ‏םִי‎— is modified—the ‏ם‎ being entirely dropped and the vowel changed. In learning the resulting forms, it is probably best to memorize the entire endings as added to the noun stem.

2. Paradigm of ‏סוּסִים‎ with suffixes:

Singular Suffixes		Plural Suffixes	
‏סוּסַי‎	my horses	‏סוּסֵינוּ‎	our horses
‏סוּסֶיךָ‎	thy (m) horses	‏סוּסֵיכֶם‎	your (m) horses
‏סוּסַיִךְ‎	thy (f) horses	‏סוּסֵיכֶן‎	your (f) horses
‏סוּסָיו‎	his horses	‏סוּסֵיהֶם‎	their (m) horses
‏סוּסֶיהָ‎	her horses	‏סוּסֵיהֶן‎	their (f) horses

D. Special Notes

1. Since a suffix makes a noun definite, an attributive adjective modifier takes the article; e.g., "his large horse" is ‏סוּסוֹ הַגָּדוֹל‎; also, ‏סוּסוֹ הַגָּדוֹל הַהוּא‎ would be translated "that large horse of his."

"nominative" forms have ‏ן‎, probably come from primitive alternative forms ‏אַךְ‎, ‏אֲכֶם‎, etc. The form ‏וֹ‎— is contracted from ‏הוּ‎—.

2. In the English sentences the solemn style is adopted for the second person pronouns, in order to show their number readily. All pronouns are masculine in gender unless they refer to a feminine noun or are marked (f).

3. Discriminate between the following terms: an *afformative* is an inflectional ending qualifying the word itself (e.g., the plural ending ‎‏ם‎‏‎‏-‎‏); a *suffix* is some other word added on (e.g., ‎‏ו‎‏‎‏—‎‏, "his"); *ending* is a comprehensive term for either or both.

4. Table of the endings analyzed to show: (1) the pronoun fragments proper; (2) the "connecting vowels" for the singular-noun suffixes, and the ‎‏י‎‏ with its several vowels for the plural-noun suffixes[1]:

Singular Suffixes to		Plural Suffixes to	
Sing. Nouns	Plu. Nouns	Sing. Nouns	Plu. Nouns
‎‏י‎‏‎‏ִ‎‏(—)	(‎‏ַ‎‏י)	‎‏נוּ‎‏(—)	‎‏נוּ‎‏(‎‏ֵ‎‏י)
‎‏ךָ‎‏(‎‏ְ‎‏)	‎‏ךָ‎‏(‎‏ֶ‎‏י)	‎‏כֶם‎‏(—)	‎‏כֶם‎‏(‎‏ֵ‎‏י)
‎‏ךְ‎‏(‎‏ֵ‎‏)	‎‏ךְ‎‏(‎‏ִ‎‏י)	‎‏כֶן‎‏(—)	‎‏כֶן‎‏(‎‏ֵ‎‏י)
‎‏ו‎‏(—)	‎‏ו‎‏(‎‏ָ‎‏י)	‎‏ם‎‏(‎‏ָ‎‏)	‎‏הֶם‎‏(‎‏ֵ‎‏י)
‎‏ה‎‏(‎‏ָ‎‏)	‎‏הָ‎‏(‎‏ֶ‎‏י)	‎‏ן‎‏(‎‏ָ‎‏)	‎‏הֶן‎‏(‎‏ֵ‎‏י)

5. All the endings are accented. The first plural suffix to singular nouns is accented on the connecting vowel, and the majority of the plural-noun suffixes on the syllable containing the ‎‏י‎‏; the rest are accented on the characteristic part of the suffix.

6. The second plural suffixes to singular nouns, and the second and third plural suffixes to plural nouns (accented on the ultima), are called *heavy suffixes;* they exert a special influence on the pointing of certain classes of nouns. All other suffixes are called *light.*

---

[1] In the form ‎‏י‎‏‎‏—‎‏, the ‎‏י‎‏ of the suffix has coalesced with the ‎‏י‎‏ of the plural afformative.

VOCABULARY

בְּהֵמָה   (f) beast; cattle   מִשְׁפָּחָה   (f) family; clan

בְּכוֹר   first-born   צֹאן   flock

דּוֹר   generation

דָּם   blood   רֵעַ   friend; neighbor
                  (*see note 2, page 27*)

יָד   (f) hand   עַתָּה   now

מִשְׁכָּן   dwelling-place   תָּפַשׂ   to seize; hold

EXERCISES

1) שָׁכַח דּוֹרְכֶם אֶת־מִשְׁכָּנִי: 2) הֲשָׁמַע בְּכוֹרָם זֹאת:
3) לָמָה לֹא לָקַח אֶת־יָדֵךְ: 4) מָלַכְתִּי עַל־גְּבוּלוֹ הַגָּדוֹל:
5) הֲלֹא מִיָּדִי תָּפַשְׂתָּ אֶת־רֹאשׁוֹ הָאִישׁ: 6) זָכְרָה אֶת־
הֶהָרִים הָרָמִים בָּאָרֶץ הַהִיא וְלֹא אֶת־יָאֳרָהּ:
7) עַתָּה לֹא עַל־יָדֵי דָּמְךָ: 8) תָּפְשׂוּ בָנֶיךָ אֶת־הַבְּהֵמָה
מִן־הַמִּשְׁפָּחָה הַהִיא: 9) יָשְׁבָה עִם רֵעֶיהָ בִּגְבוּלֵיהֶם:
10) אָמְרוּ נָשַׁי כִּי סוּסֵיהֶן טוֹבִים מְאֹד: 11) שָׁמַעְתִּי כִּי
צֹאנָיו בְּמִשְׁכָּנֵנוּ: 12) הַגָּדוֹל בָּאָרֶץ אֱלֹהֵיכֶם:

1. My first-born seized their dwelling-place. 2. Your territory is now large. 3. Thy (f) good friend is with his flock. 4. Was her hand upon thy head? 5. Your (f) generation was not wiser than ours.

6. Their God is in His dwelling-place. 7. Their (f) blood is now upon your heads. 8. Did thy sons seize their

flocks? 9. He was not with our men in this country, but he saw its high mountains. 10. His friends remembered your righteous covenant with this clan.

SUPPLEMENTARY VOCABULARY

גֵּר stranger; sojourner   מְדִינָה (f) province

חֲמוֹר ass   עֵד witness

יְרִיעָה (f) curtain   צוּר rock

כְּרוּב cherub   בָּלַע to swallow

מִגְדָּל tower   בָּקַע to cleave

SUPPLEMENTARY EXERCISES

‏1) יָדוֹ עַל־רֹאשָׁהּ: 2) מִי טוֹב מִמַּלְאָכְךָ: 3) כִּי הָלַךְ
אֶל־הַמִּשְׁפָּחָה הַהִיא רָאָה אֶת־בְּכוֹרֶךָ: 4) מַה־שָּׁמַע
אִישֵׁנוּ: 5) הֲלֹא הָלַךְ רֵעֲכֶן לְמִשְׁכָּנוֹ הָאַחֵר: 6) הֲרָאָה
אֶת־צֹאנְכֶם בְּמִשְׁכָּנָן:

‏7) זָכְרוּ עֵדֵיהֶם אֶת־מַלְאָכַי וְאֶת־בְּרִיתֵנוּ: 8) הֲשָׁמְעוּ
בָּנֶיךָ אֶת־הַכְּרוּבִים: 9) תָּפְשׂוּ אֲנָשָׁיו אֶת־הַמְּדִינָה הַזֹּאת
וְאֶת־מִגְדָּלֶיהָ: 10) לֹא הָלְכוּ בָנֵי אֶל־הַשַּׁעַר: 11) בָּקַע
אֶת־הָהָר וּבְצוּרָיו בָּנָה אֶת־מִגְדָּלָיו: 12) זָכַר אֶת־הַנָּשִׁים
הָהֵנָּה וְאֶת־רֵעֵיהֶן:

1. Did that family take the cattle from its territory to our dwelling-place? 2. Those women went to their temple. 3. Thou and thy messenger are not good.

4. Is not His temple in Jerusalem? 5. The beast swallowed their blood.

6. His good men went to the outer province. 7. Our wives are in my towers. 8. I said to those women, "They took your horses and your asses to her territories." 9. Thy witnesses, O woman, are better than his. 10. Did ye take that curtain from our sojourners?

CHAPTER XIII

THE PRONOUNS AS OBJECTS

A. Pronouns as Objects of Prepositions

1. A pronoun used as the object of a preposition became amalgamated with it and reduced to a fragmentary suffix, just as in the possessive use; e.g., "with me" is not עִם אֲנִי, but עִמִּי.

2. Some prepositions take object suffixes almost like the possessive suffixes used with singular nouns:

	את	עם	ל	ב	מֶן	כ
1cs	אִתִּי	עִמִּי	לִי	בִּי	מִמֶּ֫נִּי	כָּמֹ֫ונִי
	with me	*with me*	*to me*	*in me*	*from me*	*like me*
2ms	אִתְּךָ	עִמְּךָ	לְךָ	בְּךָ	מִמְּךָ	כָּמֹ֫וךָ
2fs	אִתָּךְ	עִמָּךְ	לָךְ	בָּךְ	מִמֵּךְ	כָּמֹוךְ
3ms	אִתֹּו	עִמֹּו	לֹו	בֹּו	מִמֶּ֫נּוּ	כָּמֹ֫והוּ
3fs	אִתָּהּ	עִמָּהּ	לָהּ	בָּהּ	מִמֶּ֫נָּה	כָּמֹ֫והָ
1cp	אִתָּ֫נוּ	עִמָּ֫נוּ	לָ֫נוּ	בָּ֫נוּ	מִמֶּ֫נּוּ	כָּמֹ֫ונוּ
2mp	אִתְּכֶם	עִמָּכֶם	לָכֶם	בָּכֶם	מִכֶּם	כָּכֶם
2fp	אִתְּכֶן	עִמָּכֶן	לָכֶן	בָּכֶן	מִכֶּן	כָּכֶן
3mp	אִתָּם	עִמָּם	לָהֶם	בָּם	מֵהֶם	כָּהֶם / כְּמֹוהֶם
3fp	אִתָּן	עִמָּן	לָהֶן	בָּהֶן	מֵהֵ֫נָּה	כָּהֵ֫נָּה

a. Note that in the first four (which are very common) Qamets is used in some places instead of Tsere or Shewa as connecting vowel.

b. A lengthened form of כְ, כְּמוֹ, is used before most of the suffixes[1]; and מִן is reduplicated in several forms.

3. Some prepositions take suffixes identical with those used with plural nouns; e.g., אֶל and עַל (note the changes in the vowels of these prepositions themselves):

	אֶל		עַל	
	Sing.	Plu.	Sing.	Plu.
1c	אֵלַי	אֵלֵינוּ	עָלַי	עָלֵינוּ
2m	אֵלֶיךָ	אֲלֵיכֶם	עָלֶיךָ	עֲלֵיכֶם
2f	אֵלַיִךְ	אֲלֵיכֶן	עָלַיִךְ	עֲלֵיכֶן
3m	אֵלָיו	אֲלֵיהֶם	עָלָיו	עֲלֵיהֶם
3f	אֵלֶיהָ	אֲלֵיהֶן	עָלֶיהָ	עֲלֵיהֶן

B. Pronouns as Objects of Verbs

1. A pronoun direct object of a verb is written as a suffix, either to the particle אֵת or to the verb itself; only the first form is given here, the other necessarily being left until the verb is more fully studied.

2. The vowel of the particle has been modified in receiving suffixes; the pronoun as direct object is as follows:

---

*[1] In poetry, this syllable מוֹ is sometimes added to בְ and לְ. And lengthened forms of the third plural suffixes occur; e.g., בָּהֵנָּה, לָהֵמָּה.

אֹתִי me		אֹתָנוּ us	
אֹתְךָ thee		אֶתְכֶם you	
אֹתָךְ thee (f)		אֶתְכֶן you (f)	
אֹתוֹ him		אֹתָם them	
אֹתָהּ her		אֹתָן them (f)	

3. A pronoun object (either direct or indirect) usually stands immediately after the verb.

VOCABULARY

חֶרֶב (f) sword		אָסַר to bind	
כֶּסֶף silver		יָצָא to go out (עַל, against)	
רִיב controversy		כָּרַת to cut, cut off;	
שְׁאוֹל Sheol		בְּרִית אֵת, make a cove-	
		nant with	
שָׁלוֹם peace		עָבַד to serve	
תּוֹרָה (f) law		שָׁלַח to send, send away	

EXERCISES

1) הֲלֹא רִיב לָהֶן עִמָּכֶן: 2) הָאִישׁ הַזֶּה תָּמִים מִמֶּנִּי:
3) נָתְנוּ לָהּ רֵעַי אֶת־הַכֶּסֶף: 4) אָמַרְתְּ לִי כִּי אָסְרוּ אֹתָךְ:
5) מַה־אָמְרוּ אֵלֶיהָ עַל־הַתּוֹרָה: 6) דָּמוֹ עֲלֵיהֶם: 7) כָּרְתוּ
אֶת־רֹאשָׁהּ בַּחֶרֶב וְלֹא שָׁלְחוּ אֹתוֹ אֵלָיו: 8) לֹא שְׁמַעְתֶּם
אֹתִי כִּי אִם שָׁמַעְתִּי אֶתְכֶם: 9) כָּרַתְנוּ בְרִית אַתֶּם לְשָׁלוֹם

כָּכֶם וְלֹא יָצְאוּ עֲלֵיהֶם: 10) הֶעָבְדוּ אֹתְךָ אַחֲרֵי הָרִיב
עִמָּנוּ: 11) בָּלַע אוֹתָם שְׁאוֹל: 12) אֲנַחְנוּ עַם גָּדוֹל מִכֶּם:

1. She gave me this law. 2. They served you, for ye ruled over them. 3. Our horse is stronger than we. 4. We made a covenant with them in peace. 5. Our God is not like us. 6. I took the sword unto her, and with it she cut off his head. 7. The silver is not his. 8. We did not send him unto you (f) for controversy. 9. If those daughters went out with thee, hast thou forgotten them? 10. Did they bind thee, O daughter, and thy friends?

CHAPTER XIV
THE RELATIVE

1. Hebrew has only one relative, אֲשֶׁר[1],—which appears sometimes to be a true relative pronoun ("*who, which*"), sometimes a mere connective particle.

2. In the simpler uses, when the English relative is either the subject of the subordinate clause or the direct object of its verb, the construction offers no difficulty; e.g., הָעֵץ אֲשֶׁר בְּתוֹךְ הַגָּן (Gen. 3:3), "The tree which is in the midst of the garden;" הַבַּת אֲשֶׁר רָאָה, "The daughter whom he saw" (אֵת is not usually used here)[2].

3. This word, however, is quite inflexible—has no possessive form, and is very seldom used as the object of a prepo-

---

*[1] Sometimes in poetry and late writings it is a simple prefixed שׁ, pointed with Segol (occasionally Pathah or Shewa) and followed by D.F.; e.g., in Eccl. 1:3. In poetry the demonstrative is frequently made to do duty for the relative (e.g., Prov. 23:22); sometimes, similarly, the article (e.g., 1 Chron. 26:28). And the relative is not infrequently entirely omitted. (Originally, אֲשֶׁר may have been a demonstrative).

*[2] Sometimes, however, an accusative personal pronoun is added (cf. section 3 above); e.g., שָׂדֶה אֲשֶׁר בֵּרֲכוֹ יְהוָֹה (Gen. 27:27), "A field which Jehovah has blessed (it)." Sometimes also a personal pronoun is introduced as subject, especially in a negative clause; e.g., Gen. 7:2; Num. 14:8.

sition. Therefore, in the more complex constructions, where the English uses a relative in an oblique case, and also in adverbial clauses, the less developed Hebrew must commonly use, in combination with the relative, a personal pronoun or a simple adverb, to express the full thought-relationship. Thus the English sentence, "I remember the man *whose* sons said this," must in Hebrew be phrased "I remember the man *who his* sons said this," ‫זָכַרְתִּי אֶת־‬ ‫הָאִישׁ אֲשֶׁר אָמְרוּ בָנָיו זאת‬[1]. Likewise, the phrase "The mountain *whither* he has gone" becomes "The mountain *which* he has gone *thither*," ‫הָהָר אֲשֶׁר הָלַךְ שָׁמָּה‬; and "All flesh *in which* is the breath of life" (Gen. 6:17) becomes "All flesh *which in it* is the breath of life," ‫כָּל־בָּשָׂר אֲשֶׁר־בּוֹ רוּחַ חַיִּים‬[2].

4. Sometimes, even as in English, the pronoun antecedent is either contained in the relative itself, or is to be supplied before it; e.g., "I remember *what* (i.e., *that which*) he did" is in Hebrew ‫זָכַרְתִּי אֶת־אֲשֶׁר עָשָׂה‬ (here the relative usually takes ‫אֵת‬)[3].

---

1 Cf. the primitive English "John Smith, his book," whence comes our ordinary "John Smith's book," by contraction.

*2 But the extra pronoun is regularly omitted from time clauses (no preposition being used), and occasionally from others; e.g., Gen. 45:6; 43:27. See Ch. XXV, 3.

*3 Less commonly the relative is thus used as subject — e.g., ‫אֲשֶׁר‬ ‫תָּאֹר יוּאָר‬ (Num. 22:6), "(He) whom thou cursest is cursed"; or as object of a preposition — e.g., ‫אָמַר לַאֲשֶׁר עַל בֵּיתוֹ‬ (Gen. 44:4), "He

5. אֲשֶׁר is used after certain prepositions and adverbs to form conjunctions; e.g., אַחֲרֵי־אֲשֶׁר, "after"; כַּאֲשֶׁר (*lit.*, according to that which), "as"[1].

6. In indirect questions the relative is sometimes used, when the substantive idea is very strong; e.g., שָׁאַל אֵת־אֲשֶׁר אָמַרְתָּ , "He asked what you said." But more commonly the question idea is more prominent, and then an interrogative introduces the clause; e.g., לֹא יֵדַע מִי אֹסְפָם (Ps. 39:7), "He does not know who will gather them."

VOCABULARY

גְּבוּרָה	(f) might; strength	כַּאֲשֶׁר	as; when
מִלְחָמָה	(f) war	שָׁם	there
מָקוֹם	place	מִשָּׁם	thence
עֲבוֹדָה	(f) servitude	עָמַד	to stand
קֶרֶן	(f) horn	עָשָׂה	to do, make
אַחֲרֵי־אֲשֶׁר	after	פָּעַל	to do, make (*a poetic word*)

EXERCISES

‫1) וּבָנֵינוּ עַל־הָהָר אֲשֶׁר שָׁמַעְנוּ אֶת־הַקּוֹל מִשָּׁם:‬
‫2) הֲזָכַרְתָּ אֶת־הַמֶּלֶךְ אֲשֶׁר עָמַד מַלְאָכוֹ בַּצּוּר הַזֶּה:‬
‫3) שָׁמַעְתִּי אֶת־אֲשֶׁר פָּעַלְתָּ אַחֲרֵי־אֲשֶׁר תָּפְשׂוּ אֹתְךָ: 4) לֹא‬

---

said to (him) who was over his house"; or conjoined to a construct— e.g., בְּיַד אֲשֶׁר שָׂנֵאת (Ezek. 23:28), "In the hand of (them) whom thou hatest."

*[1] Sometimes, also, by itself, it is a conjunction of purpose (e.g., in Gen. 11:7), of cause (e.g., in Josh. 22:31), etc.

‎5) יָצְאוּ שָׁכַחְתִּי אֶת־הַגְּבוּרָה אֲשֶׁר רָצָה אַתָּה בַּמִּלְחָמָה:
‎אֶל־מִשְׁכָּנֵינוּ כַּאֲשֶׁר אָמַרְנוּ: 6) זֶה הַמָּקוֹם אֲשֶׁר־מִמֶּנּוּ
‎הָלַכְנָה אֵלָיו: 7) הָלַךְ הַמֶּלֶךְ אֶל־הָאִישׁ אֲשֶׁר לָקַח אֶת־
‎הָאִשָּׁה: 8) מֶה הָאָרֶץ אֲשֶׁר יְשַׁבְתֶּם שָׁם: 9) מִי רָאָה אֶת־
‎צֹאנִי אֲשֶׁר בַּמְּדִינָה הַהִיא: 10) יָשַׁב הַנָּבִיא אֶת־הַבַּיִת
‎אֲשֶׁר עָשָׂה־לּוֹ הָעָם: 11) הֲלֹא זֹאת הַחֶרֶב אֲשֶׁר־בָּהּ כָּרַת
‎אֶת־רָאשֵׁיהֶם: 12) רָאָה אֶת־הַקֶּרֶן אֲשֶׁר נָתְנוּ לָכֶם:

1. This is the horn with which he made the sound.
2. We served the man whose messenger took us. 3. I remember what we said concerning the war after they went out. 4. They went to the place where the towers stood. 5. They are the women about whom ye asked. 6. This is the house whence thou wentest, O daughter. 7. This is the servitude from which they went out. 8. Hast thou not gone to the gate which the king made? 9. She made a covenant with him as I said. 10. Those are the witnesses who gave me strength in my controversy.

PART THREE
NOUNS

CHAPTER XV
THE CONSTRUCT STATE

A. Meaning and Form

1. Hebrew has no system of case endings—in fact, no real cases at all. While some thought-relations are expressed by auxiliary words[1], a *"genitival"* relation is indicated simply by closely connecting the two words involved —with, usually, a resulting modification in the form of one.

a. Thus, when an object is named (e.g., חֶרֶב, "sword"), the immediate addition of a determinative word will specify or describe the one meant; e.g., חֶרֶב הַמֶּלֶךְ, "the sword of the king"; חֶרֶב הַזָּהָב, "the sword of gold."

b. Since there was a strong tendency to throw the stress of tone toward the end of a word or phrase in Hebrew speech, the first word of such a compact phrase was passed over lightly and modified in form, while the second retained

---

[1] E.g., some "dative" ideas are indicated by לְ and עַל, some "ablatives" by בְּ and מִן, the "accusative" by אֵת. By a rather loose use of terms, Hebrew words are often said to be "in the dative case", etc., when they stand in the same kind of thought-relations as are expressed by the corresponding cases in Latin. (Only a few fragments of a primitive system of case endings remain; see Ch. XII, *B*,2; Ch. XVI, *E*,3; Ch. LV, *D*, and note).

its ordinary form; e.g., "the word of the prophet" is דְּבַר
הַנָּבִיא—the ordinary דָּבָר having been shortened to דְּבַר.

c. This special modified form is known as the *construct
state*, and a noun in this form is called a *construct*; the ordinary form is called the *absolute state*.

2. Special rules for forming the constructs of various kinds of words are given later. The general principles are:

a. *The vowels were shortened*, whenever possible.

b. *Certain endings were modified in form.*

c. *The article was not used.*

d. In words whose stem or ending cannot be modified, only the absence of the article and the position indicate the use. (This is the case in all the exercises in this chapter).

3. *The construct is not a genitive.* The following noun is sometimes so designated (cf. note 1, page 87); but there is not the same logic of syntax involved as in the Western cases, and a more fitting name would be *Conjoined Noun*[1].

B. Syntax

1. Note this idiomatic peculiarity: the object of immediate interest is regularly placed first, and hence in the Cst. or inflected form; and the qualifying or defining term (such as the owner, in the possessive use) second, and hence

---

[1] Or, *Annexed Noun*, adapting the excellent term *Annexion* with which Harper described the whole construction.

in the Abs. or primary form[1]; e.g., "the man's blood" is written דַּם הָאִישׁ. This type of construction may be partially imitated in English by using the word grouping "the-blood-of the-man," in contrast to our grouping "the-blood of-the-man."

2. Since the Cst. is not a true "case" form, the word can evidently have various syntactical relations to other words in the sentence. Thus it may be subject, direct object, object of a preposition, "vocative," or even conjoined noun to another construct preceding it; e.g.,

בְּנוֹת יִשְׂרָאֵל לָמָה לֹא זְכַרְתֶּן אֶת־דִּבְרֵי חָכְמָה אֲשֶׁר
אָמְרוּ בְּנֵי נְבִיא הָאֱלֹהִים בְּיוֹם הֶחָג

"O-daughters-of Israel, why did ye not remember the-words-of wisdom which the-sons-of the-prophet-of God spoke on-the-day-of the feast?"

a. When the construct is the subject, the verb or predicate adjective agrees with it, not with the absolute; except that the words כֹּל, "all," and מְעַט, "few," are considered to be of such minor importance that the predicate agrees with the conjoined noun which is the logical subject.

b. The construct is usually definite; hence, when used as direct object, it takes אֵת.

3. The construct is so closely united to the absolute that it cannot be separated therefrom by the interposition of any word. Therefore—

---

[1] But in a few uses (e.g., as equivalent to a partitive genitive) the word in the Cst. is of inferior logical importance.

a. If a construct is modified by an attributive adjective this must be put after the absolute instead of immediately after the word modified; e.g., "the great king of the country" would be written מֶלֶךְ הָאָרֶץ הַגָּדֹל.

b. In expressing an idea like "our spirit of peace," *the possessive pronoun cannot be affixed to the construct;* instead, it is attached to the absolute— רוּחַ שְׁלוֹמֵנוּ. Similarly, "my men of war" (i.e., my warriors) is expressed as "the men of my war"— אַנְשֵׁי מִלְחַמְתִּי.

c. Two coördinate constructs cannot be used with one absolute; the possessive idea is repeated by means of a pronoun suffix; e.g., "the head and hand of the man" is רֹאשׁ הָאִישׁ וְיָדוֹ .

d. Similarly, two coördinate absolutes are not used with one construct, but the construct is repeated with the second; e.g., "the king of Israel and Judah" is וּמֶלֶךְ יִשְׂרָאֵל וּמֶלֶךְ יְהוּדָה[1].

4. In the majority of cases the construct is definite; but, since it never has the article, this cannot be clearly indicated. When a definite construct is used with an indefinite absolute the article is sometimes placed with the latter to indicate the definiteness of the former; e. g., אַנְשֵׁי הַמִּלְחָמָה, "the men of war"[2].

VOCABULARY

אוֹר	light	דֶּרֶךְ	way, path; journey
גִּבּוֹר	mighty man; hero	חֶסֶד	mercy, kindness; good-will

---

*[1] This rule, however, is not always strictly adhered to, especially when the two absolutes are very closely related in thought.

*[2] A special application of this principle occurs in certain proper names; e.g., from בֵּית־לָחֶם, "Bethlehem," is formed בֵּית הַלַּחְמִי, "the Bethlehemite" (1 Sam. 16:18).

יֶ֫לֶד child   נֶ֫פֶשׁ (f) soul; life

כֹּל (כָּל־) all; every   קֶ֫רֶב midst

מְעַט little; few; fewness   רוּחַ (f) spirit

נְאֻם oracle   שַׂר prince

EXERCISES

1) שָׁמְעוּ כָל־אֲנָשָׁיו אֹתוֹ: 2) הָאָמְרוּ הַנָּשִׁים הָאֵ֫לֶּה כִּי
טוֹבוֹת מִיַּלְדֵי גְּבוֹרֵ֫נוּ הֵֽנָּה: 3) חֶ֫סֶד יְהֹוָה אוֹר דֶּ֫רֶךְ גּוֹיֵֽנוּ:
4) רָאָה אֶת־בֶּן הַמֶּ֫לֶךְ וְאֶת־סוּסָיו בְּקֶ֫רֶב הַכְּרָ֑ם: 5) בָּעֳנִי
רוּחִי זָכַ֫רְתָּ אֹתִי: 6) זָכְרָה אֶת־גְּבוּל הָאָ֫רֶץ הַהִיא וּמְעַט
יָאֲרִיךָ: 7) הֲלֹא רָצָה אֶת־נֶ֫פֶשׁ בְּכוֹרוֹ: 8) לֹא שָׁכְחָה
בַת־הַשַּׂר הַצַּדִּיקָה אֶת־דּֽוּחַ רִיבוֹ: 9) מִי זָכַר אֶת־נְאֻם
יְהֹוָה אֲשֶׁר אָמַר הַנָּבִיא עַל שַׁ֫עַר יְרוּשָׁלַ֫ם: 10) דֶּ֫רֶךְ
הַטּוֹבִים בְּשָׁלוֹם: 11) כָּרַת אֶת־רֹאשׁ בַּת מַלְאָכִי
הָרִאשׁוֹנָה: 12) לָמָּה לֹא שָׁמַע בְּכוֹר בָּנֶיךָ לְקוֹל אֱלֹהֵֽינוּ.

1. I heard the oracle of Jehovah. 2. The mercy of God was upon the king who walked in the path of peace. 3. The spirit of God is upon the righteous soul of our hero. 4. The prince's child and messenger are in the temple. 5. The people of Israel in the midst of the earth is the light of all the nations. 6. Our nation of heroes is stronger than you. 7. A few women remembered the poverty of the prophet and his men. 8. All of the silver of the king of Israel is for his first-born.

CHAPTER XVI

PRINCIPLES OF INFLECTION

A. Meaning of Inflection and Declension

1. The inflection of a noun includes the dual and plural absolutes, and the constructs and pronoun suffix forms in all three numbers. The following is a *skeleton paradigm* (i.e., a synopsis of the typical or leading forms, from which the full inflection can easily be filled out) of סוּס, and of the plural of the feminine noun תּוֹרָה.

	Sing.	Dual	Plu.	Fem. Plu.
Abs.	סוּס	סוּסַיִם	סוּסִים	תּוֹרוֹת
Cst.	סוּס	סוּסֵי	סוּסֵי	תּוֹרוֹת
1cs	סוּסִי	סוּסַי	סוּסַי	תּוֹרוֹתַי
	etc.	etc.	etc.	etc.
1cp	סוּסֵנוּ	סוּסֵינוּ	סוּסֵינוּ	תּוֹרוֹתֵינוּ
	etc.	etc.	etc.	etc.

2. This inflection causes various *changes in the stems* of most words. We accordingly classify nouns into five special declensions[1], besides the "unchangeables."

---

[1] This classification in the following chapters is not made on a strictly etymological basis, but with a view to helping the beginner to master readily the various inflectional changes; e.g., "fourth declension" nouns are in reality a special variety of the first declension, and most "fifth declension" words come from a segolate-form root.

B. Masculine Plural Construct

The Cst. of a Masc. Plu. is formed by *dropping the* םֹ[1] *and changing Hireq to Tsere*—i.e., by replacing םִי—with —ֵי; e.g., סוּסִים, cst. סוּסֵי.

C. Feminine Nouns

1. All nouns ending in הָ— are feminine[2]; hereafter their gender is not marked. Also, various words are feminine by meaning, especially abstract nouns and those denoting parts of the body or things considered productive.

2. Feminines in ה originally ended in ת; *this* ת *is retained in all inflectional forms,* tho lost in Sing. Abs.[3]

a. In the Sing. Cst., ה is replaced by ת and Qamets is shortened to Pathah; e.g., תּוֹרָה, cst. תּוֹרַת.

b. The Plu. is formed by replacing the הָ— with the plural ending וֹת—; e.g., תּוֹרָה, plu. תּוֹרוֹת. This וֹת— is unchangeable, both in Cst. and before suffixes.

c. Before suffixes to the singular noun, vowel changes occur, as explained later. To the plural noun are added the complete endings used with Masc. plurals, including

---

1 Cf. the elision of a final *m* in Latin poetry.

2 Two apparent exceptions are the words לַיְלָה (see note 1, page 95) and יְהוָֹה.

3 The primitive ת remains in מִשְׁמֶרֶת, דַּעַת, חַטָּאת, בְּרִית, etc. But the ת in מָוֶת, מוֹפֵת, בַּיִת, etc. (masculines) belongs to the stem.

the **י** and its vowels (altho these are really parts of the Masc. Plu. ending); e.g., תּוֹרוֹתֶיךָ, תּוֹרוֹתָיו¹.

3. Feminines which do not end in **ה** are inflected in the Sing. just like masculines. To form the Plu., the **וֹת**– is added directly to the stem; e.g., רוּחַ, plu. רוּחוֹת.

D. The Dual Number

1. Hebrew has a dual number, for nouns only²; it is used chiefly for things occurring in pairs (especially organs of the body), but sometimes also for two objects of any kind.

2. The Abs. is formed by adding **ַיִם**–to the Sing. stem; e.g., יָדַיִם, "hands"; יְרִיעָתַיִם, "pair of curtains."

3. The Cst. is formed by *replacing the* **ַיִם**– *with* **ֵי**–, just as in the Masc. Plu.; e.g., סוּסַיִם, cst. סוּסֵי.

4. Plural-noun suffixes are used, the afformative being modified just as the Masc. Plu. is; e. g., (from סוּסַיִם) סוּסָיו, סוּסֶיךָ, etc.

E. Miscellaneous Notes

1. Some masculine nouns take the Fem. Plu. ending; e.g., קוֹל, plu. קוֹלוֹת. Also, some feminine nouns take the Masc. Plu. ending; e.g., עִיר, plu. עָרִים. Of course in neither case is the actual gender of the word affected.

---

*¹ But frequently for the third person plural suffixes (and occasionally for others), the singular-noun forms are used, which is really more logical; e.g., תּוֹרוֹתָם.

² When an adjective or verb must agree with a dual noun, the plural is used.

2. Some nouns are used in what might be called an adverbial accusative construction; e.g., הַיּוֹם, "to-day."

3. There is also a remnant of an old accusative case remaining in an afformative הָ‍ֽ sometimes attached to nouns and adverbs. It indicates *direction towards*, and is called *He Locative* or *He Directive;* e.g., בָּבֶ֫לָה, "to Babel"[1]. (It is not used with names of persons).

4. All nouns in the Sing. Abs. or Cst. are accented on the ultima, except the "Segolates" (Ch. XVIII). All endings (afformatives and suffixes) are accented, except He Directive.

VOCABULARY

אָרוֹן	ark	מִצְוָה	command[2]
חֹ֫דֶשׁ	new moon; month	עוֹלָה	burnt-offering
חוּץ	street (plu. in וֹת—); Adv. Acc., outside	עִיר	(f) city (plu. עָרִים)
חֲצִי	half	עֲרָבָה	desert (Arabah)
חָצֵר	court; village	פֶּ֫שַׁע	transgression, trespass
יוֹם	day (plu. יָמִים)	שִׂמְחָה	joy; festivity
לַ֫יְלָה	(m) night	מַ֫עַל	above; up
מִנְחָה	meal-offering	שָׁ֫מָּה	thither

---

1 The הָ‍ֽ of לַ֫יְלָה is probably such an accusative ending, of which the force has been lost; the simple form לֵיל also occurs. Words are also used "in the Accusative" (sometimes with אֶת־, seldom with הָ‍ֽ, frequently with no sign) to express extent of space or time, cognate object, "Accusative of specification," etc.

2 The plu. is written מִצְוֺת; see Ch. III, A, 3, a, (3).

EXERCISES

1) נָתַן לָנוּ אֱלֹהִים בְּרָכוֹת מִמַּעַל: 2) הַלַּיְלָה הֵמָּה
עַל־חוֹמוֹת עִירְכֶם: 3) מִי שָׁכַח אֶת־הֶחָצֵר הַהוּא וְאֶת־
הַשִּׂמְחָה בְּחוּצוֹתָיו: 4) הָלְכוּ צֹאנֵי הָאָדוֹן שָׁמָּה בְּיוֹם
הַחֹדֶשׁ: 5) הֲתָפַשְׂתָּ אֶת־עוֹלוֹתֵינוּ בְּיָדֶיךָ: 6) הָלַךְ מַעְלָה
אֶל־רֹאשׁ הָהָר: 7) הֲזָכְרָה אֶת־תּוֹרַת אֱלֹהֵי גּוֹיָהּ וְאֶת־
מִצְוֹתָיו: 8) הַיּוֹם לָקַחְנוּ אֶת־עָרֵי הָעֲרָבָה: 9) יָשְׁבוּ
הָרֵעִים מְחוּץ לְחוֹמַת הָעִיר: 10) הֲזְכַרְתֶּן אֶת־פֶּשַׁע
הַנָּשִׁים הָהֵנָּה בַּמָּקוֹם הַהוּא: 11) הֶעֱמַדְתָּ בֶּחָצֵר אַחֲרֵי־
אֲשֶׁר שָׁמַעְתָּ אֶת־קוֹלוֹתֵיהֶן: 12) אָמְרוּ כִּי לָקַחְתֶּם אֶת־
חֲצִי מִנְחֹתֵיהֶם מִן־הַהֵיכָל:

1. Her sons seized the province of that clan, according to the command of the prince. 2. Did not the cities of Israel forget half the laws of Jehovah? 3. The two messengers went with presents to the heroes of the day of affliction. 4. They cut off his hands and his head near the outer boundaries of the country. 5. What did he do concerning the transgression of the prophet's servant above (*say*, from above to) the vineyard? 6. Who remembers the streets and the walls of this village? 7. This is the ark which went with us all our days in the desert. 8. Jehovah did not delight in your burnt-offerings and meal-offerings and the festivity of your generation.

Write the full inflection of גִּבּוֹר; plural of חוֹמָה.

CHAPTER XVII
FIRST DECLENSION

A. Character of the Words. Tone-Long Vowels

1. This declension consists of words having *tone-long* Qamets or Tsere, which undergo changes in the inflection (Ch. III, B, 2)[1].

2. A tone-long vowel is one which has been *heightened from an original short vowel under the influence of the accent.* The vowel in the syllable receiving the main stress, and that in the one before it (if open) were commonly thus prolonged (e.g., from the primitive מִשְׁכַּן, נַבִיא, and דַּבֵּר were developed the present נָבִיא, מִשְׁכָּן, and דָּבָר); so also a vowel separated from the tone by only a half-vowel (e.g., יָדְךָ, from the ground-form יַדְךְ; cf. note 1, page 13).

3. Conversely, the syllables preceding these were passed over lightly in speech, and a short vowel there was thinned down to Shewa whenever possible; e.g., the primitive

---

[1] These vowels occur also in other declensions (and in verbs) in combination with other peculiarities; in general they follow the principles here explained. In words of this declension Holem is always fixed. Tsere is fixed in רֵעַ, גֵּר, עֵד, and הֵיכָל (cf. note 1, page 17, and note 1, page 18); and Qamets is fixed in הָרִים, רָאשִׁים, and עָרִים.

דַּבָּרִים became דְּבָרִים, and עַרְמַת became עֲרֵמָה ("heap").

4. The beginner can probably learn the inflection and vowel changes best by deducing all forms from the present Sing. Abs., and they are so described below. It is more strictly accurate, however, to derive each form independently from its own primitive, and this is indicated in the footnotes.

B. Principles of Inflection. Ordinary Masculines

1. Full inflection of the typical noun דָּבָר:

	Singular Noun		Plural Noun	
	Abs. דָּבָר		Abs. דְּבָרִים	
	Cst. דְּבַר		Cst. דִּבְרֵי	
	Sing. Suf.	Plu. Suf.	Sing. Suf.	Plu. Suf.
1c	דְּבָרִי	דְּבָרֵנוּ	דְּבָרַי	דְּבָרֵינוּ
2m	דְּבָרְךָ	דְּבַרְכֶם	דְּבָרֶיךָ	דִּבְרֵיכֶם
2f	דְּבָרֵךְ	דְּבַרְכֶן	דְּבָרַיִךְ	דִּבְרֵיכֶן
3m	דְּבָרוֹ	דְּבָרָם	דְּבָרָיו	דִּבְרֵיהֶם
3f	דְּבָרָהּ	דְּבָרָן	דְּבָרֶיהָ	דִּבְרֵיהֶן

2. *When endings are added, a tone-long vowel usually remains long whenever it can*[1]—i. e., while in "tone position"; when two or more places from the accent it shortens; e.g., דְּבָרֶיךָ, דְּבָרוֹ, etc.[2]

---

[1] More properly, *became long whenever it could.*

[2] Groundforms דַּבָּרוֹ, etc.; the pretonic Pathah lengthened, the ante-pretonic shortened, according to A, 2 and 3 above.

a. Note especially that the *heavy* second and third plural suffixes to plural nouns move the accent *two places* to the left; then the Qamets under בּ shortens to Shewa, and the Shewa which already stood under דּ in the simple plural דְּבָרִים must be replaced by Hireq (Ch. III, B, 1, a); e.g., דִּבְרֵיכֶם, for דְּבְרֵיכֶם[1].

b. In the singular noun with a *heavy* second plural suffix, however, the Qamets under בּ reverts to the original Pathah, as in דְּבַרְכֶם. (But in one word, יָד, it is deflected to Segol, giving יֶדְכֶם).

3. *In forming constructs, the vowels are made as short as possible*—for the following absolute of course receives the principal accent of the phrase, and the whole construct is at a considerable distance from the main stress of tone.

a. *Hence the ultima becomes short*[2], *and the penult extra short;* e. g., יָד, cst. יַד; דָּמִים, cst. דְּמֵי; זָקֵן, cst. זְקַן (note that Tsere is replaced by Pathah, even tho it belongs to a different class of vowels).

b. Then the *ante-penult*, if it had Shewa, must take Hi-

---

[1] Groundforms דַּבְרֵיכֶם, etc. The Pathah under דּ, tho far from the tone, could not shorten to Shewa as the one under בּ did, for two consecutive half-vowels cannot be pronounced; but it was *attenuated* to Hireq, which is a slightly shorter or thinner sound. (If the word had a guttural, however, this caused the first Pathah to remain; e.g., נַהֲרֵיכֶם).

[2] But a long final vowel remains before א; e.g., צְבָא, טְמֵא.

req; i.e., it is *short*; e.g., דְּבָרִים, cst. דִּבְרֵי (for דְּבְרֵי)[1].

4. In applying these principles, first locate the accent; then start from the tone syllable and work towards the right. Note also that the occurrence of a fixed syllable in a word may affect the way in which preceding vowels are shortened[2].

C. Special Types of Words

1. Skeleton Paradigm:

Singular

Abs.	נָהָר	צְדָקָה	עֵדָה
Cst.		צִדְקַת	עֲדַת
3ms		צִדְקָתוֹ	עֲדָתוֹ
2mp		צִדְקַתְכֶם	עֲדַתְכֶם

Plural

Abs.	נְהָרִים	צְדָקוֹת	עֵדוֹת
Cst.	נַהֲרֵי	צִדְקוֹת	עֵדוֹת
3ms	נְהָרָיו	צִדְקוֹתָיו	עֵדוֹתָיו
2mp	נַהֲרֵיכֶם	צִדְקוֹתֵיכֶם	עֵדוֹתֵיכֶם

---

[1] In the groundform דְּבְרֵי, one Pathah was shortened to Shewa, the other attenuated to Hireq (cf. note 1, page 99).

[2] Such changing of vowels may at first sight seem strange and complicated, but it is largely *the result of natural rhythmic tendencies, made obvious by phonetic spelling*. In English there are just as great changes in vowel *quantity* in derived forms, altho the vowel *symbols*

2. Whenever a guttural must take a half-vowel, it takes Hateph Pathah instead of simple Shewa; e.g., חָזָק, plu. חֲזָקִים. And whenever such a compound Shewa is thrown before or after another Shewa, the first half-vowel heightens to Pathah, not Hireq (Ch. III, B, 1, b and c, and note 1, page 99); e.g., בְּהֵמוֹת,חֲזָקִים, cst. חַזְקֵי;בְּהֵמוֹת, cst. בַּהֲמוֹת.

3. In feminines, it must be remembered that the ה reverts to the original ת in all inflectional forms. The tone-long vowels follow the principles already described.

4. The dual also follows regular principles, and should offer no difficulty. Typical forms (from שָׂפָה) are: Abs., שְׂפָתַיִם; 3mp suf., שִׂפְתֵיהֶם.

VOCABULARY

Section B		*Section C*	
זָקֵן	old man; elder	אֲדָמָה	ground
לָשׁוֹן	(f) tongue	כָּנָף (f) wing (dual Cst. כְּנָפֵי)	
מִשְׁפָּט	judgment; justice		
יָשָׁר	upright; straight	נָהָר	river
רָשָׁע	evil	עֵדָה	congregation

---

remain the same; e.g., compare our words *telephone* and *telephony*, or *anatomy* and *anatomical*, and the Hebrew transliterations טֶלֶפֹן, אַנְטֹמְכַל, אֲנַטֹמִי, טֶלֶפָּנִי. (Of course there is also a degree of artificiality in the details of these Hebrew vowel changes, for both the tone-long vowels and the half-vowels were most probably developed in the chanting of the Scriptures in the synagogue services; such formal intoning accounts for the rigidly fixed system).

עָוֹן iniquity   שָׂפָה lip; edge

צְדָקָה righteousness   תּוֹעֵבָה abomination

EXERCISES

1) מִשְׁפַּט הָאֱלֹהִים עַל־נְשֵׁי הָאָרֶץ הַגְּדוֹלָה הַהִיא:

2) כָּרְתוּ אֶת־לְשׁוֹן מַלְאַכְכֶם: 3) יֵשְׁבוּ כָל־הַזְּקֵנִים בַּשַּׁעַר:

4) יָשָׁר מְשָׁרְכֶם נְבִיאָם: 5) רְשָׁעוֹת נְשֵׁיהֶם מִבְּנֵיהֶם:

6) דַּם הַמַּלְאָכִים הַיְשָׁרִים עַל־רֹאשָׁהּ:

7) יָצְאוּ אַנְשֵׁי עֲדָתָם מֵחֲצַר הֵיכַלְכֶם: 8) זָכַר אֶת־
עֲוֹן בְּנֵי־נְבִיאֶךָ וְאֶת־תּוֹעֲבֹתֵיהֶם: 9) רָאָה אֲדֹנִי אֶת־כַּנְפֵי
הַכְּרוּבִים בַּאֲרוֹן הַבְּרִית: 10) מִשְׁפָּטֵי נְבִיאֵנוּ שָׁמַעְנוּ אֶת־
בִּרְכָתוֹ עַל־דֶּרֶךְ הַחֲכָמִים: 11) הֲלָקְחוּ הַזְּקֵנִים אֶת־
הַחֶרֶב הַגְּדֹלָה הַהִיא בִּידֵיהֶם: 12) דַּם מַלְאֲכֵי הָרְשָׁעִים
עַל־יְדֵיהֶם:

1. Why are the judgments of this prince evil? 2. The upright messenger of our elders served us. 3. He delighted in the words of her tongue to your wives. 4. The sons of the prophets did not stand in your dwelling-place.

5. God did not forget their iniquity and their evil words concerning our congregation. 6. The edges of the rivers of this country are not straight. 7. He remembered thy (f) abominations in the court of the temple. 8. He sat on the ground after they bound his strong wings.

SUPPLEMENTARY VOCABULARY

Section B

מָשִׁיחַ anointed one; Messiah

קָצִיר harvest

רָצוֹן delight, pleasure;

לְרָצוֹן, acceptable, delightful

שׁוֹפָר trumpet(plu. in וֹת—)

שָׁלָל plunder, booty

גָּבֹהַ tall, high

כָּבֵד heavy; hard

Section C

יְשׁוּעָה deliverance; salvation

כָּתֵף (f) shoulder

מִדָּה measure

SUPPLEMENTARY EXERCISES

1) זָכַר אֱלֹהֵינוּ אֶת־יְמֵי הָעֳנִי הַכְּבֵדִים הָהֵמָה:
2) יָשָׁרִים מְשִׁיחֵי יְהֹוָה וְלֹא לָקְחוּ אֶת־שְׁלַלְכֶם: 3) רְצוֹנְךָ
בְּתוֹרַת הָאֱלֹהִים כְּמִדַּת צִדְקָתֶךָ: 4) אַחֲרֵי־אֲשֶׁר רָאָה
אֲדוֹנָם אֶת־קְצִירָיו הַגְּדוֹלִים שָׁכַח אֶת־יָמָיו הָרְשָׁעִים:
5) הֲשְׁמַעְתֶּם אֶת־שׁוֹפַר מַלְאַךְ הַמֶּלֶךְ: 6) לָקַחְתִּי אֶת־
הַיְרִיעוֹת הַכְּבֵדוֹת מִמִּשְׁכַּן הַגִּבּוֹרִים הַגְּבֹהִים הָהֵם:
7) שְׁלוֹם אֱלֹהִים וְשִׂמְחָתוֹ לִבְנוֹת הַצַּדָּקָה: 8) לֹא נָדוֹל
עָנְיָה מִגְּבוּרַת יְשׁוּעַת אֱלֹהֶיהָ: 9) יָצָאנוּ מֵהַחֲצֵרִים אֲשֶׁר
עָמַדְנוּ בְּאַדְמָתָם: 10) לֹא חָכְמָה וְלֹא לְרָצוֹן תּוֹרַתְכֶם:
11) בִּכְתֵפֵי בְנוֹתַי יָשְׁבוּ בְּנֵיהֶן: 12) חֲכָמִים מֵאַנְשֵׁיהֶם
אַנְשֵׁי עֲדָתְךָ:

1. The sound of his trumpets was delightful to the sons of
our anointed one.   2. Are their high towers in your hand?

3. He gave his gold for the harvest of the elders of the village.   4. His daughters took the heavy stone from its place.

5. The measure of your joy is greater than the misery of the days of your servitude. 6. She seized his booty from upon his shoulders. 7. Our master gave gifts of gold into the hands of those wise men. 8. After his deliverance from the tower of thy master he ruled over their congregation according to his pleasure.

CHAPTER XVIII

SECOND DECLENSION

A. Form of the Words

1. All words included in this declension have been formed from *stems ending in two vowelless consonants;* e.g., סֵפֶר from a primitive stem סְפַר, and אָזֶן from אָזְן[1].

a. The difficulty of pronouncing these basic forms occasioned the introduction of a *helping vowel*, usually Segol, between the last two consonants; this is a distinctive mark, and hence these words are known as *Segolates*.

b. Furthermore, the vowel of the primitive stem, coming thus to stand in an open syllable, was *lengthened* or *deflected*, thus producing the present forms[2].

2. Segolates fall into three main classes, according to the original vowel:

---

[1] More properly, אָזְן; but the basic *ŭ* has been so completely replaced by the derived *ŏ* that it is preferable to disregard the former in a beginners' book.

[2] These processes are entirely natural; cf. the similar formation of the English word *mēter* from the stem μετρ of the Greek word μετρον. (These stems doubtless originally had *case endings*, and the words so formed were of course pronounceable; cf., in the closely related Arabic, the forms (nominative case) of such words as *sif-run*, "book," *kal-bun*, "dog," and *rum-hun*, "spear"—Hebrew רֹמַח).

Class	Type Word	Formed from
a	יֶלֶד	יַלְד
i	סֵפֶר, also קֶרֶב	קַרְב, סֶפֶר
o	חֹדֶשׁ	חָדְשׁ

Of the words having Segol in the penult, the majority belong to the *a* class; those of the *i* class are marked (i). The original stem vowel of all others is immediately apparent.

3. *All Segolates are accented on the penult*, for that is of course where the accent fell in the primitive form, and the final vowel is purely auxiliary; e.g., קֶ֫רֶב, קֶרְב.

B. Inflection of Ordinary Forms

1. Skeleton paradigm:

Singular

Abs.} Cst.}	יֶלֶד	סֵפֶר	חֹדֶשׁ
3ms	יַלְדוֹ	סִפְרוֹ	חָדְשׁוֹ
2mp	יַלְדְּכֶם	סִפְרְכֶם	חָדְשְׁכֶם

				Dual
		Plural		
Abs.	יְלָדִים	סְפָרִים	חֲדָשִׁים	אָזְנַיִם
Cst.	יַלְדֵי	סִפְרֵי	חָדְשֵׁי	אָזְנֵי
3ms	יְלָדָיו	סְפָרָיו	חֲדָשָׁיו	אָזְנָיו
2mp	יַלְדֵיכֶם	סִפְרֵיכֶם	חָדְשֵׁיכֶם	אָזְנֵיכֶם

2. *The Sing. Cst. is identical with the Abs. But in no other forms is the auxiliary Segol used*[1].

3. *Singular-noun suffixes are added directly to the simple primitive stem*[1]; e.g., יַלְדִּי, קָרְבָּם, etc. (Since the first syllable is closed, the third letter, if a Beghadhkephath, receives D. L.).

4. *The dual is also formed directly on the primitive stem;* e.g., סִפְרַיִם, יַלְדַּיִם, etc.[2]

5. The Plu. Abs. is formed quite differently. *Qamets is introduced under the second letter; and the stem vowel shortens to Shewa*, being in an open syllable two places from the accent; e.g., the plural of יֶלֶד is יְלָדִים[3] (*not* יַלְדִּים, as might be expected).

---

[1] It is evident that, when an ending is attached, the two final consonants of the stem fall in different syllables, and the difficulty of pronunciation (which alone occasioned the insertion of Segol) disappears; cf. the formation of the English adjective *metric*. (*Occasional irregularities occur, as in בְּגְדִי, with vocal Shewa; also in such Csts. as חֲדַר from חָדָר).

[2] Comparing this with section 5, it appears that in these words the dual and plural differ considerably in the absolute and with light suffixes; but in the construct and with heavy suffixes the two forms differ only in the one having the first syllable closed and the other having it open (e.g., יְלָדַי and יַלְדַי).

[3] The obvious similarity to a first declension plural may be the result of direct imitation, or of mere coincidence; worthy of comparison are such Arabic plurals as *kilābun* and *rimāhun* (see note 2, page 105).

a. Naturally the form of the Plu. Abs. is identical in all three classes of words. Also, feminine words are quite analogous; e.g., נֶפֶשׁ, plu. נְפָשׁוֹת.

b. In deriving the Cst., and adding heavy suffixes, the Qamets, which is tone-long, of course becomes Shewa; and then the *primitive stem vowel* reappears under the first consonant (instead of Hireq as in the first declension); e.g., חָדְשֵׁיכֶם, יְלָדַי. The Qamets of course remains be-fore light suffixes to masculines.

6. The accompanying diagram summarizes the divergent uses made of the primitive stem: in its original form, and with different helping vowels.

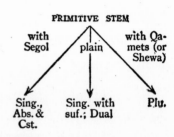

PRIMITIVE STEM

with Segol / plain \ with Qamets (or Shewa)

Sing., Abs. & Cst.　Sing. with suf.; Dual　Plu.

VOCABULARY

אֹזֶן (f) ear

בֶּגֶד (i) garment

בֹּקֶר morning

יֶתֶר (i) remnant

לֶחֶם bread

נֶגֶב the South

סֵפֶר book

צֶדֶק (i) righteousness

קֹדֶשׁ holiness

רֶגֶל (f) foot

שֵׁבֶט rod; tribe

שֶׁמֶן oil

שֶׁמֶשׁ sun

EXERCISES

1) כָּרַתְנוּ אֶת־אָזְנֵי הָרְשָׁעִים וְאֶת־רַגְלֵיהֶם: 2) יָשַׁב
יֶתֶר שִׁבְטוֹ עַל־כַּרְמוֹ: 3) נָתְנוּ לָהֶם אֶת־לַחְמָם וְאֶת־שַׁמְנָם:
4) גְּדוֹל עֲוֹן יַלְדֵי שִׁבְטְכֶם מֵחַסְדּוֹ: 5) לֹא רָאָה אֶת־כָּל־
אַרְצֵךְ כִּי אִם רָצָה אֶת־הַדְּרָכִים הַיְשָׁרִים בִּמְדִינָתָהּ
הַטּוֹבָה: 6) הֲלָקַחְתֶּם אֶת־בִּגְדֵיכֶם וְאֶת־סִפְרֵיכֶם וְאֶת־
כַּסְפְּכֶם אִתְּכֶם: 7) הָלַכְנוּ עִם יְלָדֵינוּ אֶל־הַר־קָדְשׁוֹ:
8) זָכַרְתִּי אֶת־צֶדֶק מַלְכֵי הַנֶּגֶב: 9) כָּל־בֹּקֶר הַשֶּׁמֶשׁ אוֹר
דַּרְכִּי: 10) חֲזָקוֹת חַרְבוֹתָם מִשִּׁבְטֵי: 11) עָמַד נְבִיא
הָאֱלֹהִים בְּקִרְבָּם וְלֹא לָקְחוּ אֶת־נַפְשׁוֹתֵינוּ:

1. The remnant of those tribes dwelt in the South.
2. He asked for his bread and his books. 3. I seized his
sword, with which he had cut off my ear. 4. Are your
paths paths of righteousness or paths of iniquity? 5. He
said their garments were better than hers. 6. Did they
cut off thy feet and ears? 7. The sun was high this morning when her children went out to the vineyards. 8. He
seized his horn and the holy oil (*say*, oil of holiness).

CHAPTER XIX

SECOND DECLENSION (CONTINUED)

The second declension includes many words similar to those already described, but with various differences of detail. The name *Segolate* is loosely applied to all words derived from stems ending in two vowelless consonants.

A. Words with Gutturals

1. When the last consonant, or the next to last, is a guttural, the helping vowel is regularly Pathah (for the gutturals prefer the *a* sounds); e.g., פֶּשַׁע, רֹחַב. Also, an *a* class word with a middle guttural usually retains the primitive Pathah of the stem; e.g., נַעַר.

2. A guttural always takes a Hateph vowel where another consonant has simple Shewa. This is Hateph Pathah in words of the *a* or *i* class, Hateph Qamets in words of the *o* class; e.g., אֶבֶן, plu. אֲבָנִים; חֹדֶשׁ, plu. חֳדָשִׁים; פֶּשַׁע with suf., פִּשְׁעֲכֶם; נְעָרִים, cst. נַעֲרֵי.

3. Words with a middle guttural usually take a Hateph vowel instead of a silent Shewa under the guttural when singular-noun suffixes are added (Ch. V, D, 2); e.g., נַעֲרִי and פָּעֳלִי. And before the second masculine suffixes this must of course heighten to the full vowel; e.g., נַעַרְכֶם.

*4. Words of the second class usually have Segol, not Hireq, as primitive stem vowel; e.g., חֵלֶק, חֶלְקִי (but אֵמֶר has אִמְרִי, etc.) And

110

in the plural these words have peculiar irregularities in the vowel changes; e.g., abs. חֲלָקִים, cst. חֶלְקֵי.

B. Contract Stems

1. Words having Waw as middle consonant undergo contraction in *all* inflectional forms. The Pathah of the primitive stem *coalesces* with the ו to form Holem; e.g., the stem מַוְת of מָוֶת becomes מוֹת in the Sing. Cst., forms a plural מוֹתִים, etc.[1]

2. Words with Yodh as middle consonant have Hireq as helping vowel; e.g., אַיִל. In most derived forms contraction occurs, somewhat analogous to that in the preceding class ‑יַ‑ becoming ‑יֵ‑; e.g., cst. אֵיל, suf. אֵילִי, etc.

C. Feminines in ת

Some feminines have retained in the Sing. Abs. the primitive ת (note 3, page 93), attached directly to the stem— giving rise to segolate forms; e.g., מִשְׁמֶרֶת, from a stem מִשְׁמַרְת[2] (with suf. מִשְׁמַרְתּוֹ, plu. מִשְׁמָרוֹת, etc.[3]).

---

[1] Most words with such a stem are contracted in the Sing. Abs.; e.g., קוֹל, יוֹם, דּוֹר. Quite peculiar is the word שׁוֹר, which has an uncontracted Plu. Abs., שְׁוָרִים.

[2] A guttural requires Pathah (cf. A, 1 above), as in טַבַּעַת, with suffix טַבַּעְתּוֹ (with silent Shewa, not Hateph Pathah). (חַטָּאת* is of this class, contracted from חַטַּאת. The other types of segolate stems also occur; e.g., תָּכְלַת and גִּבְרֶת—*i* class, and בֹּשֶׁת and כָּתֹנֶת— *o* class).

[3] Irregular types of plurals also occur; e.g., מַחֲלָקוֹת from מַחֲלָקֶת, and קְשָׁתוֹת from קֶשֶׁת.

D. Feminines in הָ—

1. A number of feminines have been formed by adding הָ— to such a monosyllabic stem as is the ground-form of all segolates; e.g., מַלְכָּה, "queen," from מֶלֶךְ, and מִנְחָה from the obsolete root מֶנַח.

2. In the Sing. they are exactly parallel to the first declension forms. But the Plu. is formed like the Plu. of other segolates—i.e., Qamets is introduced under the second letter, and the stem vowel becomes Shewa; e.g., the Plu. of מַלְכָּה is מְלָכוֹת (*not* מַלְכוֹת). The further inflection follows regular principles.

E. Allied Words

1. Several feminines ending in הָ—ָ, which in the Plu. follow regular first declension forms, have borrowed Sing. forms from the segolates. They are mostly nouns formed by prefixing מ to a verb root; e.g., מִלְחָמָה, "war," from לָחַם, "to fight"[1]. All inflectional forms in the Sing. come from a primitive stem ending in two consonants, such as מִלְחַמְת[2], and hence resemble the words in C above; e.g., cst. מִלְחֶמֶת, suf. מִלְחַמְתּוֹ; with a final guttural, מִשְׁפַּחְתִּי, מִשְׁפַּחַת, etc. (cf. note 2, page 111).

2. Nouns ending in י have a peculiar form in the Sing.

---

[1] The somewhat irregular noun בְּהֵמָה is partly similar to these words; cst. בֶּהֱמַת, suf. בְּהֶמְתּוֹ, plu. בְּהֵמוֹת.

[2] The other forms of course are from a stem of the type מִלְחַמַת.

Abs., tne stem vowel being shortened to Shewa; e.g., פְּרִי
(primitive stem פִּרְי), אֲרִי (stem אַרְי), עֲנִי (stem עָנְי).
Suffix and plural forms are made according to regular
segolate principles; e.g., אֲרָיוֹת, פִּרְיוֹ, etc.

*3. A few words have the stem vowel with the second consonant;
e.g., דְּבַשׁ (suf. דִּבְשִׁי), בְּאֵר (plu. בְּאֵרוֹת), מְעַט, etc.

*4. A few words retain the primitive monosyllabic form in the Sing.
Abs.; e.g., שָׁוְא, קְשֹׁט, חַטְא (plu. חֲטָאִים), etc.

*5. A few first declension words have a segolate form in the Sing.
Cst. only; e.g., כָּתֵף, cst. כֶּתֶף.

VOCABULARY

Section A

אֹהֶל tent

זֶבַח (i) sacrifice

נַחַל brook; torrent

נַעַר lad; attendant

עֶצֶם (f) bone

פֶּתַח (i) door

Section B

אַיִל ram

חַיִל strength

מָוֶת death

עַיִן (f) eye

תָּוֶךְ midst

Section C

מִשְׁמֶרֶת custody; charge

תִּפְאֶרֶת beauty; splendor

Section D

מַלְכָּה queen

שִׂמְלָה garment

Section E

מְלָאכָה work, labor, business

מַמְלָכָה kingdom

פְּרִי fruit

EXERCISES

1) גְּדוֹלִים נַחֲלֵי הָאֲרָצוֹת הָהֵנָּה: 2) עָמְדוּ הַנְּעָרִים
אֲשֶׁר־לָהֶם מִשְׁמֶרֶת אָהֳלוּ אַחֲרֵי פִּתְחוֹ: 3) בֵּית הָאֱלֹהִים
חֵיל הָהָר הַזֶּה: 4) בְּתוֹךְ זְבָחָיו זָכַר אֶת־עַבְדֵי בֵיתוֹ:
5) עֵינַיִם לוֹ וְלֹא רָאָה אֶת־תִּפְאַרְתָּהּ: 6) אַחֲרֵי פִּשְׁעֵי
עֲבָדָיו מִחוּץ לַשְּׁעָרִים שָׁאַלְנוּ אֶת־מוֹתָם:

7) הֶעָשָׂה אֶת־מְלַאכְתּוֹ בְּתוֹךְ מִשְׁפַּחְתְּךָ: 8) גָּדוֹל חֵיל
הַמְּלָכוֹת מֵחֵיל אַנְשֵׁי מִלְחַמְתּוֹ (See Ch. XV, B, 3, b):
9) פִּשְׁעֵיהֶם פְּרִי עֲנְיָם: 10) שָׁמַעְתִּי עַל־זִבְחֲכֶם הַגָּדוֹל
לְמַמְלֶכֶת רֵעֲכֶם: 11) שָׁם רָאָה אֶת־שִׂמְלוֹת מַלְכַּתְכֶם
וְאֶת־עַצְמוֹתֶיהָ: 12) שָׁכַח מַלְכְּכֶם אֶת־מוֹתָם בְּמִלְחֲמוֹת
מַמְלַכְתּוֹ:

1. Was not their lad in my custody all the months since
(מֵאָז) their death?　2. She gave sacrifices of rams at the
door of her tent.　3. His bones are in the midst of the
brook.　4. With his eyes he saw the splendor of the
strength of your lad.

5. Thy family is the greatest in their kingdom.
6. Did ye take our fruit?　7. The work of his warriors
was delightful to our queen.　8. In his need he took
those garments from thy door.

SUPPLEMENTARY VOCABULARY

אָוֶן	nothingness; vanity; iniquity	חֵלֶק	portion
אֲרִי	lion (plu. in וֹת—)	מַחֲשֶׁבֶת	counsel, purpose, plan
בַּעַל	master	נַעֲרָה	maiden; maid-servant
גִּבְעָה	hill	עֵמֶק	valley

SUPPLEMENTARY EXERCISES

‏1) שָׁאַל לְמוֹת אֵילָיו בַּנַּחַל: 2) מִי אָסַר אֶת־הָעֲצָמוֹת
עַל־פִּתְחֶךָ: 3) הַהֲרָבוֹת הָהֵנָּה בְּמִשְׁמַרְתֶּךָ כָּל־הֶחָדָשִׁים
הָאֵלֶּה: 4) עֵינָיו עֲלֵיכֶם הַנְּעָרִים וּמִתּוֹכְכֶם שָׁלַח אֶת־
הָרְשָׁעִים: 5) כָּבֵד לַחְמָה כָּאֲבָנִים הָהֵנָּה: 6) זֶה לֹא
פִשְׁעֲךָ הָרִאשׁוֹן אֲשֶׁר־בּוֹ לָקַחְתִּי אֹתְךָ:

‏7) הָלְכוּ בְעָלֵינוּ אֶל־הַנָּבִיא וְלֹא שָׁמְעוּ לְמַחֲשַׁבְתּוֹ:
‏8) בְּעֵינָיו רָאָה אֶת־תּוֹעֲבַת אוֹנָם: 9) הֲלֹא הַנְּעָרוֹת אֲשֶׁר
רָצָה אֹתָן בְּמַמְלַכְתֵּנוּ: 10) יָשְׁבוּ הָאֲרָיוֹת בַּגְּבָעוֹת הָהֵנָּה:
‏11) בָּנָה אֶת־אָהֳלֵיהֶם בְּחֵלֶק עֶמְקֵי אֲשֶׁר הַנְּחָלִים שָׁם:
‏12) חָזְקָה יָדִי מֵחֵיל כָּל־אַנְשֵׁי מִלְחַמְתְּכֶם:

1. Did they forget your (f) beauty and your sacrifice?
2. Her servants seized the swords in thy house.   3. The
stones cut the eyes of his ram.   4. She remembered the
death of your servants in the brook.

5. The family of their masters shall have the strength
of lions.   6. Our warriors are on the hills in the midst of

his kingdom.   7. Our masters gave us our portion (*see A, 4, above*) according to their purpose.   8. He saw your iniquity, O maidens, in those valleys.

CHAPTER XX
THIRD AND FOURTH DECLENSIONS[1]

A. Forms of the Words

1. The third declension consists chiefly of words having tone-long Tsere in the ultima and a fixed vowel in the penult; this includes all participles ending in Tsere (Ch. XXXV, A), as well as many nouns formed from participles. There are also a number of monosyllables in Tsere.

2. The fourth declension comprises words ending in הָ—; this includes, besides nouns and adjectives derived from verbs ending in ה, the participles of these verbs (Ch. XLIV, B).

B. The Third Declension

1. The Sing. Cst. is the same as the Abs. in almost all words. In a few, however, it shortens; e.g., מִזְבֵּחַ, cst. מִזְבַּח; בֵּן, before Maqqeph בֶּן־.

2. In *dissyllables*, the Tsere shortens when *any* ending is

---

[1] N.B. Instead of following thru the other regular and special types of nouns at once, the simpler forms of the regular verb may be studied at this point, if desired; for the exercises in Chs. XXVI–XXX are arranged so as to be practically independent of Chs. XX–XXV —only a few nouns from these intervening vocabularies being used, and in forms which will cause no confusion.

added, even tho it would still stand in tone position[1].

 a. It ordinarily becomes Shewa (under a guttural, Hateph Pathah)[2]; e.g., from שָׁפַט שָׁפְטוּ, שֹׁפְטִים; from כֹּהֲנִים ,כֹּהֵן.

 b. But before the second person suffixes, which take Shewa as connecting vowel, it becomes Segol (under a guttural, Pathah); e.g., שֹׁפֶטְךָ (in place of שֹׁפְטְךָ), כֹּהֶנְךָ; אֹיֵב, however, takes Hireq (אֹיִבְךָ).

 3. *Monosyllables*, however, usually retain the Tsere before light suffixes and in Plu. Abs.; e. g., עֵץ, עֵצוֹ, עֵצִים. But in בֵּן and שֵׁם it shortens before suffixes; e.g.,בְּנוֹ, שִׁמְךָ (note the Hireq), etc.

C. The Fourth Declension

 1. The Sing. Cst. is very peculiar in that the final vowel is lengthened; e.g., רֹעֶה, cst. רֹעֵה.

 2. *The* ֶה *is dropped before all endings;* e.g., from רֹעֶה is formed רֹעֶךָ, רֹעִים, etc.[3]

---

[1] This shortening of a pretonic vowel is in accordance with the principle followed in verbs, to which these words are so closely related, rather than with that followed in most nouns; cf., e.g., the form קָטְלוּ, plu. of קָטַל.

[2] Note the occasional loss of D.F. over the Shewa, as in עֹרְרִים (Ch. IV, A, 2, b); and the further loss of vocal Shewa itself in כִּסְאֲךָ.

*[3] Occasionally the ה, instead of being entirely dropped before suffixes, is replaced by י, just as in some forms of the root verbs— making the noun appear plural altho really singular, as shown by the agreement; e.g., מַעֲשָׂיו, מַעֲשֵׂה; מִקְנֶיךָ; מִקְנֶה ;מַרְאֵיהֶם; מַרְאֶה.

a. Two suffixes to the singular noun have a special form; e. g., 3ms, רֵעֵהוּ; 3fs רֹעָהּ. The הּ is *not* a part of the noun, but of the suffix in its more primitive form (note 1, page 70).

b. In the feminine of the adjectives (and participles), after the ־ֶה is dropped and ־ָה added, the further inflection is like the first declension; e.g., feminine forms of יָפֶה are: abs. יָפָה, cst. יְפַת, plu. abs. יָפוֹת.

VOCABULARY

Third Decl.

אֹיֵב enemy

יֹשֵׁב inhabitant

כֹּהֵן priest

כִּסֵּא throne

מוֹעֵד appointed time; assembly place

מִזְבֵּחַ altar(Cst. has ־ַ; plu. in וֹת—)

עֵץ tree

שֵׁם name (plu. in וֹת—)

שֹׁפֵט judge

Fourth Decl.

מַחֲנֶה camp; army

מַטֶּה rod; tribe (plu. in וֹת—)

מַעֲשֶׂה work, deed

מַרְאֶה appearance

פָּנִים (*plu. of the unused form* פָּנֶה) face

שָׂדֶה field (plu. in וֹת—)

יָפֶה fair, beautiful

EXERCISES

1) הָעִמְדוּ כֹהֲנֵיכֶם אַחֲרֵי מִזְבַּח הָאֱלֹהִים: 2) כָּרַת שֹׁפְטְךָ אֶת־עֲצֵי כַרְמוֹ: 3) רָאָה אֶת־יֹשְׁבֵי הָעִיר הַזֶּה בְּמוֹעֲדָם: 4) הָלַךְ מַלְאַךְ שֹׁפְטֵינוּ אֶל־מִזְבַּחֲכֶם הַכֹּהֲנִים:

5) הַיּוֹם שָׁמַעְתִּי אֶת־שִׂמְחוֹתֵיכֶם רֵעִי: 6) מֶלֶךְ בָּנָה עַל־
אֹיְבָיו מֵעַל כִּסְאָם:

7) חֲזָקִים מִמַּטֵּךְ מַחֲנָיו: 8) נָשֵׁי הַיָּפוֹת בְּכָל־יִשְׂרָאֵל:
9) עָשָׂה אֶת־מַעֲשֵׂהוּ בִּשְׂדֵה בַעֲלִי: 10) רָאָה אֶת־פָּנֶיהָ
וְלֹא לְרָצוֹן לוֹ מַרְאָם: 11) הַגְּדוֹלִים בִּמְדִינוֹתַי שָׂדֵיכֶם
הַיָּפִים: 12) זָכְרוּ יֹשְׁבֵי הַחֲצֵרִים אֶת־מַרְאִי:

1. Who built his throne by those high trees? 2. I
sent my son to all the assembly places. 3. He asked the
priests whether I was thy judge. 4. Your enemy saw
you when we stood with you near your altar.

5. His name is evil in all the tribes. 6. That is the
camp of our enemies to which she went out. 7. He did
not do his work because he did not take his rod. 8. Her
face is not fair, but her work is good. 9. I remembered
thy appearance among the inhabitants of our village.

SUPPLEMENTARY VOCABULARY

Third Decl.

מוֹפֵת miracle

מוֹקֵשׁ snare

מַעֲשֵׂר tithe (Cst. has —;
plu. in וֹת־)

עִוֵּר blind

Fourth Decl.

חֹזֶה seer

מִקְנֶה substance, wealth;
cattle

קָנֶה reed

קָצֶה end

רֹעֶה shepherd

קָשֶׁה hard; stubborn

SUPPLEMENTARY EXERCISES

1) גְּדוֹלִים מְאֹד מוֹפְתֶיהָ אֲשֶׁר לָהֶם שָׁאֲלָנוּ: 2) לֹא
בָדְעוּ אֶתְכֶם מוֹקְשֵׁי אֹיְבְכֶם כִּי לֹא עִוְרִים שֹׁפְטֵינוּ:
3) רָאָה אֶת־סְפָרָיו בְּתוֹךְ הָעֵצִים הָהֵם: 4) הַשְׁכַחְתָּן
אֶת־שְׁמוֹ בְּנוֹת הַמִּזְבְּחוֹת: 5) לָקְחוּ אֹיְבָיו אֶת־כִּסְאוֹ מִמֶּנּוּ:
6) לֹא נָתְנוּ אֶת־מַעֲשַׂרָם לְכֹהֲנֵנוּ:

7) הֲנָתְנוּ אֶת־כָּל־מִקְנָם לַחִיִּים אֲשֶׁר שָׁמְעוּ זֹאת מֵהֶם:
8) קָשָׁה מְאֹד רוּחוֹ: 9) הֲיָשְׁבָה אִתָּךְ בִּקְצֵה שָׂדֵהוּ:
10) הֲשָׁמְעוּ הָרָעִים הַטּוֹבִים הָהֵמָּה אֶת־הַמִּצְוֹת אֲשֶׁר
נָתְנוּ לְמַעֲשָׂם: 11) מִי לָקַח אֶת־קְנֵה הַמִּדָּה: 12) לִמְעַט
מִשְׁפְּחוֹת הַמַּטִּים הָאֵלֶּה כָּל־מִקְנֵה הָעָם הַזֶּה:

1. Who served their blind priests? 2. They sent all
the tithe of their trees to the altar of Jehovah. 3. He
did his miracles for the delight of the inhabitants. 4. I
did not hear the name of your son. 5. Did your priest
make snares of death for your enemies?

6. The shepherds are in the fields of their master.
7. The end of these hard works is delightful. 8. How
great is our wealth! 9. They took their reeds from thy
fields.

CHAPTER XXI
FIFTH DECLENSION

A. Form of the Words

1. This declension consists of words which *double the final letter* when endings are added[1]. These words can, in general, not be distinguished from those of other declensions, except as their derivation or the forms in actual use are known. Words of this declension previously given are הַר, עַם, גָּמָל, כֹּל, and שַׂר.

2. In most of these words the vowel has been lengthened in the Sing. Abs.; e.g., לֵב, stem לִבְּ; חֹק, stem חֻקְּ; יָם, stem יַמְּ (cf. Ch. 4, A, 2, a).

B. Inflection

1. *D. F. is inserted in the last letter before all endings* (except in the words noted below); e.g., עַם with suf., עַמִּי; אַף, dual אַפַּיִם; etc. *And then any vowel which was lengthened in the absolute is shortened;* Qamets becomes

---

[1] This includes: (a) words derived from verb roots in which the last two letters are the same (e.g., עַם from עָמַם); (b) words in which a root letter has been lost by assimilation (e.g., אַף from the stem אַנְף; עֵת from עֶדֶת); (c) Gentilic names, etc., in ־ִי (e.g., לֵוִי; cf. Ch. IV, A, 1, c); and (d) some words derived from strong verbs, in which the doubling seems artificial (e.g., גָּמָל).

Pathah, Holem becomes Qibbuts (rarely Qamets Hatuph), and Tsere becomes Hireq (rarely Segol); e.g., לְבוֹ, לֵב; חֻקּוֹ, חֹק; יַמִּים, יָם.

2. Words which have a final guttural or ר of course cannot take the D.F. They therefore retain the long vowel of the absolute before the endings, or lengthen it if it was not long (e.g., פָּר, פָּרִים; רָע, רָעָה); except that before כֶם and כֶן, the vowel is short, just as in the first declension nouns (e.g., שָׁרְכֶם).

3. Words which have a Qamets in the Abs. usually shorten it to Pathah in the Cst.; e.g., גָּמָל, cst. גְּמַל; but יָם retains its Qamets. Words with Tsere or Holem are usually unchanged in Cst.; except that, when united by Maqqeph to the conjoined noun, the vowel shortens (Holem to Qamets Hatuph, Tsere to Segol; e.g., חָק־).

4. Several words have special peculiarities.

a. Suffix forms with חֹק are חֻקִּי, חֻקְּךָ (the ק refusing D.F. over the Shewa).

b. כֹּל takes pronoun suffixes, which are not possessive but resemble the partitive genitive in Latin; e.g., "all of you" is כֻּלְּכֶם.

*c. חִי has an irregular construct, חֵי.

VOCABULARY

אֵם (f) mother

אַף nose; anger

חֵן grace, favor

חֵץ arrow

חֹק (*also* חֻקָּה) statute

יָם sea

כַּף (f) palm (of hand)

לֵב heart (plu. in וֹת—)

מָגֵן   shield (*fixed* —ָ)   שַׁבָּת   (f) rest; Sabbath

עֵת   (f) time (plu. in ־ים)   חַי   alive, living

פַּר   bullock

צַר   adversary   רַב   much, many, numerous

רֹב   abundance; multitude;   רַע   evil, bad
       greatness

EXERCISES

‫1) מַעֲשֵׂי אִמּוֹתֵיהֶן הַטּוֹבוֹת לֹא בִלְבָבֹתֵיהֶן הָרָעִים:‬
‫2) נָתַן רָב־פָּרִים בְּזִבְחוֹ: 3) שָׁמַעְנוּ לְחֻקּוֹת יְהֹוָה כַּאֲשֶׁר‬
‫אָמַר לָנוּ שָׂרֵנוּ: 4) בְּחִצָּיו בָּקַע אֶת־מָגִנֵּיהֶם: 5) לָקְחוּ‬
‫אֶת־כָּל־צָרֵיהֶם חַיִּים: 6) גָּדוֹל חֲנוּ מֵאַפּוֹ: 7) לֹא שָׁכְחָה‬
‫אִמֵּךְ אֶת־שַׁבַּת אֱלֹהֶיהָ אוֹ אֶת־חֻקָּיו בְּעִתָּהּ: 8) לוֹ גְמַלִּים‬
‫רַבִּים מִלְּכָלָנוּ: 9) הֲלֹא רָצָה לֵב שַׂרְכֶם אֶת־מַרְאֵה עַמּוֹ:‬
‫10) דָם חָזִינוּ עַל־כַּפֵּי הַצָּרִים הָהֵמָּה: 11) בָּנָה שָׂרָם‬
‫חוֹמוֹת רַבּוֹת כְּחָק־מַלְכָּם:‬

1. My mother was not alive at that time.   2. Jehovah gave many statutes concerning the sabbath of His people. 3. Anger was in the hearts of the evil princes many times. 4. Your adversaries have many shields.   5. My grace is sufficient (*say*, an abundance) for all of them.   6. He had arrows in the palms (*use Plu.*) of his hands.   7. He went with his camels and bullocks to the great sea of the desert. 8. In their anger they sent the multitude of their servants against the shepherds on their mountain.

CHAPTER XXII

IRREGULAR NOUNS

Many very common nouns in Hebrew are irregular.
Several of these have already been given, in full or in
part, but are listed here for ready reference. The salient
forms only are given; other forms are either derived regularly, or are too rare to be included. (Numbers 6, 17,
and 19 are rather rare; but the others should be learned
thoroly).

1. אָב, "father." Cst., אֲבִי; suf., אָבִי, אָבִיו or אֲבִיהוּ,
אֲבִיכֶם; plu., אָבוֹת.

2. אָח, "brother." Thruout Sing. like אָב; plu., אַחִים;
cst., אֲחֵי; suf., אָחִיךָ, אָחִיו אֲחִיכֶם.

3. אָחוֹת, "sister." Plu., אֲחָיוֹת.

4. אַחֵר, "other, another." Fem., אַחֶרֶת; plu., אֲחֵרִים,
אֲחֵרוֹת.

5. אִישׁ, "man." Plu., אֲנָשִׁים.

6. אָמָה, "maidservant." Plu., אֲמָהוֹת.

7. אִשָּׁה, "woman." Cst., אֵשֶׁת; suf., אִשְׁתּוֹ; plu.,
נָשִׁים.

8. בַּיִת, "house." With ה Directive, בַּיְתָה; plu.,

בָּתִּים (fixed ־ָ; it is not certain whether this is a Qamets or Qamets Hatuph).

9. בֵּן, "son." Cst., בֶּן־; suf., בְּנִי; plu., בָּנִים.

10. בַּת, "daughter." Suf., בִּתִּי; plu., בָּנוֹת.

11. גַּיְא, "valley." Cst., גֵּיא; also written without the א.

12. יוֹם, "day." Plu., יָמִים.

13. כְּלִי, "vessel, implement, weapon." Plu., כֵּלִים.

14. מַיִם, "water." This is a Plu.; cst., מֵי (or, reduplicated, מֵימֵי); suf., מֵימֵיכֶם.

15. עִיר (f), "city." Plu., עָרִים (fixed ־ָ).

16. פֶּה, "mouth." Cst., פִּי; suf., פִּיךָ, פִּיו or פִּיהוּ.

17. פֶּחָה, "governor." Plu., פַּחוֹת.

18. רֹאשׁ, "head." Plu., רָאשִׁים (fixed ־ָ).

19. שֶׂה, "sheep, goat." Cst., שֵׂה; suf., שֵׂיוֹ or שֵׂיהוּ.

20. The following Masculines have וֹת— in the Plu.:

אָב, אֲרִי, חוּץ, חֲלוֹם, כִּסֵּא, לֵב (לֵבָב), לַיְלָה, מִזְבֵּחַ, מַטֶּה, מַעֲשֵׂר, מָקוֹם, עָוֹן, עָפָר, צָבָא, קוֹל, קִיר, שָׂדֶה, שׁוֹפָר, שֵׁם.

21. The following Feminines have ־ִים— in the Plu.:

אֶבֶן, אִשָּׁה, חִטָּה, עִיר, עֵת, פַּעַם, שָׁנָה.

EXERCISES

1) יָשַׁב אָבִיהוּ בְּתוֹךְ גֵּיא הַמֶּלַח: 2) הָלְכָה אֲמָתָם בֵּיתָה כִּי בֵיתָהּ בְּעֵנִי הוּא: 3) כָּרַת אֶת־יְדֵי אִשְׁתּוֹ וְאֶת־

יָדֵי אֲחוֹתָהּ: 4) יָצָא שֶׂה אֲחִי מִשָּׂדֵהוּ: 5) רָצָה אֶת־בְּנִי
וְאֶת־בִּתִּי: 6) הֲשָׁלַחְתָּ אֶת־כְּלַי אֶל־מֵימֵי הַיְאֹר הַזֶּה:
7) זָכַרְתִּי אֶת־הַנָּשִׁים הַיָּפוֹת הָאֲחֵרוֹת אֲשֶׁר־לָהֶן בָּנָה אֶת־
הַבָּתִּים הַגְּדוֹלִים: 8) מָלַךְ עֲלֵיהֶם אֲבִי פֶחָתֵנוּ: 9) בִּימֵי
תִפְאֶרֶת אַחְיוֹתַי עָבְדוּ אֹתָן אֲמָהוֹת רַבּוֹת: 10) בָּנָה
לַמַּלְכָּה אֶת־עָרֶיהָ בְּפִי הַגַּי: 11) מִי שָׁמַע אֶת־אִשְׁתִּי
וְאֶת־אַחֱיהָ:

1. By the word of his mouth our fathers went. 2. This is my brother's wife. 3. His maidservants had other implements. 4. The heads of the houses of their cities remembered my daughter. 5. His sisters took their weapons to the valley of the sons of Hinnom (הִנֹּם). 6. Did your brothers go to our governors? 7. Our water is better than yours. 8. I did not hear the voice of the mouth of thy father.

CHAPTER XXIII

NUMERALS

A. The Cardinals[1]

	With Masculine Nouns		With Feminine Nouns		Sym-bol
	Absolute	Construct	Absolute	Construct	
1	אֶחָד	אַחַד	אַחַת	אַחַת	א
2	שְׁנַיִם	שְׁנֵי	שְׁתַּיִם	שְׁתֵּי	ב
3	שְׁלֹשָׁה	שְׁלֹשֶׁת	שָׁלֹשׁ	שְׁלֹשׁ	ג
4	אַרְבָּעָה	אַרְבַּעַת	אַרְבַּע	אַרְבַּע	ד
5	חֲמִשָּׁה	חֲמֵשֶׁת	חָמֵשׁ	חֲמֵשׁ	ה
6	שִׁשָּׁה	שֵׁשֶׁת	שֵׁשׁ	שֵׁשׁ	ו
7	שִׁבְעָה	שִׁבְעַת	שֶׁבַע	שְׁבַע	ז
8	שְׁמֹנָה	שְׁמֹנַת	שְׁמֹנֶה	שְׁמֹנֶה	ח
9	תִּשְׁעָה	תִּשְׁעַת	תֵּשַׁע	תְּשַׁע	ט
10	עֲשָׂרָה	עֲשֶׂרֶת	עֶשֶׂר	עֶשֶׂר	י
11	אַחַד עָשָׂר		אַחַת עֶשְׂרֵה		יא
12	שְׁנֵים עָשָׂר		שְׁתֵּים עֶשְׂרֵה		יב
13	שְׁלֹשָׁה עָשָׂר		שְׁלֹשׁ עֶשְׂרֵה		יג

---

[1] There are several peculiarities in the forms: (1) the Dagesh in שְׁתַּיִם, etc., is the only exception to Ch. IV, B, 1, b; (2) the constructs and plurals of the segolate-form nouns for 7, 9, and 10 are irregular;

128

With any Noun	Symbol		With any Noun	Symbol[1]
20	עֶשְׂרִים	כ	100	מֵאָה[2]	ק
30	שְׁלֹשִׁים	ל	200	מָאתַיִם	ר
40	אַרְבָּעִים	מ	300	שְׁלשׁ מֵאוֹת	שׁ
50	חֲמִשִּׁים	נ	400	אַרְבַּע מֵאוֹת	ת
60	שִׁשִּׁים	ס	1000	אֶלֶף	אֵ
70	שִׁבְעִים	ע	2000	אַלְפַּיִם	
80	שְׁמֹנִים	פ	3000	שְׁלֹשֶׁת אֲלָפִים	
90	תִּשְׁעִים	צ	10000	רְבָבָה	

1. With the exception of אֶחָד, which is an ordinary
adjective[3], the units properly are nouns; but, from a quasi-
adjectival use, separate forms arose for the two genders.
Peculiarly enough, the original abstract feminine forms
are used with Masc. nouns; while the forms used with Fem.
nouns have been shortened therefrom, and look like masculines.

---

(3) the א in the number 4 is not a proper part of the root, but is "pros-
thetic"—merely added to facilitate the pronunciation; it is dropped in
the ordinal form.

*1 In symbols, 600 is תר, 947 is תתקמז, etc. For 15 and 16, יה
and יו are not used, as they indicate the Divine Name; טו and טז are
substituted.

*2 A Cst. form מְאַת occurs occasionally.

*3 Rarely it is used as a substantive, in the Cst.

2. *Twenty* is the plural of *ten* (one wonders why a dual is not used, as in 200 and 2000); the other "tens" are Masc. plurals of the corresponding units. In the higher hundreds and thousands, the Cst. of the unit is used with the plurals מֵאוֹת and אֲלָפִים[1]. These are all invariable in form.

3. In the numerals 11-19, the units are followed by special forms of *ten*, without any conjunction[2]. The unit is in the Cst. when used with Fem. nouns, in the Abs. when used with Masc. nouns (except in 11 and 12, which are somewhat irregular, even as in English[3]).

4. In the higher compound numbers, the usual order is thousand, hundred, unit (always in the Abs.), ten. The unit and ten are always joined with וְ, the others may be; e.g., אַרְבַּע מֵאוֹת וּשְׁנַיִם וַחֲמִשִּׁים, "452"; also עֶשְׂרִים וְשָׁלֹשׁ, "23."

B. Syntax

1. The numerals 2-10 are commonly used in the Cst., and then must precede their noun, which must be plural[4]; e.g., "five men" is חֲמֵשֶׁת אֲנָשִׁים (*lit.*, a quintet of men).

---

[1] Sometimes the singular אֶלֶף follows the Abs. of the unit (cf. B, 2, below, and footnote); e.g., 2 Sam. 10:18.

[2] Cf., in English, the special form "teen" used after the unit in a single word—*fourteen, sixteen*, etc.

[3] In place of the regular unit in 11, עַשְׁתֵּי is often used. שְׁנֵי and שְׁתֵּי occur a few times in 12.

[4] But occasionally a collective singular noun is used.

But the Abs. may be used, in apposition to the noun—usually preceding it, occasionally following; e.g., חֲמִשָּׁה אֲנָשִׁים (*lit.*, a quintet, men), or אֲנָשִׁים חֲמִשָּׁה.

2. With all the higher numerals, the following common words are usually used in the singular: אִישׁ, שָׁנָה, נֶפֶשׁ, שֵׁבֶט, אַמָּה, בָּקָר, יוֹם, and שֶׁקֶל[1]; e.g., חֲמִשִּׁים אִישׁ, "50 (times a) man." Other nouns are usually in the plural (altho the singular is not infrequently used after the even tens, and occasionally with other numerals).

3. The numerals 11-19 almost always precede the noun, and the even tens, hundreds, and thousands usually do. But numerals compounded of a unit and a ten usually follow the noun (unless it be one of the words given above in 2); or, especially with numbers including hundreds or thousands, the noun may be put in the plural following the unit, and repeated in the singular following each of the higher numbers.

C. Special Uses

1. A special idiom is used in expressing age; e.g., הָאִישׁ בֶּן־שְׁלֹשִׁים שָׁנָה, (*lit.*, The man is the son of 30 years), "The man is 30 years old"; so for women, בַּת, "daughter of," is used.

2. The article is used with either the numeral, or the noun, or both, when definite; e.g., זָכַר אֶת־שְׁלֹשֶׁת הָאֲנָשִׁים, "He remembered the three men."

---

[1] So also often אֶלֶף, כֹּר, כִּכָּר, צֶמֶד, מַצֵּבָה, רַגְלִי.

3. The cardinals above 10 serve also as ordinals; so do the absolute forms of the cardinals 1-10 with the two words יוֹם and שָׁנָה; e.g., בְּחֹדֶשׁ שְׁנֵים עָשָׂר בִּשְׁנַת שְׁתַּיִם, "in the twelfth month in the second year." These ordinals usually follow the noun, which is then in the Cst.; if the noun follows, it is in the Abs.

4. There are also the following special ordinal adjectives for 1-10:

	Masc.	Fem.		Masc.	Fem.
1st	רִאשׁוֹן	רִאשׁוֹנָה	6th	שִׁשִּׁי	שִׁשִּׁית
2nd	שֵׁנִי	שֵׁנִית	7th	שְׁבִיעִי	etc.
3rd	שְׁלִישִׁי	שְׁלִישִׁית	8th	שְׁמִינִי	
4th	רְבִיעִי	etc.	9th	תְּשִׁיעִי	
5th	חֲמִשִּׁי / חֲמִישִׁי		10th	עֲשִׂירִי	

5. *Multiplicatives* are regularly expressed by using the word פַּעַם (as in sentence 2 in the Hebrew exercises below)[1].

*6. *Distributives* are commonly expressed by repeating the numeral, sometimes by using לְ.

*7. The numerals sometimes have suffixes; e.g., חֲמִשָּׁיו, "his fifty"; שְׁלָשְׁתְּכֶם, "you three"; שְׁנֵיהֶם, "those two."

VOCABULARY

אַמָּה	cubit	פַּעַם	(f) time (plu. in ־ים)
בָּקָר	cattle	שָׁנָה	year (plu. in ־ים)
כֶּבֶשׂ	he-lamb	שֶׁקֶל	shekel
מִסְפָּר	number		
נָשִׂיא	prince	רַק	only

---

*[1] Or, sometimes, by the *dual* of the numeral; or by the simple numeral, פַּעַם being understood.

EXERCISES

1) לָקְחוּ שְׁלֹשֶׁת מַלְאֲכֵי אַרְבַּע מֵאוֹת יְרִיעוֹת: 2) שֵׁשׁ
פְּעָמִים עָשָׂה עוֹלוֹת חָמֵשׁ וְעֶשְׂרִים: 3) רָמָה הַחוֹמָה הַהִיא
רַק עֶשְׂרִים אַמָּה: 4) שֵׁשׁ וְאַרְבָּעִים וּמֵאָה מְדִינוֹת בָּאָרֶץ
אֲשֶׁר־שָׁם יָשַׁבְנוּ: 5) מִסְפַּר נְשִׂיאֵיכֶם שִׁבְעָה: 6) הַזָּקֵן
בְּבָנָיו הַשִּׁבְעָה הֶעָשָׂר בֶּן־שְׁמֹנֶה שָׁנִים וַחֲמִשִּׁים שָׁנָה:
7) הֲלֹא אֲלָפַיִם וּשְׁלֹשׁ מֵאוֹת וְתִשְׁעָה וְשִׁשִּׁים חֻקִּים בְּתוֹרַת
אֱלֹהֵינוּ: 8) שָׁמַע כִּי נָשַׁי בְּנוֹת אַרְבַּע שָׁנִים וּשְׁלֹשִׁים שָׁנָה:
9) לֹא שְׁמֹנִים אִישׁ בַּעֲדַתְכֶם אֲשֶׁר צַדִּיקִים הֵמָּה: 10) כִּי
בֶן־מֵאָה שָׁנָה הוּא נָתַן שִׁבְעִים שֶׁקֶל זָהָב לַהֵיכָל:

1. He saw those ten men four times. 2. He had only
nineteen he-lambs and three rams. 3. Seven hundred
sixty one cattle were in our prince's fields. 4. The number of my days is ninety six years. 5. He is forty years
old, and his second wife is thirty eight years old. 6. There
are now three thousand five hundred shekels of gold in
the temple of God. 7. That gate is twelve cubits high.
8. He had twenty five manservants and nine maidservants.

SUPPLEMENTARY EXERCISE

Read the Fifth Chapter of Genesis, omitting verses 1, 2, 24, and
29. In addition to the forms וַיִּקְרָא (vs. 3), "and he called," and

וַיִּתְהַלֵּךְ (vs. 22), "and he walked," five irregular verb forms occur frequently:

וַיְחִי, from חָיָה, "And (he) lived."

וַיִּהְיוּ, from הָיָה, "And (they) were."

וַיָּמָת, from מוּת, "And he died."

וַיּוֹלֶד, from יָלַד, "And he begat."

הוֹלִידוֹ, from יָלַד, "He begat" (used in subordinate clauses).

CHAPTER XXIV

SPECIAL WORDS

A. Verbal Particles

1. This is a convenient group name for several words which, along with an earlier nominal or adverbial meaning, have frequently a partial verbal force. They definitely imply some form of the verb *to be*—a conjoined noun, or pronoun suffix (see below in ‏ֵ‎), indicating that which we would use as the subject of the sentence.

a. ‏יֵשׁ‎ (Cst. ‏יֵשׁ‎ or ‏יֶשׁ־‎) originally meant "existence, being," and its proper use is to assert existence in the abstract, "there is, there are"[1]; e.g., ‏יֵשׁ גֹּאֵל קָרוֹב מִמֶּנִּי‎ (Ruth 3:12), "There is a kinsman nearer than I"; ‏הֲיִשְׁכֶם‎ ‏בְּעָלֵינוּ‎, "Are ye our masters?" It may also be used with simple copulative force, giving more emphasis to the statement than does a plain nominal sentence; e.g., ‏יֶשְׁנוֹ‎ ‏פֹּה עִמָּנוּ‎, "He is here with us."

b. ‏אַיִן‎ (Cst. ‏אֵין‎) originally meant "nothingness, non-existence." It became the negative parallel to ‏יֵשׁ‎, meaning "there is not" (‏לֹא יֵשׁ‎ is not used); e.g.‏,‎ ‏אֵין הַמֶּלֶךְ‎ ‏בְּיִשְׂרָאֵל‎, (*lit.*, The nothingness of a king was in Israel)

---

[1] This is equivalent to the German *es gibt*, French *il y a*, or Greek εἰμι (the verb ‏הָיָה‎ being more nearly equivalent to γιγνομαι).

"There was no king in Israel"; הַאֵינֶנָּה לָהֶם, (*lit.*, Is the nothingness of it to them) "Don't they have it?"

c. עוֹד, properly "continuance, duration," used as an adverbial accusative, came to mean "yet, still"; e.g., הַעוֹד אָבִי חַי, (*lit.*, Is the continuance of my father living) "Is my father yet alive?"; הָלַךְ בְּעוֹדֶנִּי בַבַּיִת, "He went while I was yet in the house" (*lit.*, in the duration of me being in the house).

d. הִנֵּה (also written הֵן) is an interjection meaning "Lo! Behold!"; e. g., הִנְּנוּ בְיָדְךָ, "Behold, he is in thy hand." There are secondary forms of the first person suffixes, used only in a special idiom: הִנְנִי, "Here am I"; הִנֶּנּוּ, "Here we are"[1].

2. The particle usually stands first in the sentence or clause. The time may be past, present, or future. In this chapter these words are used only in nominal sentences; verbal action after any of them is regularly expressed by the participle (Ch. XXXV, B, 3, b)[2].

3. Many of the suffixes used with these words are of special form, being made emphatic by the insertion of a נ; the inflection is:

---

[1] A pronoun is sometimes written in full after הִנֵּה, instead of as a suffix. Also, to these four words here given may be added some rarer words, such as אֵי, "Where?"; e.g., אַיּוֹ (Ex. 2:20), "Where is he?"

[2] So always after יֵשׁ and אֵין. But הִנֵּה is often used with simple interjectional force before a finite verb, and עוֹד similarly with simple adverbial force (in which case it may also mean "again").

	אַיִן		עוֹד		הִנֵּה		יֵשׁ
	Plu.	Sing.	Plu.	Sing.	Plu.	Sing.	Sing.
1c	אֵינֶ֫נּוּ	אֵינֶ֫נִּי	עוֹדֶ֫נּוּ	עוֹדֶ֫נִּי	הִנְנוּ	הִנְנִי	
2m	אֵינְכֶם	אֵינְךָ	etc.	עוֹדְךָ	etc.	הִנְּךָ	יֶשְׁךָ
2f	אֵינְכֶן	אֵינֵךְ		עוֹדָךְ		הִנֵּךְ	
3m	אֵינָם	אֵינֶ֫נּוּ		עוֹדֶ֫נּוּ		הִנּוֹ	יֶשְׁנוֹ
3f	אֵינָן אֵינֶ֫נָּה		עוֹדֶ֫נָּה		הִנָּה	2mp	יֶשְׁכֶם

B. Nouns Used as Prepositions

Most prepositions are really nouns in the construct state—the word we call the object being the conjoined noun. While many words so used have entirely lost the nominal idea, and may properly be called prepositions, some are still construed as nouns,—being used either in the construct with a conjoined noun as "object," or with a pronoun suffix. The most common are:

1. פָּנִים, with a prefixed ל (*lit.*, to the face *of*), is used in the sense of "before, in front of"; e.g., לִפְנֵי הַמֶּ֫לֶךְ, "in front of the king"; לְפָנֶ֫יךָ, "before thee."

2. אַחֲרֵי (*lit.*, the rear *of*[1]), is used for "behind; after." The pointing of the stem is invariable; e.g., אַחֲרָיו, "behind him"; אַחֲרֵיכֶם, "behind you."

3. תַּ֫חַת (*lit.*, the lower part *of*), is commonly used for

---

[1] This is an abstract plural. The singular, אַחַר, occurs occasionally with a noun object, never with a pronoun suffix.

"under." When a pronoun is its object, it takes, quite irregularly, plural-noun suffixes to the singular stem; e.g., תַּחְתָּיו, "under him." This may also be used figuratively to mean "where he is"; and a second figurative meaning is "instead of, in place of."

4. בֵּין (*lit.*, separation) is used for "between." It has two peculiarities: it is used with *each* of its objects, and it takes a suffix of the singular-noun form when an object pronoun is singular but of the plural-noun form when the pronoun is plural; e.g., בֵּינוֹ וּבֵינֵינוּ וּבֵין הַיָּם, "between him and us and the sea."

VOCABULARY

אָדָם	man, mankind	לֵבָב	heart (plu. in וֹת—)
בַּד	separation; לְבַדִּי by myself, etc.	נְחֹשֶׁת	(f) brass; copper
זֶרַע	seed	עַמּוּד	column; pillar
חָכְמָה	wisdom	שְׁבוּת	(f) captivity; *coll.*, captives
יַיִן	wine	שֶׁקֶר	(i) lie, falsehood; deceit
יָמִין	(f) right hand	קָדוֹשׁ	holy

EXERCISES

1) עוֹדָם בִּשְׁבוּת בְּמִגְדָּל בַּגִּבְעָה בֵּינִי וּבֵין הַגּוֹיָא: 2) יֵשׁ
נְבִיאִים קְדוֹשִׁים רַבִּים לִפְנֵי מֶלֶךְ יִשְׂרָאֵל: 3) אֵין מִקְנֶה
לָנוּ וְאֵין נְחֹשֶׁת בְּאַרְצֵנוּ: 4) הִנְנוּ בְשִׂמְחָה כִּי יֶשְׁנוֹ פֹּה
לִימִינֵנוּ: 5) שָׁאֲלוּ לָנוּ לְיַיִן וְתַחְתָּיו נָתְנוּ לָנוּ מָיִם: 6) הַאֵינָן

אַחֲרֵינוּ בְּמִשְׁמַרְתּוֹ וְגַם סִפְרֵי חָכְמָתָן: 7) הֲיֶשְׁכֶם עֲדֵי
שְׁקָרָיו בְּעוֹדֶנּוּ שָׁם בְּתוֹכְכֶם: 8) הֶאָסַרְתָּ אֹתוֹ לְבַדְּךָ
תַּחְתֶּיךָ: 9) הִנֵּה יָפָה וּלְבָבָהּ קָשָׁה וְעוֹדֶנָּה נַעֲרָה:
10) יֶשׁ־מִדָּה אַחַת לְכָל־הָעַמּוּדִים:

1. There is a spirit of falsehood in the heart of man.
2. He is still in captivity where he was, for there is no deliverance for him.   3. Behold we are before thee, O God,
only the seed of thy people.   4. He is behind them by
himself in our place.   5. While she was at his right hand
he said to the messenger, "Here am I."   6. Is she not between you and your daughter?   7. Is there a God holier
than ours and greater in wisdom?   8. They are not in
front of the pillars of brass.

CHAPTER XXV

FURTHER USES OF THE CONSTRUCT

As indicated in Ch. XV, the construct state is used in stating various other relations besides possession. Below are listed all the more important constructions in which two words are so closely related in thought that the first takes the construct form.

1. Common "genitival" uses; i.e., in which the conjoined noun is equivalent to—

a. A *subjective* genitive of ownership (e.g., הֵיכַל הַמֶּלֶךְ, "the king's palace"), or of source (e.g., נְאֻם יְהֹוָה, "the oracle of Jehovah"), or of action (as with יֵשׁ, etc.).

b. An *objective* genitive; e.g., חֲמַס אָחִיךָ (Obad. 10), "the violence to thy brother"; also with הִנֵּה.

c. A *partitive* genitive, as with מְעַט, כֹּל, etc.; also when the Cst. is an adjective used substantively, either in expressions like חַכְמֵי הָעִיר, "the wise men of the city" (note 1, page 62), or in the circumlocution for the superlative (e. g., קְטוֹן בָּנָיו, "his youngest son"—note 1, page 63).

2. Uses generally known as *Epexegetical Genitives;* i.e., in which the conjoined noun in some special way describes or characterizes the Cst., and is—

a. Equivalent to a genitive of *material* or of *quality;*

e. g., כְּלֵי כֶסֶף, "vessels of silver"; דַּרְכֵי שָׁלוֹם, "paths of peace."

b. A substitute for an attributive adjective; e.g., בְּרִית עוֹלָם, "an everlasting, or continual, covenant"; שְׁנַת שָׁלֹשׁ, "the third year." The words אִישׁ and בֵּן are specially common in this usage; e.g., אִישׁ דְּבָרִים, "eloquent man"; and in expressions of age.

c. A statement of purpose; e.g., צֹאן טִבְחָה (Ps. 44:23), "sheep for slaughter."[1]

d. A proper name; e.g., נְהַר־פְּרָת (Gen. 15:18), "the river Euphrates."

e. A loosely associated idea; e.g., מֵי־נֹחַ (Isa. 54:9), "the waters of Noah."

f. Used with an adjective or participle:

(1) In a descriptive sense; e.g., יְפֵה־תֹאַר (Gen. 39:6), "beautiful of (i.e., in respect to) form."

(2) In statements of agency; e.g., הֲלוּמֵי יָיִן (Isa. 28:1), "overcome of (i.e., by) wine."

(3) As a substitute for an accusative with a participle; e.g., מְאִירַת עֵינָיִם (Ps. 19:9), "enlightener of the eyes (or, enlightening . . .)."

3. By a very special idiom, a word defined by a prepositional phrase or a relative clause may take the construct state; e.g., יֹשְׁבֵי בָאָרֶץ (Isa. 9:1), "the dwellers in a land"; מְקוֹם אֲשֶׁר יָשַׁב, "the place where he dwelt"; בְּיוֹם דִּבֶּר יְהוָה (Ex. 6:28), "on the day that Jehovah spoke" (cf. note 2, page 81).

4. A pronoun suffix is in every respect analogous to a noun conjoined

---

[1] Cf. also בֶּן־מָוֶת (2 Sam. 12:5), "worthy to die."

to a construct; and, besides being a possessive, it may have practically
any genitival use described above; e.g., כֹּל and חֲצִי take *partitive*
suffixes; an *objective genitive* suffix occurs in חֲמָסִי (Gen. 16:5), "the
wrong against me"; a genitive of *purpose* occurs in a suffix in יִשְׁלַח
עֶזְרְךָ (Ps. 20:3), "He will send thy help (i.e., help for thee)"; etc.[1]

VOCABULARY

בָּשָׂר	flesh	מַצָּה	unleavened; *plu. as sub.*, unleavened bread
זְרוֹעַ	(f) arm; might, power	סָבִיב	circuit; *Adv. Acc.*, *plus* לְ, around, about
חַג	feast (*5th decl.*)	עוֹלָם	eternity
חַטָּאת (f) sin (plu.חַטָּאוֹת)		עָפָר	dust
יוֹבֵל	jubilee	צָבָא	host (plu. in וֹת —)
כָּבוֹד	glory, honor, majesty	בַּעֲבוּר	on account of, for the sake of

EXERCISES

1) יָצְאוּ אַנְשֵׁי הַכָּבוֹד מִבֵּית הַמָּוֶת: 2) אֵינָם לְשָׁלוֹם כִּי
צִבְאוֹת אֹיְבֵיהֶם סָבִיב לָהֶם: 3) בְּעוֹדֶנּוּ אִתְּכֶם בָּאֲרָצוֹת
אֲחֵרוֹת כָּרְתוּ חִזְקֵי עֲבָדָיו אֶת־זְרוֹעַ אַנְשֵׁי חַטָּאת: 4) עָשָׂה
אֶת־כָּל־מִצְוֹת הֶחָג בְּעִיר יְרִיחוֹ: 5) יָצְאוּ אַנְשֵׁי שְׁקָרִים

---

[1] The noun having the suffix is practically a Cst., in form as well
as in use. The vowel pointing has minor differences, for the pronoun
fragment is usually so small, and is so very closely united with the noun,
that it affects the pronunciation, and therefore the form, less than
does a separate noun; after the *heavy* suffixes, however, the noun is
always pointed exactly as in the Cst., for these greater additions have
as strong an influence as a separate noun.

מִלִּפְנֵי שָׂרָם בַּעֲבוּר אַפּוֹ: 6) הִנָּם עֲדִי עָוֹנוּ בִּשְׁנַת הַיּוֹבֵל:
7) קְשֵׁי לֵבָב כֹּהֲנֵי בְהֵיכַלְכֶם: 8) יֵשׁ־זְרוֹעַ אֲשֶׁר גְּדוֹלָה
מִזְּרוֹעַ הַבָּשָׂר לְעוֹלָם: 9) תָּפְשָׂה אֶת־שֶׁקֶל הַזָּהָב מֵעֲפַר
אַחֲרָיו: 10) הַיְפוֹת פָּנִים בְּנוֹתֶיהָ אֲשֶׁר עָמְדוּ לְפָנֶיךָ:
11) עָמְדוּ כָל־הַמַּטִּים לִפְנֵי הַנָּבִיא לְבִרְכַת צְבָא מַחֲנָם:

1. Behold, we are only a few men (*say*, men of number), and their host is like the dust of the earth. 2. All the people kept (שָׁמַר) the feast of the unleavened bread before the Holy One of Israel. 3. Did they cut off the flesh of those honored men with their swords? 4. The priests gave a continual burnt-offering on account of the sins of our people. 5. There are tall men (*say*, men of measure) about him, and they are hard of heart. 6. My brother's strong men (*use only the adjective*) are behind him in the midst of their journey. 7. The sons of might heard the trumpets of jubilees in front of them. 8. A lying tongue said that that mighty miracle was not the greatest of his deeds.

PART FOUR

REGULAR VERBS, VERB
AND SENTENCE SYNTAX

CHAPTER XXVI

TENSE. THE IMPERFECT

A. Meaning of Tense

1. The basis of tense distinction in Hebrew is the *completeness or incompleteness of action*. The fundamental thought is not whether the action occurs in a time antecedent to, contemporaneous with, or subsequent to the present, but whether or not it is finished at the time referred to.

2. Since, then, the Hebrew has only these two time relations to state, there are only two tenses, called the *Perfect* and the *Imperfect*. *The Perfect indicates action or state as completed; the Imperfect indicates it as incomplete.*

3. It is to be specially noted, however, that the "completeness" of an action does not depend so much upon the degree of its actual accomplishment, but *on the writer's mental conception of it as finished or not;* and this may, or may not, coincide with actual facts. Hence, while the Perfect more commonly refers to past time, and the Imperfect to future time, either tense may refer to past, present, or future time[1].

---

[1] The tense names Preterite (or Past) and Future, sometimes used, are evidently both inaccurate and inadequate designations.

B. Use of the Tenses[1]

1. The perfect tense.

a. As an indication of actually completed action, this may be the equivalent of the aorist, the pluperfect, or the present perfect; e.g., בָּנוּ אֶת־הַבַּיִת כַּאֲשֶׁר צִוָּה הַמֶּלֶךְ וְלֹא רָאָה אֹתוֹ, "They *built* the house as the king *had commanded*, but he *has not seen* it."

b. In the freer use according to the writer's conceptual viewpoint, it may stand or an imperfect, a simple present, or a future perfect; e.g., כֹּה אָמַר הַמֶּלֶךְ יָכְלוּ לָדַעַת אֶת־מַחְשְׁבוֹתֵינוּ וְלָכֵן חֻזַּק הַמָּקוֹם, "Thus *saith* the king, 'They *were able* to discover our plans, and therefore the place *will have been fortified.*'"

2. The Imperfect tense.

a. This may indicate simple action in either the present or the future; e.g., יִשְׁפֹּט אֶתְכֶם יְהֹוָה כִּי יִרְאֶה עַל־הַלֵּבָב, "Jehovah *will judge* you, for He *looks* upon the heart."

b. It also may express continued or repeated action at any time; e.g., יִבְעַר הַבַּיִת, "The house *is burning*"; יְסַפֵּר אֶת־מִצְוֹתַי, "He *kept declaring* my commands."

c. It is regularly used after certain particles and conjunctions; e.g., פֶּן, לְמַעַן, and (usually) טֶרֶם.

---

[1] A more comprehensive classification of the uses of the tenses is given in the Appendix, Ch. LVI. See Ps. 10:11 for a remarkable example of variety in the rendering of Perfects.

C. Form of the Imperfect

	Singular	Plural
3m	יִקְטֹל	יִקְטְלוּ
3f	תִּקְטֹל	תִּקְטֹלְנָה
2m	תִּקְטֹל	תִּקְטְלוּ
2f	תִּקְטְלִי	תִּקְטֹלְנָה
1c	אֶקְטֹל	נִקְטֹל

1. Note that this inflection, in contrast to that of the Perfect, is accomplished principally by means of preformatives (but, like the afformatives of the Perfect, these are chiefly fragments of the personal pronouns).

2. The Shewa under the first root letter is silent; so the second, if a Beghadhkephath, takes D.L. For the use of Segol rather than Hireq as preformative vowel in the first singular, compare Ch. V, D, 3.

VOCABULARY

אָז then	לָכֵן ⎫
אַיֵּה where?	עַל־כֵּן ⎬ therefore
אֵיךְ how?	לְמַעַן in order that
אַךְ only; wholly	עַד־אֲשֶׁר until
בְּטֶרֶם (less commonly טֶרֶם) before	עַד־מָתַי how long?
יַחְדָּו together	פֶּן lest, so that not

EXERCISES

1) עַד־מָתַי לֹא יִשְׁמְעוּ לִי: 2) עַל־כֵּן עָבַדְתִּי בְּבֵיתוֹ
לְמַעַן יִזְכֹּר אֶת־מְלַאכְתִּי הַטּוֹבָה: 3) הָלְכוּ אֶל־בֵּיתָם
בְּטֶרֶם נִתְפֹּשׂ אֹתָם: 4) לָכֵן יִמְלְכוּ עַל־הֶעָרִים הָאֵלֶּה
עַד־אֲשֶׁר שָׁמַעְנוּ לָהֶם: 5) לֹא יָצְאוּ מִשָּׁם יַחְדָּו פֶּן תִּשְׁמְעוּ
אֹתָם: 6) אָז תִּזְכֹּר בַּת רֵעֵנוּ אֶת־כְּבוֹד הַמִּלְחָמוֹת אֲשֶׁר
אֲלֵיהֶן יָצָא מִמֶּנָּה: 7) אֵיךְ תִּשְׁלְחִי אֶת־שָׁלָלֵךְ אֶל־אֲדוֹנֵךְ
בַּחֲצַר הַחִיצוֹן: 8) אַיֵּה אֶתְפֹּשׂ אֶת־עֶדְיֵיהֶם: 9) אַךְ
תִּשְׁכְּחוּ אֹתִי אַחֲרֵי־אֲשֶׁר שְׁמַעְתֶּם אֹתִי: 10) הַשָּׁלַחְתֶּן־לוֹ
בְּרָכוֹת לְמַעַן תִּכְרֹתְנָה אֶת־הַבְּרִית אִתּוֹ:

1. Now I will seize the prince, but how long will I rule
over the people of his kingdom? 2. Therefore our prophet
did not say a word until we had gone as far as his house.
3. Then they sat down there together so that they might
make the covenant. 4. Oh women, why did ye not
hearken to me before ye seized him? 5. The prince was
cutting off the heads of his evil servants. 6. How will
they hear your commands? 7. They did not ask for his
good-will, lest he should remember only their counsels of
iniquity. 8. Where did they dwell after they had gone
out thence?

CHAPTER XXVII

VOICE

A. Primary Meanings and Forms of the Voices

1. *Voice* is a term of wide signification in Hebrew, including various special qualities of action. The Hebrew verb has, or can have, seven voices[1]: a *simple active* voice (already given), and *its passive;* a voice denoting *intensity* of action, and *its passive;* one indicating a *causative* influence on action, and *its passive;* and a *reflexive*[2].

This remarkable manipulation of the verb is based on the fact that the *radicals*, as the three consonants of a verb stem are called, signify a generic root idea; and this consonantal root can be variously vocalized, augmented with prefixes, etc., to express the several modifications of thought[3].

---

[1] There are very few good examples of all voices of a verb in use; see in lexicon בָּקַע, גָּלָה, יָדַע, יָלַד. Out of 280 of the most common verbs, as listed by Harper, 250 occur in Qal a total of approximately 32,000 times; 160 in Ni. 2,570 times; 150 in Pi. 4,670 times; 75 in Pu. 330 times; 170 in Hi. 6,400 times; 60 in Ho. 280 times; and 95 in Hithp. 550 times.

[2] For traces of such specialized forms in English, compare the force of certain prefixes, suffixes, and variations of vowels in related verbs; e.g., *bedeck* and *reassure*, intensives of *deck* and *assure; stabilize,* *lay,* and *fell*, causatives of *be stable, lie,* and *fall.*

[3] These various forms are sometimes called the *conjugations* of the verb. Verbs are usually listed in the lexicon in the simplest form, 3ms Perf. Qal; sometimes as an unpointed stem.

2. The voices, except the first, are named from the form which the verb פָּעַל has in the 3ms Perf. of each, as follows[1]:

In the 3ms Perf. of the	the form of פָּעַל is	hence the voice is called	Forms of קָטַל[2]
Simple active	פָּעַל	Qal [3]	קָטַל
Simple passive	נִפְעַל	Niph'al	נִקְטַל
Intensive active	פִּעֵל	Pi'el	קִטֵּל
Intensive passive	פֻּעַל	Pu'al	קֻטַּל
Causative active	הִפְעִיל	Hiph'il	הִקְטִיל
Causative passive	הָפְעַל	Hoph'al	הָקְטַל
Reflexive	הִתְפַּעֵל	Hithpa'el	הִתְקַטֵּל

3. To form the respective voices (3ms Perf.) of any regular verb, the preformatives and vowel pointings

---

[1] The use of this verb is quite arbitrary, but nearly universal; sometimes the forms of קָטַל are used, on account of the D.F.

[2] If all these forms actually occurred, their probable meanings would be: *Qal*, he killed; *Ni.*, he was killed; *Pi.*, he slaughtered (i.e., brutally or wholesale), or assassinated; *Pu.*, he was slaughtered, etc.; *Hi.*, he incited to murder, or hired assassins; *Ho.*, he was caused or hired to kill; *Hith.*, he committed suicide.

[3] This name is a Hebrew adjective meaning "light"—used in reference to the simplicity of the voice in meaning and form.

shown above with קָטַל are used[1]; note especially the
use of *D.F. in the middle radical of Piel, Pual, and Hithpael*[2] (an important point which does not appear in פָּעַל
on account of the guttural).

B. Special Voice Uses

The voices sometimes have other meanings besides the principal
ones described above.

1. The Niphal often has a reflexive meaning, like the Hithpael[3]; e.g.,
טָמֵא, "to be unclean"; Ni., "to defile oneself." Sometimes, also, it is
the equivalent of the Greek *Middle*; e.g., רָאָה, "to see"; Ni., "to
appear."

2. The Niphal, as the main passive voice, is sometimes used in
place of a Pual or Hophal for the passive of a Piel or Hiphil; so, e.g.,
in מָלַט and שָׁמַד. But unless specially stated, each voice has its
own proper passive. After any passive the agent may be expressed
by one of the prepositions לְ, מִן, or בְּ.

3. The Piel often has the causative meaning that properly belongs
to Hiphil; e.g., טָמֵא in Pi. means "to pollute."

4. A verb is often used in Piel or Hiphil in exactly the same sense
as in Qal; e.g., גֵּרֵשׁ, Q. and Pi., "to drive out"; תָּמַם, Q. and Hi.,
"to complete, finish." On the other hand, the meaning may be quite
remote from that of Qal; e.g., חָטָא, "to sin"; Pi., "to atone."

*5. The Piel sometimes, and the Hiphil more frequently, is used to

---

[1] Also, the Shewas are all silent; so the following letter, if Beghadhkephath, takes D.L.; e.g., Ni. of תָּפַשׂ is נִתְפַּשׂ.

[2] Because of the similarity of formation, Hithpael is often called
an intensive voice.

[3] Indeed, this was probably the primary meaning, from which the
passive use was evolved.

form a verbal idea from a nominal—i.e., to "turn a noun thought into action"; e.g., from עָפָר is formed עִפֵּר, "to dust"; and from אֹזֶן comes הֶאֱזִין, "to give ear, hear." This is called the *denominative* use[1].

*6. The Hithpael is sometimes used in a reciprocal sense; e.g., הִתְרָאָה, "They looked at one another." Also, it may convey the idea of pretended action, as in playing a part; e.g., הִתְאַבְּלִי (2 Sam. 14:2), "Feign thyself a mourner."

VOCABULARY

דָּבַר Pi., speak; Hith. or Ni., converse

זָכַר Hi., bring to remembrance, commemorate, make mention of; record; celebrate

מָלַט Pi., deliver; Ni., be delivered; escape

מָלַךְ be *or* become king; Hi., make king; crown

סָפַר count; Pi., narrate, declare; recount

פָּקַד visit; charge; Hi., appoint, set over; make overseer

קָרַב draw near, approach; Hi., bring near; offer (gifts)

שָׁלַךְ Hi., cast, throw

שָׁמַר keep, observe; watch, guard; Ni., beware, take heed; refrain

EXERCISES

1) מְלַט אַתָּה מֵהֶחָצֵר פֶּן יִפְקְדוּ אֶת־עֲוֹנָה עָלֶיהָ:
2) דְּבַר הַנְּאֻם מִלְּבָבְךָ וְלֹא לִישׁוּעָתָם: 3) הִשְׁלִיךְ אֶת־חֲצִי
בִגְדֵיהֶם לָאֲדָמָה בְּטֶרֶם יִקְרְבוּ אֶל־אָהֳלָם: 4) לֹא נִסְפַּר
מִסְפַּר מִשְׁפְּחוֹת בְּנֵי־יִשְׂרָאֵל: 5) הַזְכֵּר חֵיל גִּבּוֹרָיו הַיְשָׁרִים

---

[1] A similar result is achieved in English by certain prefixes and suffixes; e.g., accredit, beautify, belittle, lengthen, luxuriate, victimize.

אַחֲרֵי־אֲשֶׁר שָׁמְרוּ אֶת־הֵיכָלוֹ: 6) נִשְׁאַל דָּבָר קָשֶׁה
מִשִּׁבְטָהּ: 7) הִפְקִיד אֶת־בָּנָיו עַל־מַעֲשַׂר מְדִינָתֵינוּ:
8) נִשְׁמַר מִפִּשְׁעֵי הַתּוֹרָה אַחֲרֵי־אֲשֶׁר סִפֶּר־לוֹ מִשְׁפַּט
הָרְשָׁעִים: 9) הָפְקַד הַשַּׂר הַזֶּה עַל־מַחֲנֶה מַמְלַכְתּוֹ:
10) סִפֵּר לַנָּשִׂיא הַתָּמִים אֶת־חֵיל שְׁבָטָיו וְאֶת־תִּפְאַרְתָּם
בַּמִּלְחָמָה אֲשֶׁר־בָּהּ נִמְלַט מִמַּחְשְׁבוֹת צָרוֹ:

1. We did not observe the commands until he brought them to remembrance. 2. A wise word was spoken by the stranger whose master was made king. 3. He took heed lest they should count all his sins. 4. He brought his children near to the prophet after he declared Jehovah's laws. 5. He delivered from death the remnant of their (f) tribe over which he had been appointed by his king. 6. He made his first-born king over half the nation. 7. Our book was sent to the wisest men of your city. 8. Did he cast his sword upon your table?

CHAPTER XXVIII

FULL INFLECTION OF THE TENSES

A. Skeleton Paradigm

	Qal	Ni.	Pi.	Pu.	Hi.	Ho.	Hith.
Perf. 3ms	קָטַל	נִקְטַל	קִטֵּל	קֻטַּל	הִקְטִיל	הָקְטַל	הִתְקַטֵּל
2ms	קָטַלְתָּ	נִקְטַלְתָּ	קִטַּלְתָּ	etc.	הִקְטַלְתָּ	etc.	הִתְקַטַּלְתָּ
3cp	קָטְלוּ	נִקְטְלוּ	קִטְּלוּ	קֻטְּלוּ	הִקְטִילוּ		הִתְקַטְּלוּ
Impf. 3ms	יִקְטֹל	יִקָּטֵל	יְקַטֵּל	יְקֻטַּל	יַקְטִיל	יָקְטַל	יִתְקַטֵּל
1cs	אֶקְטֹל	אֶקָּטֵל	אֲקַטֵּל	אֲקֻטַּל	אַקְטִיל	etc.	etc.
3fp	תִּקְטֹלְנָה	תִּקָּטַלְנָה	תְּקַטֵּלְנָה	תְּקֻטַּלְנָה	תַּקְטֵלְנָה		

B. General Principles of Verb Inflection

1. *Vowel afformatives*, i. e., those beginning with a vowel sound, are preceded by vocal Shewa under the second radical in all voices except Hiphil—where the Long Hireq remains before all vowel endings.[1]

2. The accent, in general, is on the syllable containing the second radical; e. g., קָטַ֫לְתָּ, יִקְטִ֫ילוּ. But it is on the ultima—

a. When the second radical has Shewa; e.g., נִקְטְלָ֫ה[2].

---

[1] All consonantal afformatives are of course preceded by silent Shewa under the last radical.

[2] The vowel under the first radical, if long, receives Metheg; e.g., Pf. Qal, קָ֫טְלוּ; Impf. Ni., יֵ֫קָטְלוּ.

b. With the heavy second plural afformatives in the Perf.; e.g., קְטַלְתֶּם. (In Qal this of course results in the shortening of the tone-long Qamets in the first syllable to Shewa; e.g., קְטַלְתֶּם).

3. The afformatives in all the voices are the same as in Qal; so also are the consonants of the preformatives in the Impf.

4. When the last radical of the verb is the same as the first letter of an afformative, it is written with a D.F. instead of being repeated; e.g., נָתַנּוּ for נָתַנְנוּ, and כָּרַתָּ for כָּרַתְתָּ (but a ט does not thus assimilate; e.g., מִלַּטְתִּי).

5. The stems of verbs, as of nouns, frequently retain primitive vowel pointings in the inflected and derived forms.

a. The vowel under the second radical in both tenses of all voices (except Impf. Qal) was originally Pathah. The present vowels of the 3ms probably were developed simply to secure some variety of sound in the leading forms; the Pathah remains before all consonantal afformatives except in Impf. Piel and Hiphil (and sometimes Hithpael), where Tsere is used.

b. In Piel, Pathah originally stood under the first radical; e.g., קִטֵּל, יְקַטֵּל (see below in C). And the preformative of Hiphil originally had Pathah—Perf., הַקְטֵל.

c. In some forms of Niphal, a ה originally stood before the נ (see below in C, 1, b).

C. Deriving the Imperfect

1. The preformative יְ, which was attached to the voice-stem to form the 3ms Impf.[1], had vocal Shewa in the

---

[1] The other persons were similarly formed, and each preformative

ground-forms (except in Qal); this remained in Piel (יְקַטֵּל)
and Pual, but elsewhere was changed.

a. In Hi., Ho., and Hith., the voice preformative הַ was
elided and the י took the vowel which this had in place of
its own Shewa[1]; e.g., יְהַקְטֵל became יְקַטֵל, etc.

b. In the ground-form of Ni., יְהִנְקָטֵל, the נ was
assimilated, the הַ elided, and the vowels lengthened,
giving יִקָּטֵל.

2. The vowel pointings of the stems are in some cases
closer to those of the primitive forms than is the case in
the Perfect. Note especially the primitive Pathah under
the first radical in Pi. and under the preformative in Hi.
(B, 5, b, above), in contrast to the Hireq in the Perfect
of each.

D. Special Notes

1. In the intensives of בקשׁ and some other words, D.F. is dropped
when the letter has vocal Shewa (Ch. IV, A, 2, b); e.g., בְּקַשׁוּ for בִּקְשׁוּ.

2. The preformative of Hith. is modified in two cases:

a. When the first radical is a sibilant (ס, צ, שׁ), it and the
ת of the preformative change places (doubtless in order to facilitate
pronunciation); e.g., שָׁמַר, Hith. הִשְׁתַּמֵּר. And when the first radical
is צ, a further change occurs, ת becoming ט; e.g., צָדַק, הִצְטַדַּק.

b. When the first radical is ד, ט, or ת, the ת of the preformative

---

is pointed just as the י is (except that א has Segol instead of Hireq, and
Hateph Pathah instead of simple Shewa).

[1] The הַ, being a weak letter, easily drops out; cf. the similar process with the article after בְּ, כְּ, and לְ.

is assimilated into it and represented by D.F.; e.g., הִטַּהֵר, הַדִּבֵּר, יְהַתַּמֵּם[1].

3. There is a secondary form of Pi. which has the primitive Pathah in the second syllable in the Perf.; so, e.g., in שָׁלַם, קָדַשׁ, and some weak verbs. Also, there are three verbs which have final Segol in the Perf.: דבר, כפר, and כבס. In the Impf. all these verbs usually have the regular Tsere.

*4. A secondary form of Hophal, with Qibbuts under the preformative, occurs in a few regular verbs and certain classes of irregulars.

*5. Thruout the Pentateuch the Fem. Plu. Impf. is written without the ה; e.g., תִּקְטֹלָן. And the 2ms Perf. is sometimes written תָּה—.

*6. A *paragogic* Nun is frequently added to the Masc. Plu. Impf., especially when the word is emphatic; e.g., יִקְטְלוּן.

VOCABULARY

בקשׁ Pi., search, search for, seek after; inquire of (Jehovah)

סתר Hi., hide, conceal; Ni., be hid; hide oneself (so also Hith.)

צָדַק be just, righteous; Hi. (also Pi.), justify, make righteous; Hith., justify oneself

קָדַשׁ be pure, holy; Ni., be sanctified; Pi. (also Hi.), sanctify, consecrate; keep holy;

Hith., purify *or* sanctify oneself

רָחַק be distant; Hi., remove

שׂכל Hi., be wise, act wisely; make wise

שָׁלַם be whole; be at peace; Pi., make whole; perform (vows); recompense; Hi., make peace

נֶדֶר vow

עֶרֶב evening

---

*1 This also occurs occasionally before כ or נ; e.g., הִנָּבֵּא; and even before ז or שׁ (in place of transposition); e.g., הִשָּׁמֵּם.

EXERCISES

1) נִסְתְּרוּ נְבִיאֵי יְהֹוָה בָּהָרִים: 2) הִתְקַדְּשָׁה אַחֲרֵי־
אֲשֶׁר דִּבֶּר לָהּ: 3) הִצְדַּקְנוּ אֹתוֹ לְאָבִיו עַל־הַנְּדָרִים אֲשֶׁר
לֹא שָׁלַם לַיהֹוָה: 4) הֲלֹא בִקַּשְׁתָּ אֶת־דַּם הַשָּׁבוּת מִיַּד
הַכֹּהֵן: 5) הַהִשְׁכַּלְתֶּם כִּי לֹא קִדַּשְׁתֶּם אֶת־הַשַּׁבָּת וְאָז
הִצְטַדַּקְתֶּם:

6) אַקְרִיב אֹתָךְ לִימִין מַלְכָּתֵךְ: 7) אַיֵּה תְשַׁלֵּם אֶת־
נְדָרֶךְ אֲשֶׁר־בּוֹ אָסְרוּ אֹתָךְ: 8) הֲתַרְחֵקְנָה נְשֵׁי הַנְּעָרִים
אֶת־מוֹקְשֵׁיהֶם אֲשֶׁר הִסְתִּירוּ הַיּוֹם בִּשְׂפַת הַנָּהָר: 9) לֹא
יִלָּקְחוּ אַנְשֵׁי מִלְחַמְתֵּנוּ מִמְּלַאכְתָּם בְּטֶרֶם נַשְׁלִים: 10) לֹא
תִמָּלֵט כִּי לֹא תִשָּׁכַחְנָה חַטֹּאותֶיהָ:

1. The old men sanctified themselves after they removed his abominations. 2. Why did not the prophets inquire of Jehovah this evening? 3. Thou (f) hast performed thy vows, and therefore I have justified thee. 4. Ye were cut off from your friends, but were not removed from your house.

5. Wilt thou hide me, O maiden, until they make peace? 6. Ye were acting wisely before your friends. 7. We are hidden here so that we may escape from the judgment of their congregation. 8. How will she perform her vows before she is sanctified?

SUPPLEMENTARY VOCABULARY

אוֹת (f) sign   מִגְרָשׁ pasture

אֱמֶת (f) truth   צָפוֹן north

דַּעַת (f) knowledge

חֹשֶׁךְ darkness   קֶדֶם east

כֹּחַ strength   קָהָל congregation

SUPPLEMENTARY EXERCISES

1) הַהִסְתַּתַּרְתָּה עִמָּךְ תַּחַת הַצּוּר: 2) הִסְתַּרְתִּי אֶת־אַפִּי
מִמֶּנָּה: 3) הֲבִקַּשְׁתֶּם אֶת־מוֹתוֹ אַחֲרֵי־אֲשֶׁר הִשְׁלַמְתֶּם אִתּוֹ:
4) נִמְלְטוּ צִבְאוֹת אֹיְבֵיהֶם נֶגְבָּה: 5) הֲזָכַרְתִּי אֶת־הַנְּדָרִים
אֲשֶׁר עָלָיו:

6) הִרְחִיקוּ כָל־אַנְשֵׁי הַקָּהָל אֶת־תּוֹעֲבֹתֵיהֶם וְעַתָּה
יִקְדָּשׁוּ: 7) הֲתִתְקָרְבִי לְבַעְלִי לְמַעַן נַשְׁלִים: 8) יִתֵּן הָאוֹר
לָעַמִּים אֲשֶׁר בַּחֹשֶׁךְ: 9) הַאַסְתִּיר אֶת־פָּרוֹ בָּעֵצִים בְּתוֹךְ
הַמִּגְרָשׁ: 10) תַּשְׂכִּילוּ אֶת־יַלְדֵיכֶם אִם תַּזְכִּירוּ אֲלֵיהֶם
אֶת־הַתּוֹרוֹת הָאֵלֶּה:

1. We hid the bones of his ram under our tent.
2. That evening all the servants were sanctified, and in the morning they were brought near to the altar.   3. Have ye searched for the men with whom the daughter of your delight spoke?   4. Did I act wisely after we made peace?

5. We are seeking for knowledge of the tribes of the north and east. 6. If thou wilt make mention of this sign, thou wilt escape in the darkness. 7. We were recounting the number of his strong hills (*say*, hills of his strength). 8. Ye have not concealed the truth, and therefore ye shall be justified by your congregation.

CHAPTER XXIX
THE IMPERATIVE

A. Forms

1. Skeleton Paradigm.

	Qal	Ni.	Pi.	Hi.	Hith.
2ms	קְטֹל	הִקָּטֵל	קַטֵּל	הַקְטֵל	הִתְקַטֵּל
2mp	קִטְלוּ	הִקָּטְלוּ	קַטְּלוּ	הַקְטִילוּ	הִתְקַטְּלוּ
Coh	קָטְלָה	הִקָּטְלָה	קַטְּלָה	הַקְטִילָה	הִתְקַטְּלָה

2. The Impv., 2ms, is formed by dropping the preformative of the Impf., and restoring ה in the forms from which it was elided[1]; also, in Hi., Long Hireq is changed to Tsere.

    a. The Shewa left under the first radical in Qal is of course vocal.

    b. Pu. and Ho. Impv. do not occur in strong verbs.

3. The inflectional forms closely correspond to those in the second person of the Impf., the afformatives being the same and the vowel changes in the stem usually so. However—

    a. When the vowel afformatives are added to Qal,

---

*1 More strictly, the Impv. is like the Inf. (Ch. XXXIV), and the Impf. is formed from this by attaching the preformatives.

two Shewas are thrown together; the first heightens to Hireq.

b. When vowel afformatives are added to Hi., the final Tsere gives way to the characteristic Long Hireq.

4. A special form of the 2ms, called the *Cohortative Imperative*, is made by adding the ending הָ‎֑. Note that in Qal the Shewa under the first radical heightens not to Hireq, but to Qamets Hatuph — presumably out of a desire to retain an *o* sound[1].

B. Syntax

1. The Impv. is used only in giving positive commands; for prohibitions, see next Chapter.

2. The Cohortative Impv. may either give a less brusque tone to the command, or add more insistence, according to the context. The note of entreaty may commonly be expressed in English by adding "now"; e.g., הַשְׁקִיפָה מִן הַשָּׁמַיִם (Dt. 26:15), "Look down now from heaven"[2].

3. The particle נָא, "prithee," is frequently joined to the simple or cohortative Impv.

---

[1] The קְטָלָה of the 3fs Perf. is distinguished from this קָטְלָה by the Metheg.

[2] Note three different uses of our word "now:" (1) temporal— Hebrew עַתָּה; (2) to add a note of entreaty, as here; (3) to introduce a statement of incidental detail (as, e.g., in Num. 12:3; Dan. 6:10)— for which, in Hebrew, see Ch. XXXII, B.

VOCABULARY

דָּרַשׁ seek (Jehovah); require, seek from; in-
quire, ask

כפר Pi., ᵓcover; expiate,
atone for; forgive

לחם Ni., fight, wage war
(בְּ, against)

רָדַף pursue

שָׂרַף burn

שׁאר Hi., leave, let remain;
Ni., be left, remain

שָׁפַךְ pour out

דֶּבֶר pestilence

נַחֲלָה inheritance

פָּרָשׁ horseman (*first—fixed*)

רֶכֶב (i) chariot

רָעָב famine

EXERCISES

1) פָּקְדָה־דִנָּא אֹתִי וְכַפְּרָה אֶת־פְּשָׁעַי: 2) הַשְׁאֶר־נָא לָנוּ
אֶת־נַחֲלָתֵנוּ בְּשָׁלוֹם: 3) הִלָּחֲמוּ בְרִכְבֵּיהֶם וְשָׁפְכוּ אֶת־דַּם
פָּרָשֵׁיהֶם: 4) הִסְתַּתְּרָנָה כְּמַחֲשַׁבְתָּה בָּעֵמֶק הַהוּא אֲשֶׁר
לֹא יִרְדֹּף אֶתְכֶן הַנָּשִׂיא שָׁמָּה: 5) הַרְחִיקָה אֶת־הַדָּבָר
הַגָּדוֹל הַזֶּה מִמֶּנּוּ פֶּן יִשָּׁאֵר רַק חֲצִי גּוֹיֵנוּ: 6) הִשָּׁמֶר־לְךָ
פֶּן יִפְקְדוּ כָל־חַטֹּאותֶיךָ עָלֶיךָ: 7) רִדְפָנָה שָׁלוֹם עִם
אַנְשֵׁי קְצִירְכֶן: 8) בַּקְּשׁוּ אֶת־מִזְבַּח הָאֱלֹהִים הַנָּעֳרִים:
9) דַּבְּרִי־נָא אֶת־נְאֻם יְהֹוָה: 10) דִּרְשׁוּ אֶת־יְהֹוָה בְּעוֹדְכֶם
פֹּה:

1. Seek ye Jehovah, for He has come near unto you.
2. Atone for your elder's transgressions, ye attendants of
his. 3. Fight, O prince, against those horsemen, pursue
them to the hills. 4. Leave my chariots, I pray thee,

near this tower. 5. Sanctify yourselves, O daughters of Israel, on account of this famine. 6. Deliver us, O God, from this pestilence. 7. Pour out thy spirit upon us, O God. 8. Hide your chariot from the enemies of your king, lest they burn it.

CHAPTER XXX

JUSSIVE AND COHORTATIVE

A. Modal Forms

1. Hebrew has only a partially developed system of moods. There are two special modifications of the Impf. which regularly express certain modal ideas[1]: the *Jussive*, used only in the second and third persons; and the *Cohortative*, used only in the first person[2].

2. To express the Jussive[3] idea, the Impf. was spoken quickly, with a tone of decision; this gave rise, in some cases, to distinct, shortened forms.

a. In the 3ms, 3fs, and 2ms Hi. of all verbs, *the Long Hireq was replaced by Tsere* (just as in the Impv.); e.g., יַשְׁלֵם, "Let him make peace."

b. But in all other voices of the strong verb, and always in forms with afformatives, the Jussive is identical in form with the simple Impf.[4]; the context must decide the use.

---

1 The Perfect, in all voices, indicating completed action, is practically excluded from any modal usages.

*2 Rarely the Jussive occurs in the first person and the Cohortative in the other persons.

3 From Latin *jussum*, supine of *jubeo*, "to order."

4 Some weak verbs have special Jussive forms in these other voices; see Chs. XLIII, C, 1; **L,** B, 1.

3. The Cohortative is formed by adding to the first person Impf. the hortatory ending הָ‎ֶ; e. g., אֶקְטְלָה‎ "Let me kill"; נַשְׁלִיכָה‎, "Let us throw."

B. Syntax

1. These modal forms have their own special negative—אַל‎; לֹא‎ is not used with them (cf. the μη and οὐ in Greek). When the particle נָא‎ is used in a negative sentence, it is usually joined to the אַל‎.

2. The principal uses of the Jussive include:

a. Commands given in the third person; e.g., יְהִי אוֹר‎ (Gen. 1:3), "Let there be light"; תִּכְבַּד הָעֲבוֹדָה עַל‎ הָאֲנָשִׁים‎ (Ex. 5:9), "Let the work be made heavy upon the men."

b. Exhortations or suggestions; e.g., תָּגֵל הָאָרֶץ‎ (1 Chron. 16:31), "Let the earth rejoice"; יַפְקֵד פְּקִדִים‎ (Gen. 41:34), "Let him appoint overseers."

c. Entreaty, including simple wishes or prayers and blessings or imprecations; e.g., אַל יִחַר אַפְּךָ‎ (Gen. 44:18), "Let not thine anger burn."

d. Prohibitions (a substitute for a negative Impv.); e.g., אַל תִּקְרַב הֲלֹם‎ (Ex. 3:5), "Do not draw nigh hither."[1]

3. The Cohortative is in large measure the counterpart of the Jussive for the first person.

---

[1] Sometimes, however, the simple Impf. with לֹא‎ is used. This is properly an emphatic declaration, to which absolute agreement is expected, rather than a dissuasive warning, and is practically confined to formal commands from Deity; e.g., לֹא תִרְצָח‎ (Dt. 5:17), "Thou shalt not kill."

a. Thus it is used to ask permission or make other entreaty, or to state a wish, purpose, or resolution; also for self-encouragement, or exhortation; e.g., אֶעְבְּרָה־נָּא בְאַרְצֶךָ (Jg. 11:17), "Let me, I pray thee, pass through thy land"; נֵלְכָה וְנַעַבְדָה אֱלֹהִים אֲחֵרִים (Dt. 13:14), "Let us go and serve other gods."

b. It can also express determination or assuredness of statement (equal to our *I will* as vs. *I shall*); e.g., וַאֲגַדְּלָה שְׁמֶךָ (Gen. 12:2), "And I will make thy name great."

4. The Jussive and Cohortative are the equivalents of practically any English verb with *let*—whether that "let" be simply an auxiliary verb, as in "Let the earth rejoice," or an independent verb equal to "permit," as in "Let me pass through." Note that in all cases the subject is the following noun or pronoun (as in Latin, Greek, etc.), and not an understood "you" as in the English idiom with "let."

5. These forms are also used in certain instances without conveying any modal idea; see next chapter.

VOCABULARY

כָּתַב	write	עֵבֶר	the region beyond;
מָשַׁל	rule, have dominion (בְ, over)	אֶל־עֵבֶר	across, beyond (*of motion*);
פָּרַשׂ	spread, spread out	בְּעֵבֶר	id. (*of location*)
שָׁבַר	break	רֵאשִׁית	(f) beginning; first-fruits
תָּקַע	strike, drive; pitch (tent); blow (trumpet)	גַּם	also
חָרְפָּה	reproach	הֵנָּה	hither

EXERCISES

1) אַל תְּשַׁבְּרוּ אֶת־מִצְוֹתַי פֶּן בְּאַפִּי אַךְ תְּבָלְעוּ:
2) נִכְתְּבָה סֵפֶר גָּדוֹל מִזֶּה: 3) יַקְרֵב הֵנָּה לְבַדּוֹ אֶת־
הָאֲבָנִים הָהֵנָּה מֵעֵבֶר הַנַּחַל: 4) אַל־תַּזְכֵּר זֹאת לַזְּקֵנִים:
5) יִפְרְשׂוּ־נָא אֶת־אָהֳלֵיהֶם וְיִתְקְעוּ אֹתָם בִּקְצֵה מִגְרָשְׁכֶם:
6) אַל יַשְׁלֵךְ חֲרָפוֹת עָלֵינוּ: 7) אֶשְׁמְרָה גַּם אֶת־חַג רֵאשִׁית:
8) יִרְדֹּף רַע אֶת־דַּרְכְּךָ וְיִמְשֹׁל רָעָב בְּמִשְׁכָּנְךָ וְאַל יִשָּׁאֵר־
לְךָ שֶׁקֶל אֶחָד: 9) אַל־נָא יַזְכִּרוּ שְׁקָרָיו עָלָיו: 10) תִּלָּחֶם־
נָא אִשְׁתּוֹ לִבְכוֹרָה:

1. Let these laws concerning the first-fruits be written in those books. 2. Do not thou have dominion over our land. 3. Let us spread out our garments before them. 4. Let the priests blow the trumpet for the beginning of our feast. 5. Let them not escape hither from his kingdom. 6. Let me, I pray thee, break their swords and burn their chariots. 7. Let her also hide our gold beyond that river. 8. Let him remove our reproach from upon us.

CHAPTER XXXI

WAW CONSECUTIVE

A. Meaning and Use

1. In expressing time relations, Hebrew is handicapped by its limited tense system and the paucity of subordinate clauses. The simple verbal forms have therefore been supplemented by two special constructions: one to indicate consecutive events, as explained in this chapter; and another to indicate antecedent or attendant circumstances (which must of course be differentiated from the main narrative), as explained in Ch. XXXII, B.

2. The construction used in a *simple past series* is to be explained on the principle that the use of the Hebrew tenses is largely a matter of the point of view (Ch. XXVI, A, 3). Here the view-point regularly adopted is that of *the first action in the series,*—the other actions then being only in process or prospect of accomplishment, and so not completed. Hence, while the first verb takes the Perf., each subsequent action is expressed by a verb in the *Imperfect tense*, joined by the conjunction וֹ to the preceding verb; e.g., יָצְאוּ וַיִּשְׁמְעוּ אֹתוֹ וַיִּשְׂמְחוּ, "They went out and heard him and rejoiced."

   a. The conjunction in this usage, which is called "Waw Consecutive with the Impf.," is always *pointed like the article*—i.e., ordinarily with Pathah followed by D.F. (the D.F. being omitted, however, from the י of the third Masc. Pi. and Pu.—Ch. IV, A, 2, b), with Qamets before א.

b. An Impf. with Waw Consec. is therefore always equal to a Perf.; and it is always used instead of a Perf. for the second and all succeeding verbs in a series of past actions (unless the series be interrupted; see below in 4).

3. The construction used in a *simple future series* closely corresponds, in a formal way, to that just described for a past series. The first verb is of course in the Impf.; but each subsequent verb is regularly placed in the *Perfect tense*, joined to the preceding one by a ו pointed with simple Shewa (or one of the other forms described in Ch. IX, B)[1]; e.g., יִזְכֹּר אֹתָם וְהָלַךְ וְדִבֶּר לָהֶם, "He will remember them and will go and speak to them." A Perf. with such a Waw Consec. is therefore always equal to an Impf.; and it is always used instead of an Impf. for the second and all succeeding verbs in a series of future actions (unless the series be interrupted).

---

[1] This construction is usually explained as simply a false analogy to, and an illogical imitation of, the construction in a past series. Among other theories proposed, we suggest that, since the first verb is in the Impf., obviously no subsequent action could be completed; and hence for the following verbs the *simpler* Perf. is used—merely stating the verb action, to which the presiding genius of the first verb, perpetuated by the closely connecting Waw, imparts the "imperfect" quality.

4. This special construction can be used only when a verb is directly joined by וֹ to the preceding verb or clause. Therefore, when any word except the verb stands first in the clause, so that the וֹ cannot be attached to the verb, *the immediacy of consecution is broken, and the verb takes the form proper to it in its own meaning;* e.g., עָמַד פֹּה וַיְדַבֵּר וְאַחֲרֵי־כֵן בָּרַח, "He stood here and spoke, and afterwards fled."

Dependent words or clauses *following* a verb, however, have no effect; the central train of thought leaps across these subordinate ideas, and the next main verb can take the consecutive construction just as when the verbs are immediately contiguous; e.g., see various sentences above.

B. Influence on Form

1. *Waw Consec. with the Impf. always takes the Jussive form*, instead of the simple Impf.; e.g., הָלַךְ וַיַּשְׁלֵם, "He went and made peace." With the first person, the simple Impf. is usually used[1].

2. When the penult of an Impf. is long and open, Waw Consec. draws the accent from the ultima onto this penult, and then the vowel of the ultima is shortened, being no longer in tone; e. g., in Ni., וַיִּשָּׁמֶר.

---

[1] But sometimes the Cohortative occurs, as a parallel to the Jussive; very occasionally also a first person Jussive. The Jussive (or Cohortative) after Waw Consec. has no modal force whatever.

3. Waw Consec. with the Perf. usually causes the accent to be thrown onto the ultima in the forms which had it on the penult; a tone-long vowel in the ante-penult is not thinned down to Shewa, however, but given a secondary accent (Metheg); e.g.,   יְכָתֹב וְזָכַרְתִּ֫י.

C. Special Uses

1. The verb הָיָה, "to be, become," is commonly used in narration in the sense "to come to pass." The next verb is coördinate, joined with Waw Consec., instead of being subordinated by the conjunction "that" as in the English idiom; e.g., יִסָּתְרוּ וְהָיָה אַחֲרֵי־כֵן וְנִמְלָטוּ, "They will hide, and it will come to pass afterwards that they will escape." In the Impf. with Waw Consec. this verb has an irregular form, וַיְהִי, "And it came to pass."

2. The Waw Consec. construction need not depend on a simple Perf. or Impf. It may depend on an Impv. or Participle; or upon a nominal sentence; or even an assumed verbal idea. Thus in grammar exercises some sentences are given beginning with "and"—implying that they are parts of series altho the first verbs of the series are not given. Also, a past series may depend on a frequentative Impf.; and a future series on an action in past time.

3. Waw Consec. most commonly indicates chronological sequence, and is translated "and." But sometimes there is an idea of logical sequence, and then the translation is "then," or "and so." Or some idea of contrast may be involved, indicated by translating it "but," or "and yet." Also, this construction is frequently used where we would use a temporal or other subordinate clause, and then the best translation is as a complex rather than a compound sentence.

4. A rather curious but very important construction occurs in conditional sentences, where the apodosis is commonly (tho not always)

introduced by a Waw Consec. (indicating logical sequence); e.g.,
אִם אֶשָּׁאֵר פֹּה וַעֲבַדְתִּי אֹתָךְ, "If I remain here, then I will serve you."

*5. Since a frequentative or progressive action takes the Impf. in its own right, it will be represented in a series by a Perf. with Waw Consec. (see, e.g., 1 Sam. 16:23); i.e., this construction has become established as the equivalent of the Impf., whatever the temporal meaning of the Impf. may be. Similarly a present action which might take the Perf. in its own right would, in a series, take an Impf. with Waw.

VOCABULARY

בָּרַח	flee	שבע	Ni., swear (בְּ, by; לְ, to); Hi., bind, adjure
זָרַע	sow	שָׁבַת	rest, cease; Hi., give rest to
לָכַד	take, capture	זָכָר	male
סָגַר	shut, close; Hi., deliver over	קֶשֶׁת	(f) bow

EXERCISES

1) נִשְׂרֹף אֶת־הַזֶּרַע הַזֶּה וְזָרַעְנוּ אֶת־זַרְעֲכֶם הַטּוֹב:

2) נִרְדְּפוּ וַיִּבְרְחוּ מֵהַמָּקוֹם הַהוּא: 3) נִשְׁבַּעְתִּי כִּי אַסְגִּיר אֹתוֹ וַתִּזָּכֵר אֶת־נִדְרִי אֵלָי: 4) יְכַפֵּר אֶת־שְׁקָרָיו אֲשֶׁר דִּבֶּר וְהַצַּדִּיק: 5) הָלַכְתִּי אֶל־בֵּיתוֹ וָאֶשְׁבֹּת וּמִשָּׁם בָּרַחְתִּי:

6) אִם גְּדוֹלָה חָכְמָתוֹ מֵחָכְמַת אֹיְבָיו וְשָׁבַר אֶת־חֵילָם:

7) וַיְהִי בָּעֶרֶב הַהוּא וַיְבַקְשׁוּ אֶת־קַשְׁתִּי בַּשָּׂדֶה סָבִיב לְמַחֲנָם וַיִּשָּׁבֵר: 8) אִם נַשְׂכִּיל מִמֶּנּוּ נִלְכַּד אֹתוֹ: 9) לֹא

נָתְנָה לָהֶם חֶסֶד וַיִּבְרְחוּ מִלְּפָנֶיהָ: (10 אִם לֹא תִשְׁבַּתְנָה
בְּתֵיכֶם מִשְׁקְרֵיהֶן וְהִסְגַּרְנוּ אֹתָן לַשֹּׁפְטִים:

1. Ye visited his fields and sowed bad seed in them.
2. All the males will remain and swear that they will fight.
3. He went to this large gate, and it was closed.   4. They
did not rest on the sabbath day, and did not keep it holy.

5. And it shall come to pass, if the peace be broken,
that the city shall be shut up (*Pu.*).   6. But it came to
pass after we had captured her master that she gave rest
to his other servants.   7. The shepherds were resting
under their trees and were watching their flocks.   8. If
they shall pitch tent here this evening, we will flee from
them and escape.

SUPPLEMENTARY VOCABULARY

בָּדֵל	Hi., separate, select, choose out; Ni., *Pass.*	כְּסִיל	fool
בָּצַר	cut off; fortify	מִקְדָּשׁ	sanctuary
גָּנַב	steal	תְּהִלָּה	praise
קָצַר	reap, harvest	תְּפִלָּה	prayer

SUPPLEMENTARY EXERCISES

(1 הָלְכוּ לְאָחִיו וַיִּשָּׁבְעוּ־לוֹ כִּי יִמְשֹׁל בָּם: (2 יִשְׂרֹף
אֶת־עָרֵיכֶם וְשָׁפַךְ אֶת־דָּמְכֶם: (3 הָלַךְ אֶל־פִּתְחוֹ וַיִּסָּגֵר
עָלָיו: (4 יִזְכֹּר אֶת־הַחֲקִּים הָהֵמָּה וְלֹא יִקָּטֵל בַּקֶּשֶׁת:
(5 נִלְחַם בְּכָל־הַזְּכָרִים וְלָכַדְנוּ אֶת־חֲצֵרָם:

6) וְהָיָה הַשָּׁנָה הַזֹּאת וְנָתַן בַּעֲלֵנוּ חֵלֶק בַּשָּׁלָל לַעֲבָדָיו
וְנָתְנוּ אֵלָיו כֻּלָּם תְּהִלּוֹת: 7) וַיִּסְגֹּר יְהֹוָה אֶת־אָזְנָיו
מִתְּפִלַּתְכֶם בַּמִּקְדָּשׁ כִּי גְנַבְתֶּם אֶת־דְּבָקַר רֶעֲכֶם וַתִּשְׁמְרוּ:
8) אִם נִכְרֹת בְּרִית אִתְּךָ וְנָתַנּוּ לְךָ אֶת־הַמִּגְרָשִׁים וְהַשַּׁבָּת
אֹתָנוּ מִמְּלַאכְתֵּנוּ: 9) וַיְהִי בַּעֲבוּר חַטֹּאותָם וַיִּפָּרְשׁוּ
הַכְּסִילִים עַל־פְּנֵי הָאָרֶץ: 10) זֶרַע הַנַּעַר אֶת־זַרְעוּ וַיִּקְצֹר
הַזָּקֵן אֶת־פִּרְיוֹ:

1. They will flee, and their fields will their enemies harvest (*preserve this emphatic order*). 2. He broke her bow and cast it at her feet. 3. Their men of war acted wisely and captured the fool. 4. They will only speak lies, and therefore we will charge them and adjure them not to (פֶּן) hide the truth.

5. And we will remember thy kindness and will give thee praise. 6. And it came to pass, because he stole the sacred vessels from the sanctuary, that he was cut off from before the face of God. 7. And it will come to pass in the morning that I will select my horsemen. 8. And he spoke his prayers and delivered his soul over unto God.

CHAPTER XXXII

SIMPLE WAW

A. Modal Ideas in Series

1. When Jussives, Cohortatives, or Imperatives occur in series, they regularly retain their own proper form, and are joined with a simple Waw—i.e., וֹ pointed with Shewa or one of the other forms given in Ch. 9, B; e. g., יֵרֶא פַּרְעֹה אִישׁ. . . וְיַפְקֵד פְּקִדִים (Gen. 41 : 33–34), "Let Pharaoh look out a man . . . and let him appoint overseers, etc." This is commonly called *Weak Waw*, in distinction from the consecutive use in which the tense form is affected.

a. Distinguish a Jussive with simple Waw, which is a real Jussive (future time and modal), from a Jussive form with Waw Consec., which is the idiomatic equivalent of a Perf. (past time and simple).

b. An Impf. form with simple Waw is thereby shown to be a Jussive.

2. Two modal ideas thus joined may be coördinate, as above. But frequently the second is subordinate, giving the purpose of the first; e.g., הַעְתִּירוּ אֶל־יְהֹוָה וְיָסֵר הַצְפַרְדְּעִים וַאֲשַׁלְּחָה אֶת־הָעָם וְיִזְבְּחוּ (Ex. 8: 4), "Pray to Jehovah, that He may remove the frogs (*lit.*, and let Him remove); and I *will* send the people away that they may sacrifice (*lit.*, and let them sacrifice)." Purpose after any "voluntative" (as Jussives, Cohortatives, and Imper-

178

atives are called) is usually thus expressed by a simple Waw with the Jussive or Cohortative (according to person), instead of by לְמַעַן with the simple Impf.

3. A second form of connecting modal ideas grows out of the very complete establishment of the Waw Consec. construction in the language. Instead of using the modal form with simple Waw, it is not uncommon for a Waw Consec. with the Perf. to represent a Jussive or even an Impv. in a series (the idea of futurity having predominated over that of determination); e.g., יְהִי מְאֹרֹת . . . וְהָיוּ לְאֹתֹת (Gen. 1:14), "Let there be lights . . . and let them be for signs"; or Ex. 3:16.

B. Circumstantial Clauses

1. The conjunction וְ finds another special use when it is desired to introduce some explanatory statement, or some antecedent or attendant circumstance into a narrative. The Waw in such clauses has a certain *subordinating* force; this may be rendered by a subordinate clause or a participle, by "now" (cf. note 2, page 164), or by a nominative absolute; the context will usually show the relation and suggest the proper translation.

2. When such a circumstantial clause is purely descriptive, it usually takes the form of a nominal sentence, and shows no special peculiarity; e.g., וּלְרִבְקָה אָח וּשְׁמוֹ לָבָן (Gen. 24:29), "Now Rebekah had a brother, whose name was Laban."

3. When some verbal action is to be thus introduced, it is differentiated from the main consecutive events by put-

ting the subject instead of the verb first—thus separating the event from the main course of the narrative[1].

a. If there is no noun subject, the pronoun subject is expressed; e.g., וַיָּמֹת . . . וְהוּא שָׁפַט אֶת־יִשְׂרָאֵל אַרְבָּעִים שָׁנָה (1 Sam. 4:18), "And he died . . .having judged Israel forty years."

b. While sometimes a finite verb is used in such a clause, more commonly a Participle is used—see further in Ch. XXXV, B.

VOCABULARY

זֶבַח	sacrifice	שׁכם	Hi., rise early
זָעַק	cry, exclaim	שָׁפַט	judge
צָעַק	cry, implore	בָּמָה	high place (first — fixed)
קָבַץ	collect, gather, assemble	יַעַר	forest
קָרַע	rend, tear	מוּסָר	chastisement; admonition

EXERCISES

1) יִזְבְּחוּ לַיהוָֹה וִישַׁלְּמוּ אֶת־נִדְרֵיהֶם כְּמוּסָרֵנוּ:
2) לָקַח הַנַּעַר אֶת־חֶרֶב אָבִיו וְלוֹ כֹחַ גָּדוֹל וַיִּכְרֹת אֶת־
הָעֵץ: 3) קִצְרוּ אֶת־שְׂדֵיכֶם וְהִשְׁאִירוּ מְעַט לִבְנֵי עָנִי:
4) נַשְׁבִּיתָה אֶת־עֲבָדֵינוּ וְיִזְבְּחוּ לֵאלֹהֵיהֶם בַּבָּמוֹת:
5) הַשְׁכִּימִי וְתִקְבְּצִי אֶת־חֵלֶק לַחְמֵךְ בַּיַּעַר: 6) זָעַקְנוּ עַל־
עֲבוֹדָתֵנוּ וּכְבֵדָה הִיא וַיֵּשֶׁב אֹתָנוּ בְּעָלֵנוּ: 7) קָרְעוּ אֶת־

---

[1] This usage is of course to be discriminated from the placing of the subject first for special emphasis, or in strictly coördinate statements (e.g., in Isa. 17:7). And compare note 1, page 46.

שְׂמְלוֹתֵיכֶם וּצְעַקְתֶּם לֵאלֹהֵיכֶם: 8) יִשְׁפֹּט אֶת־עַמּוֹ
בִּצְדָקָה וְיִמְשֹׁל בָּם בְּחֶסֶד: 9) פָּקְדוּ אֶת־קְהָלֵנוּ וְהֵם
שָׁמְעוּ כִּי לֹא גָדוֹל הוּא וַיְקַדְּשׁוּ אֶת־זְקֵנֵינוּ: 10) הַזְכֵּר
אֵלֶיהָ אֶת־מַחְשֶׁבֶת כֹּהֵן אֹיְבֶיהָ הָרַע וְתִמָּלֵט מֵעֲוֺנָיו:

1. Let her arise early and escape to that sanctuary.
2. Take heed, I pray thee, to thy words, that they may not judge our congregation. 3. He sacrificed three bullocks on the high-place in the forest (an ancient altar stood there), and did not go to the temple. 4. Collect all your tribes, that ye may capture the strong tower. 5. He went to the hill, having remembered its strength, and shut himself up (*Ni.*) in the tower. 6. Let them rend their garments and cry in the streets (*use Waw Consec.*). 7. Let us rise early, that we may collect all the clans. 8. Heed his admonition, spread out your hands unto your Gods, and atone for your iniquities.

CHAPTER XXXIII

VERBAL SUFFIXES

A. Tabular View

1. Suffix forms with Hi. Perf. (since the Hi. *stem* is not modified, it shows the other peculiarities without confusion).

with	3ms הִקְטִיל	3fs הִקְטִילָה	2ms הִקְטַלְתָּ	1cs הִקְטַלְתִּי	3cp הִקְטִילוּ
1cs	הִקְטִילַנִי	הִקְטִילָתְנִי	הִקְטַלְתַּנִי		הִקְטִילוּנִי
2ms	הִקְטִילְךָ	הִקְטִילָתְךָ		הִקְטַלְתִּיךָ	הִקְטִילוּךָ
2fs	הִקְטִילֵךְ	הִקְטִילָתֶךְ		הִקְטַלְתִּיךְ	הִקְטִילוּךְ
3ms	הִקְטִילָהוּ / הִקְטִילוֹ	הִקְטִילַתְהוּ / הִקְטִילַתּוּ	הִקְטַלְתָּהוּ / הִקְטַלְתּוֹ	הִקְטַלְתִּיהוּ / הִקְטַלְתִּיו	הִקְטִילָהוּ
3fs	הִקְטִילָהּ	הִקְטִילָתָהּ	הִקְטַלְתָּהּ	הִקְטַלְתִּיהָ	הִקְטִילוּהָ
1cp	הִקְטִילָנוּ	הִקְטִילָתָנוּ	הִקְטַלְתָּנוּ		הִקְטִילָנוּ
2mp	הִקְטִילְכֶם			הִקְטַלְתִּיכֶם	הִקְטִילוּכֶם
3mp	הִקְטִילָם	הִקְטִילָתָם	הִקְטַלְתָּם	הִקְטַלְתִּים	הִקְטִילוּם

2. Skeleton paradigm of other forms.

with	Perfect			Imperfect		Imperative	
	Qal 3ms קָטַל	Qal 3mp קָטְלוּ	Pi. 3ms קִטֵּל	Qal 3ms יִקְטֹל	Pi. 3ms יְקַטֵּל	Qal 2ms קְטֹל	Hi. 2ms הַקְטֵל
				(Emph.)			
3ms	קְטָלוֹ	קְטָלֻהוּ	קִטְּלוֹ	יִקְטְלֶנּוּ	יְקַטְלֵהוּ	קָטְלֵהוּ	הַקְטִילֵהוּ
3fs	קְטָלָהּ	קְטָלוּהָ	קִטְּלָהּ	יִקְטְלֶנָּה	יְקַטְלָהּ	קָטְלָהּ	הַקְטִילָהּ
2mp	קְטַלְכֶם			יִקְטָלְכֶם	יְקַטֶּלְכֶם	קְטַלְכֶם	
3mp	קְטָלָם	קְטָלֻם	קִטְּלָם	יִקְטְלֵם	יְקַטְלֵם	קָטְלֵם	הַקְטִילֵם

3. Complete list of the suffixes.

	No Connecting Vowel	With Vowel in Perf.	With Vowel in Impf.	Emphatic
1cs	—נִי	—ֵנִי	—ֵנִי	—ֵנְיָ
2ms	—ךָ	—ְךָ	—ְךָ.	—ֶךָּ
2fs	—ךְ	—ֵךְ, —ָךְ	—ֵךְ	
3ms	—הוּ, —ִו, —ֹו, —וֹ	—ְהוּ	—ֵהוּ	—ֶנּוּ
3fs	—ָהּ, —ָה, —ָהּ	—ָהּ	—ָהּ, —ֶהָ	—ֶנָּהּ
1cp	—נוּ	—ֵנוּ	—ֵנוּ	—ֶנּוּ
2mp	—כֶם	—ְכֶם	—ְכֶם	
2fp	—כֶן	—ְכֶן	—ְכֶן	
3mp	—ם	—ָם, —ֵם	—ֵם	
3fp	—ן	—ֵן, —ָן	—ֵן	

B. The Suffixes

1. The forms of pronoun objects directly affixed to verbs resemble, in general, the singular-noun suffixes; however—

a. The 1cs suffix is —נִי, not —ִי; and the 3ms and 3fs may be —הוּ (or —וֹ) and —ָהּ, as well as —ֹו and —ָה (cf. note 1, page 70)[1].

b. With verbs having no afformative, the characteristic part of the suffix is preceded by a "connecting vowel"— usually Qamets in the Perf., Tsere in the Impf.[2]; but with

---

[1] With verbs in the Perf., the shorter form of the 3ms suffix is usually used; with the Impf. it is never contracted.

[2] These doubtless are remnants of primitive personal endings (cf. Ch. XII, B, 2).

a verb form ending in a vowel this is unnecessary—in fact impossible; e.g., הִסְתִּירָנוּ, "He has hidden us"; תַּסְתִּירִינוּ, "Thou (f) wilt hide us."

c. Special suffixes, made emphatic by the insertion of נ as connecting letter, are sometimes used with the Impf.— chiefly at the end of a sentence.

2. The suffixes נִי, הוּ, הָ, and נוּ are never accented—the tone falling on the connecting vowel or the ultimate of the verb; and ךְ is not accented after an afformative. All other suffixes are accented, except that in the 3fs Perf. the accent is always on the syllable תָ— (תָ—).

C. Changes in the Afformatives

1. Several of the afformatives in the Perf. revert to more primitive forms before suffixes (cf. Ch. XI, A, 1, c and note 2, page 67):

a. The 2fs ended in תִּי—. Hence it is identical with the 1cs before suffixes; only the context can decide between them.

b. The 2mp ended in תּוּם—; the final ם is dropped from this, so that the forms occurring with it are quite analogous to those with the 3cp—as are also those with the 1cp.

c. The 3fs ended in ת—. Even tho this ends in a consonant, no connecting vowel is used with it before three of the suffixes; and before three others the Pathah heightens to Qamets. The ה of the third singular suffixes is assimilated into the ת and represented by D.F.—the second form given for the 3ms being thus contracted from the first, and that of the 3fs similarly from הִקְטִילַתְהָ.

d. Note also that the Qamets is dropped from the 2ms in two instances.

2. Verbs in the plural very seldom have the Shureq of the afformative written fully before the suffixes הן and נו.

3. In the Impf. the Fem. Plu. afformative ‏נָה‎— is never used before a suffix; the Masc. ending ‏וּ‎— is substituted for it. Also, the ‏הָ‎— of the Cohortative is dropped.

D. Qal Perfect with Suffixes

1. The 3ms departs entirely from the analogy of verb inflection and has forms similar to those of first declension nouns. The Pathah under the second radical does not shorten to Shewa, but heightens to tone-long Qamets (except before the heavy second plural suffixes, where Pathah remains); and then, since a suffix draws the tone to the left, the tone-long Qamets under the first radical must shorten to Shewa; e.g., from קָטַל, קְטָלוֹ[1].

2. In the 3cp the Shewa has been shortened from a primitive Pathah (ground-form קָטְלוּ); this is restored and becomes tone-long, just as in the 3ms. Also, the first vowel must shorten to Shewa; e.g., from קָטְלוּ, קְטָלוּךָ. Similarly the 3fs, from a ground-form קָטַלַת, becomes קְטָלַת before suffixes.

---

[1] The ground-form was קָטַלוֹ; cf. Ch. XVII, A, 2 and 3.

3. In the other persons there is no change in the stem proper except the necessary shortening of the first Qamets to Shewa.

E. Other Forms

1. In Qal Impf. the Holem shortens to Shewa before all suffixes, except that before the second person suffixes it must become Qamets Hatuph; e.g., from יִקְטֹל, יִקְטְלֵנִי and יִקְטָלְךָ.

a. The Impv. is analogous; when the Holem becomes Shewa, the Shewa under the first radical heightens to Qamets Hatuph.

b. In all forms which have a vowel afformative, the Holem has already become Shewa, and that Shewa always remains.

2. In Pi. Perf. and Impf., the 3ms is treated like a third declension noun; i.e., the Tsere becomes Shewa before all suffixes, except that before the second person suffixes it must of course become Segol; e.g., from קִטֵּל, קִטְּלַנִי and קִטֶּלְךָ. In 3mp the Shewa always remains.

3. The Hi. Impf. stem is immutable. In the 2ms Impv. the Tsere is replaced by Long Hireq, just as before all other endings.

VOCABULARY

כָּעַס	Hi., provoke	מָשַׁח	anoint
לָבַשׁ	put on, clothe oneself; Hi., put on (another; *two Accus.*)	שִׁחֵת	Hi., overthrow, destroy; corrupt
		שָׁמַד	Hi., cut off, destroy, lay waste; Ni., *Pass.*
לָמַד	learn; Pi., teach	חֵמָה	heat, anger, wrath
מָכַר	sell	שֶׁלֶם	peace offering

EXERCISES

1. I made thee overseer. 2. His peace offerings only provoked us. 3. She hid me from his anger. 4. He took the shield and will put it on his son. 5. Ye destroyed them. 6. Thou (f) didst corrupt her. 7. We crowned him. 8. Thou didst not justify them (f) didst thou? (*see Ch.*IX, *A, 3*). 9. I remembered the statutes, but did not make mention of them.

10. They sold me. 11. He will teach you (f). 12. Watch thou (f) them. 13. And we visited thee. 14. Justify thou me. 15. She learned about their reproach and covered it (*emph*). 16. We learned it. 17. She anointed thee (f). 18. Judge thou us. 19. He will remember thee (*emph*). 20. I will judge you.

SUPPLEMENTARY VOCABULARY

זָמַר	Pi., sing	אֶרֶז	cedar
מָשַׁךְ	draw, pull, drag	אָשָׁם	guilt offering
קָדַם	Pi., precede	חִטִּים	(*Plu. of* חִטָּה) wheat

מִזְמוֹר song, psalm   קָרְבָּן gift

מְנַצֵּחַ precentor, chief mu-   שִׁיר song, hymn
    sician

SUPPLEMENTARY EXERCISES

1. He gave you rest. 2. Didst thou adjure him by Jehovah? 3. She took the swords, and will leave them here. 4. Did they select thee (f)? 5. Did ye leave your guilt offerings and not offer them? 6. If he offers her this gift she will throw it from her. 7. We left the trees of cedars there and will remove them.

8. Will ye send them (f)? 9. Deliver thou her. 10. And thou wilt collect them. 11. He preceded you. 12. And we will hear the admonition, and to you will we recount it (*emph*). 13. Ye pursued us. 14. The precentor heard the psalms and hymns and sang them. 15. Do not thou drag him from his chariot. 16. Search ye for him. 17. Did I cut thee? 18. And she searched for him in the days of wheat harvest.

CHAPTER XXXIV

INFINITIVES

The term "Infinitive" is applied to two different forms, which have an outward similarity: the so-called *Infinitive Construct* resembles our Infinitive; the so-called *Infinitive Absolute* has a quite different use.

A. Form of the Infinitive Construct

1. In its simple form the Inf. Cst. is identical with the Impv.; except that in Hi. the final vowel is Long Hireq.

2. A preposition, most frequently לְ, is commonly used with it. With the Qal this לְ naturally has Hireq (לִקְטֹל for לְקְטֹל); and, by a special peculiarity, the Shewa under the first radical is silent (note, e.g., the D. L. in לִזְכֹּר).

> a. But after בְּ, כְּ, or מִן, the vocal Shewa remains; e.g., בִּזְכֹר[1].
>
> *b. Occasionally the preformative ה of Hi. or Ni. is elided after the לְ, exactly as after the י in the Impf.; e.g., לַקְטִיל, לְקַטֵּל.

3. The Inf. takes pronoun suffixes—sometimes as objects, more frequently as subjects. The 1cs suffix has two forms —a nominal, used as subject, and a verbal, used as object[2].

---

[1] The Inf. never takes לְ in addition to another preposition.

[2] There is, however, no distinction in the use of the two forms of the second person suffixes.

a. The Qal Inf. resembles an *o* class segolate noun, except that the first syllable is usually open instead of being closed. The full inflection of כְּתֹב is:

	Singular	Plural
1c	כָּתְבִי / כָּתְבֵנִי	כָּתְבֵנוּ
2m	כָּתְבְּךָ / כְּתָבְךָ	כָּתְבְכֶם / כְּתָבְכֶם
2f	כָּתְבֵךְ	כָּתְבְּכֶן / כְּתָבְכֶן
3m	כָּתְבוֹ	כָּתְבָם
3f	כָּתְבָהּ	כָּתְבָן

b. The Hi. stem is unchangeable. The Ni., Pi., and Hith. are exactly like third declension nouns; e.g., הַקְטְרִי, קַטְּלָךְ, etc. In Ni. the Qamets is fixed; e.g., הִקָּטְלְכֶם.

B. Syntax of the Infinitive Construct

1. The Inf. with לְ is most commonly *complementary* to a verb meaning *begin, cease, be able, wish, seek, permit, command,* or some similar idea. It is also commonly used to express purpose—especially when the subject of the main verb and of the intended action are the same; e.g., וָאִמָּלְטָה לְבַדִּי לְהַגִּיד לָךְ (Job 1:15), "And I only am escaped to tell thee."

2. The Inf. serves as a verbal noun, and as such may stand in various syntactic relations. It may be subject of a sentence, object of a preposition or verb, or conjoined noun to a Cst.; e.g., לֹא כָבֵד הִצְטַדֵּק אַחֲרֵי הַשְׁלִימְךָ בִּשְׂדֵה הַלָּחֶם כִּי רָצָה הַמֶּלֶךְ כְּרֹת בְּרִית, "To justify yourself after making peace on the field of fighting was not hard, for the king delights in the making of a covenant."

In English grammar the substantive in -ing is variously designated as a gerund, a verbal noun, or an infinitive (it is not to be confused with a participial form); it will be found convenient in translating many Hebrew Infinitives.

3. The Inf. is much used to define (either exactly or approximately) the time of an action, being often preferred to a subordinate clause or participial phrase (especially after הָיָה); e.g., וַיְהִי כְּזָכְרוֹ אֶת־הַתּוֹרָה וַיִּשְׁמְרָה, "And it came to pass, when he remembered the law (lit., at his remembering...), that he kept it"; יָשַׁב בְּיִשְׂרָאֵל בִּמְלֹךְ דָּוִד שָׁם, "He dwelt in Israel when David was king there (lit., in David's being king)"; בְּיוֹם הִמָּלְטוֹ, "on the day that he escapes (lit., of his escaping)"[1]. Note the D.L. in the preposition after וַיְהִי; there is a considerable pause between the words.

---

[1] Note the peculiar jumble of syntactic relations. The Inf. is a noun in being the object of a preposition or conjoined to a Cst., a verb in taking a direct object. And it has as the subject of its verbal action a genitival modifier—either a possessive suffix or a noun conjoined to it as to a Cst.

4. The Inf. with מִן is used in several idioms:

a. After יָרֵא; e.g., יָרֵא מֵהַשְׁלִים, "He was afraid to make peace."

b. After חָלִילָה: this is an adjective meaning "unholy," and is commonly followed by an "ethical dative" and the Inf. of a tabooed action (altho other constructions occur); e. g., חָלִילָה לִי מִקְּטֹל, "God forbid that I should kill, or, Far be it from me to kill."

c. In comparative statements; e. g., וַתִּכְהֶיןָ עֵינָיו מֵרְאֹת (Gen. 27:1), "And his eyes were too dim to see" (cf. note 2, page 62).

5. Instead of the negative לֹא, the equivalent בִּלְתִּי (or בְּלִי)[1] is used. A preposition is prefixed to this adverb, not to the Inf. itself; e.g., אָמַר לָנוּ לְבִלְתִּי דַבֵּר, "He told us not to speak."

C. The Infinitive Absolute

1. In most forms of the verb, its essential meaning (determined by the stem consonants) is defined with reference to person, time, nature of action, etc., by various inflectional vowels and formative letters. But when a simple statement of the abstract verbal notion, without any such specific coloring, is desired, this is expressed by the uninflected *Inf. Absolute.*

2. In most voices, the form closely resembles the Inf. Cst.:

---

[1] Originally nouns meaning "nothingness"; cf. אַיִן.

| Qal | Ni. | Pi. | Pu. | Hi. | Ho. | Hith. |

$$\left.\begin{array}{ll}\text{קָטֵל} & \text{נִקְטַל} \\ \text{קַטֹּל} & \text{הִקָּטֵל}\end{array}\right\} \qquad \left\{\begin{array}{l}\text{קָטוֹל}\end{array}\right.$$ הָקְטֵל קַטֵּל הַקְטֵל קָטֹל הִתְקַטֵּל

Of the two forms of Ni. and Pi., the first is more common. The only forms that occur at all frequently are Qal and Hi.

3. There are three principal uses of the Inf. Abs.:

a. The most common use is to emphasize a verb action. Frequently, instead of using an adverb such as *truly* or *certainly*, the Hebrew would repeat his verb—using the Inf. Abs. followed by the proper tense or mood form[1]; e.g., הַצְדֵּק אַצְדִּיקֵהוּ וּמַלֵּט אֲמַלֵּט, "I will surely justify and deliver him."

b. It is sometimes used in place of a finite verb in vivid narration (or even of an Impv.)—a close parallel to the familiar Historical Infinitive in Latin.

c. In some cases it has degenerated into an adverbial use. This occurs chiefly in certain Hiphils; e.g., הַרְחֵק, "far off"; הַשְׁכֵּם, "early"; מַהֵר (Pi.), "quickly."

VOCABULARY

דָּבַק cleave to (*plus* בְ *or* לְ)   נָתַן (*plus Accus. and Inf.*), permit

מָאַס refuse; despise   קָבַר bury

---

[1] But occasionally the finite form precedes (so always an Impv. or Part.) The Inf. regularly is in the same voice as the main verb; but occasionally the Qal Inf. Cst., as the simplest form, is used with a finite form in another voice (e.g., Isa. 40:30).

קטר Pi., burn incense   שָׂמַח rejoice, be glad; Pi.,
                                              rejoice, make glad
רָגַל walk; Pi., spy out   מֵאָז since

EXERCISES

1) מָאַס הַפָּרָשׁ לְהִשָּׁאֵר לְהִתְקַדֵּשׁ:   2) לֹא נְתָנוּנִי
לְהַשְׁכִּים: 3) וְהָיָה בְּקָבְרוֹ אֶת־בְּנוֹ הַבְּכוֹר וְזָכַר אֶת־דְּבָרַי:
4) אַל־נַשְׁמִידָה אֶת־הַבַּיִת אֲשֶׁר־בּוֹ הִבְדִּילוּ לְהִשָּׁאֵר:
5) וְלֹא דָבַק לְאִשְׁתּוֹ מֵאָז הֲלָכְדָם: 6) שָׂמַחְתִּי לְלָמְדוֹ:
7) פְּקַדְתִּיו לְשָׁמְרֶךָ:
8) שָׁאַל אֹתָנוּ לְבִלְתִּי שָׂרְפָם: 9) וְהָיָה בְּקַטְּרִי לַיהוָֹה
וְרָצָה וְכִפֶּר אֲכַפֵּר: 10) חָלִילָה לָהֶם מֵהַשְׁמִיד אֶת־
עִירֵנוּ: 11) תָּקְעוּ אֶת־אָהֳלָם בָּעֵמֶק הָרָחֹק מֵהָחָצֵר:
12) יָרְאָה מִבַּקְשֵׁנִי:

1. And I will refuse to burn incense. 2. And it came to
pass as we drew near that he threw a great stone. 3. We
permitted her to remain. 4. And it shall come to pass
when our children remember these things that they will
justify our judgment.

5. He strictly charged me not to bury him in this land.
6. Far be it from thee to make him king over them. 7.
After we hear (*use Inf.*) the laws, let us learn to walk
according to them and not to break them. 8. Thou (f)
surely wilt not cleave to him if thou dost not rejoice in him.

SUPPLEMENTARY VOCABULARY

יָרֵא	fear, be afraid	רֹחַב	breadth
אֹכֶל or אָכְלָה	food	רֵיחַ	odor
אֹרֶךְ	length	שׁוֹר (plu. שְׁוָרִים)	ox
חֵלֶב	fat	אֶבְיוֹן	poor, needy

SUPPLEMENTARY EXERCISES

1) שָׁמַע אֶת־קוֹלְכֶם בִּצְעָקְכֶם בְּעָנְיְכֶם: 2) הֲתִשָּׁבְעוּ
לְרָדְפָה עַד־אֲשֶׁר תִּלְכְּדוּהָ: 3) וַיְהִי בְּהַקְרִיבְכֶם שְׁוָרִים
עַל־מִזְבַּחֲכֶם וָאֶשְׁבֹּת מֵחֲמָתִי: 4) אַל תִּשְׁכְּחוּ לְהַרְחִיק
אֶת־אֹתוֹת מַעֲשֵׂנוּ (See A, 2, b, above) 5) בַּקֵּשׁ לַמְלִיכֵנִי
תַּחְתָּיו: 6) וַיְהִי בְּהִמָּלֵט הָרֵיחַ מִבֵּיתוֹ וְלֹא הָלְכוּ רֵעָיו
שָׁמָּה: 7) בְּקַשְׁתִּי לְמַלֶּטְכֶם:

8) שָׁבַת הַשֵּׁכֶם מִמַּעֲשֵׂהוּ: 9) מָאַס לִכְרֹת אֶת־הַחֵלֶב:
10) וְהָיָה בְּהַשְׁלִימוֹ אֶת אֹיְבָיו וּמִלֶּטְךָ מַלֵּט מִידֵי צָרֶיךָ:
11) יָרֵא מֵהַמְּכָרָם: 12) זָכוֹר יִזְכֹּר יְהוָֹה אֶת־הָאָוֶן אֲשֶׁר
בִּלְבָבְךָ: 13) יָרְאוּ מִבְּלִי שָׁפְטוֹ אֶת־הָאֶבְיוֹנִים:

1. The horsemen went to spy out the length and breadth of the land. 2. And it came to pass when he brought the maiden near that his son did not cleave to her. 3. Will ye not rejoice to put on their beautiful garments? 4. He has not given us food since they were buried (*use Inf.*).

5. He was afraid to rise early. 6. I will surely visit upon you all your iniquity. 7. Her making their hearts glad was better than your teaching them to fight. 8. And it will come to pass when ye burn incense that the odor will go to God.

CHAPTER XXXV

PARTICIPLES

A. Form and Inflection

1. Masc. Sing. forms:

Qal	Ni.	Pi.	Pu.	Hi.	Ho.	Hith.
קֹטֵל	נִקְטָל	מְקַטֵּל	מְקֻטָּל	מַקְטִיל	מָקְטָל	מִתְקַטֵּל

a. The Qal and Ni. are derived from the Perf. stem; all the rest are from the Inf. (or Impf.) stem, and are characterized by a preformative מ.

b. Note that the three Passives have Qamets in the ultima.

c. There is another participle, known as the *Qal Passive;* the Masc. Sing. form is קָטוּל. It is the sole remnant of an ancient passive voice. It sometimes has a slightly different meaning from the Ni.

2. Inflection:

a. Masculines: The forms having Tsere (i.e., Qal , Pi., and Hith.) are third declension; e.g., מְקַטְּלִים, קֹטְלוֹ (see Ch. XX). All Passives are first declension; e.g., Ni. Cst., נִקְטַל; Ho. Plu., מָקְטָלִים. The Hi. stem is unchangeable.

b. Feminines: The Sing. Absolutes are sometimes formed by adding the ordinary הָ—; but far more frequently

the primitive תּ is added, making a segolate form in תּ—ֶ֖
(a class; see Ch. XIX, C). The singulars in הָ—֥ and the
plurals follow the same declensions as the corresponding masculines; e.g.,

	Sing.		Plu.
Qal active	קֹטְלָה	קֹטֶלֶת	קֹטְלוֹת
Qal passive	קְטוּלָה		קְטוּלוֹת
Niphal	נִקְטָלָה	נִקְטֶלֶת	נִקְטָלוֹת
Hiphil	מַקְטִילָה	מַקְטֶלֶת	מַקְטִילוֹת

B. Syntax

1. The Part. is most commonly used as an attributive
adjective. Note one special idiomatic use in the Cst.
state with an "epexegetical genitive," as in אֲנָשִׁים נִשְׁבְּרֵי
רוּחַ, "men broken of spirit."

2. It is frequently used as a simple substantive; e.g.,
סֹפֵר, "scribe"; with possessive suffix, קֹצְרָיו, "his har-
vesters."

3. As a pure verb, it is especially adapted to describe a
continuous action or state (such as the flowing of a river),
in contrast to the use of the Impf. for continued or repeated action. It also frequently indicates an action as
contemporaneous with the main narrative[1].

---

[1] As a special case of this, it is sometimes used with הָיָה exactly
as we use the progressive form in English; e.g., וּמֹשֶׁה הָיָה רֹעֶה (Ex.
3:1), "Now Moses was shepherding."

a. It is commonly used in circumstantial clauses (see Ch. XXXII, B). It makes an action less prominent than does a finite verb (forming a nominal clause); e. g., וַיֵּרָא אֵלָיו יְהוָה וְהוּא יֹשֵׁב (Gen. 18:1), "And Jehovah appeared to him as he sat."

b. It is regularly used after the "verbal particles"; it may then make either an independent sentence or a circumstantial clause.

(1) The negative לֹא is not commonly used with Participles; אֵין is used instead.

(2) Note two constructions with עוֹד: עוֹדֶנּוּ מְדַבֵּר בְּעוֹדֶנּוּ מְדַבֵּר תְּפַשְׂנָהוּ or וַנִּתְפְּשֵׂהוּ, "While he was speaking we seized him."

4. It may have a combined verbal and nominal force. As in Greek, the Part. with the article is often used as the equivalent of a relative clause; e.g., הַנִּסְתָּרִים פֹּה , "those who are hiding here." Quite similar is the use with an objective suffix (e.g., דֹּרְשִׁי, "those who seek me"); also in the Cst. with a conjoined noun (e.g., רָאָה אֶת־מַרְחִיקֵי הַיַּיִן, "He saw those who removed the wine")[1].

VOCABULARY

בָּחַר choose

כָּבַס Pi., wash, cleanse; Qal Part., fuller

כָּשַׁל be weak; totter, stumble (used in Qal in Perf., in Ni. in other forms)

---

[1] Sometimes, likewise, before a prepositional phrase; e.g., מְשָׁרְתַי בַהֵיכָל, "those who minister in the temple" (cf. Ch. XXV, 3).

שָׂחַק laugh (לְ, at)

שָׁכַן lie down; dwell

אֱמוּנָה faithfulness

חָמָס violence, wrong, oppression

תָּמִיד perpetuity; *Adv.*, continually

חָדָשׁ new

טָהוֹר clean

EXERCISES

1) הִנֵּה נִכְשֶׁלֶת בַּעֲבוּר הָעֲבֹדָה הַקָּשָׁה: 2) הֲלֹא בְחָרוּךְ מִשְׁלֶשֶׁת הָאֲנָשִׁים קְרוּעֵי בִגְדֵיהֶם: 3) הַאֵינֶנּוּ שֹׂחֵק לְלֶכְדָּיו: 4) טְהוֹרָה הַשִּׂמְלָה הַהִיא וְעוֹדֶנָּה מְכֻבָּסָה אַתָּה: 5) לְכַדְנוּם לְכָרְתֵי עֵצִים: 6) עַל־הַשָּׂרִים הַמָּשְׁחָתִים פָּקַדְתִּי אֶת־חֲמָסָם: 7) וַתְּבַקֶּשְׁנָה הַנָּשִׁים הַנִּשְׁאָרוֹת לִשְׁכֹּן תָּמִיד בָּעִיר הַבְּצוּרָה: 8) הֲיֵשׁ דָּרְבִּים מַבְדִּילִים אֶת־מְלַמְּדֵיהֶם: 9) וּלְמַחֲנָם אֵין נָשִׂיא לְמוּד מִלְחָמָה: 10) נִשְׁכַּח הַזָּהָב בַּהֵיכָל מִשֹּׁמְרָיו הַבֹּרְחִים: 11) הָלַכְתִּי לְדַבֵּר לַכֹּהֲנִים הַחֲדָשִׁים וְהֵמָּה מְקַטְּרִים וָאֶשָּׁאֵר בַּחוּץ: 12) הַאֵינָם לְבֻשִׁים:

1. Are we not continually recounting the faithfulness of our God? 2. Those who make peace shall dwell in safety. 3. Behold, the chosen (*Qal Pass.*) of Jehovah is inquiring for thee. 4. Our watchmen did not fear those men of violence. 5. Those who are fighting us shall stumble, and we shall laugh at them. 6. He who sold me the clean oil gave me a new book written (*Qal Pass.*) in his (own)

hand.   7. I went to the fuller's house, but she was not hiding there.   8. He saw your abominations while they were standing on this high hill.

CHAPTER XXXVI
STATIVES

A. Meaning and Form

1. Most of the verbs thus far studied are transitive, and indicate action. But there are many verbs which regularly describe a condition or state, and hence are intransitive. These are known as *Statives*. This difference in character and meaning is reflected in a difference in form thruout Qal; in the other voices the distinction naturally disappears.

2. The simple stem in 3ms Qal Perf. may have one of three forms, having as second vowel—

    a. Most frequently Tsere; e.g., כָּבֵד.

    b. Occasionally Holem; e.g., קָטֹן, יָכֹל.

    c. In many cases Pathah, just like ordinary verbs; of these, the following have already been given: צָדַק, דָּבַק, שָׁלַם, שָׂמַח, רָחַק, קָרַב, קָדַשׁ.[1]

3. A few verbs which are transitive are inflected like statives; e.g., לָבֵשׁ, לָמֵד. Such words doubtless were originally intransitive, but later acquired a transitive meaning.

4. The use of the tenses is somewhat looser than in other verbs.

---
[1] Numerous words sometimes have Tsere, sometimes Pathah.

By their very nature statives show continuation; hence the Perf. is often used where the strict principles of tense would seem to require an Impf. The distinction is not sharply drawn in actual usage; much is left to the predilection of the writer. The Part. is frequently used to describe general conditions or present states.

B. Inflection

1. Skeleton paradigm:

	Perf.		Impf.	Impv.	Inf.	Part.
3ms	כָּבֵד	כָּבַד	יִכְבַּד קָטֹן		כְּבֹד	כָּבֵד
2ms	קָטֹנְתָּ	כָּבַדְתָּ		כְּבַד		
2mp	תִּכְבְּדוּ קְטָנְתֶּם	(Coh. כִּבְדָה)				

2. In the Perf., Tsere becomes Pathah before all consonantal afformatives. Before unaccented afformatives Holem remains; but in the second plural it becomes Qamets Hatuph.

3. In the 3ms Impf., statives regularly have Pathah instead of Holem in the second syllable[1]; the other persons and numbers are easily derived. This Impf. with Pathah is found also in some classes of irregular verbs; we shall refer to all such verbs as *type A*, and to those with Holem as *type O*.[2]

---

[1] A few, however, have Holem; e.g., שָׁכַן, מָלַךְ; the distinction of types is not absolute.

*[2] There is a third way of forming the Impf., with Tsere; this *type E* occurs only in a few irregular verbs.

4. In the 2ms Impv. practically all *type A* verbs retain the Pathah. Then before the Cohortative ending the first Shewa heightens to Hireq, not to Qamets Hatuph.

5. Most *type A* verbs have the ordinary form of Inf., with Holem, and are inflected regularly. However—

a. A very few have the Pathah in Inf. also; e.g., שְׁכַב. In inflection, then, the first Shewa heightens to Hireq, not to Qamets Hatuph; e.g., שְׁכְבִי.

*b. Another type of Inf., having a feminine-noun form, occurs in some statives (also in a few other strong verbs and several weak verbs); e.g., דָּבְקָה; אַשְׁמָה; שִׂנְאָה or שְׂנֹא; and with the primitive קְרֹאת, יְכֹלֶת, ת.

6. The Part. of verbs having Tsere or Holem in the Perf. is identical with the Perf., and follows the first declension; those with Pathah in the Perf. have a Part. like that of other verbs; e.g., שָׁכַב, קָטֹן, זָקֵן.

7. A few statives take suffixes. They follow the analogy of ordinary Qal Perfects: in the Impf. and Impv., a Pathah (or a Shewa shortened therefrom) is lengthened to Qamets; and in the Perf., a Tsere is retained (corresponding to a lengthened Qamets).

VOCABULARY

בָּטַח   trust

גָּדַל   be, become great; grow up; Hi., make great

זָקֵן   be, become old

כָּבֵד   be heavy; Ni., be honored; Pi., honor; Hi., make heavy

קָטֹן   be little; Hi., make little

רָכַב ride   שָׁכַב lie, lie down

שָׂנֵא hate   שָׁכֹל be bereaved; Pi., be-
                 reave

EXERCISES

1) וְתִכְבַּד יַד הָאֱלֹהִים עֲלֵיכֶם: 2) וַיְהִי בְּרָכְבֵנוּ בַיְתָה
וַנִּקְרַב אֶל־עִיר גְּדוֹלָה: 3) דִּבְקָה לָאִשָּׁה הַזֹּאת וּבְטַח
בָּהּ: 4) שְׂנֵאָנוּ וַיִּכְבִּידוּ אֶת־מְלַאכְתֵּנוּ: 5) וַתִּשְׂמַח כִּי
שָׁכֹלְנוּ וַנִּשְׁכַּב בָּעֳנִי: 6) לָמַד אֶת־הַסְּפָרִים הָאֵלֶּה וְתִגְדַּל:
7) אָבְטַח בֵּאלֹהֵי בְזִקְנִי: 8) עַד־מָתַי תַּגְדִּילוּ אֶת־הַשֶּׁקֶל
וְהִקְטַנְתֶּם אֶת־הָאֵמָה: 9) וַיְהִי בְּצִדְקָן וַתִּשְׁלַמְנָה:
10) וַתִּקְדַּשׁ בִּתְּךָ בְּעֵינֵי הָאֲנָשִׁים הָהֵם: 11) וָאֶקְטַן מִלְּבֹשׁ
אֶת־שִׂמְלַת אָבִי:

I. And the iniquity of my sin was heavy upon me day and night. 2. Wilt thou ride, or hast thou chosen to lie down? 3. Put on this sword, for it is small. 4. Have ye grown old and also been bereaved? 5. My soul hateth your new moons and your meetings. 6. He was growing up when David was king in Jerusalem. 7. And it came to pass when he lay down that he trusted in Jehovah. 8. And it came to pass when he became old that he was honored.

CHAPTER XXXVII
REVIEW OF REGULAR VERBS

A. Identification Marks of Verb Forms

1. Preformative ה:

   a. Usually Hi. (Perf., Impv., Inf.).

   b. Sometimes Ni. (Impv., Inf.) or Ho. (Perf., Impv., Inf.)

2. Preformative נ:

   a. Usually Ni. (Perf., Part.).

   b. Sometimes personal preformative of first plural Impf. of any voice.

3. Preformative מ: Part. (Pi., Pu., Hi., Ho., Hith.).

4. D.F. in first radical:

   a. Usually Ni. (Impf., Impv., Inf.).

   b. Occasionally Hith.

5. D.F. in second radical: Pi., Pu., Hith.

6. Vowel under preformative:

   a. Shewa: Pi., Pu. (Impf., Part.).

   b. Pathah: Hi. (Impf., Impv., Inf., Part.).

7. Vowel with first radical:

   a. Pathah: Pi. (Impf., Impv., Inf., Part.); also Hith.

   b. Holem: Qal Part.

8. Final Vowel:

   a. Long Hireq: Hi. (except Juss., Impv., Inf. Abs.).

b. Qamets: Part. (Ni., Pu., Ho.).

B. Primitive Forms of the Verb

1. Present verb forms are the outgrowth of earlier ones. With the following list of the supposed primitive forms, the student may trace the changes which gave rise to the present regular forms (cf. Ch. XXVIII, B, 5, Ch. III, B, 2 and 3):

	Qal	Ni.	Pi.	Pu.		Qal Perf.
3ms Perf.	קָטַל	נִקְטַל	קַטַּל	קֻטַּל קָטַל		קָטַל
Impf.	¹יִקְטֹל	יְהִנְקָטֵל	יְקַטֵּל	יְקֻטַּל etc.		קָטַלְת
Part.	קָטֵל	נִקְטַל	מְקַטֵּל	מְקֻטַּל		קָטַלְתָּ

	Hi.	Ho.		Hith.		
						קָטַלְתִּי
Perf.	הַקְטֵל	הָקְטַל הָקְטַל		הִתְקַטֵּל		קָטַלְתִּי
Impf.	יְהַקְטֵל	יְהָקְטַל etc.		יְהִתְקַטֵּל		קָטַלוּ
Part.	מְהַקְטֵל	מְהָקְטַל		מְהִתְקַטֵּל		קָטַלְתּוּם
						קָטַלְתּוּן
						קָטַלְנוּ

2. From such ground-forms were also developed the present forms of the irregular verbs, special types of changes occurring in them. Explanations of the irregular verb forms in Section Five will therefore necessarily depend on the above table.

---

¹ Stative יִקְטַל.

EXERCISES

Locate fully, and translate, the following forms:

39	מִקְדָּשׁ	20	וַנִּשְׁכַּב	1	סְפַרְנוּ
40	וְנִמְשַׁךְ	21	בְּטוּחִים	2	הַשְׁלִים
41	תִּתְלַכֵּדְנָה	22	גְּנָבוּם	3	הִשָּׁכֵנוּן
42	אֹלְחֶם	23	קִדַּמְתִּי	4	מַלְטָה
43	הִכְבַּדְתָּ	24	תְּבַקְעוּ	5	הִכָּתְבָה
44	תִּשָּׁבְעוּ	25	כִּפְּרֻהוּ	6	הַשָּׁבֵת
45	כַּבְּסוּ	26	נִשְׁמְרוּ	7	אֲקַטְּרָה
46	הִצְטַדְּקָתֶּן	27	נִגְדַּל	8	וְהִשְׁחַתֶּם
47	אֶשְׁנָאֵךְ	28	קְטָנְתֶּם	9	בְּרָדְפְּכֶם
48	יַסְגֵּר	29	נְקַבְּצָה	10	מְבַקְשׁוֹת
49	שְׂמַחְנָה	30	יָזְכַּר	11	וַתַּקְרֵב
50	וְנָתְנָה	31	מַשְׁמֶדֶת	12	תְּדַבְּרוּ
51	שָׂרְפָה	32	זַמֵּר	13	נִדְרָשׁ
52	שָׁפוֹךְ	33	הִבָּדֶלְכֶם	14	מְשֵׁל
53	הִתְמַכְּרוּ	34	הָפְקַדְתְּ	15	תִּתְפַּשְׂנָה
54	הִשָּׁאֲרִי	35	זָקַנּוּ	16	יְלַמַּד
55	קָבְרֵנִי	36	מְשָׁלָךְ	17	פִּרְשׁוּ
56	הָרְחַקְתֶּם	37	וַתִּשָּׁבֵר	18	לְבָשְׁתוּ
57	הִסְתַּתַּרְנוּ	38	וַתַּמְלִיכֵךְ	19	תַּשְׂכִּילִי

CHAPTER XXXVIII
READINGS IN DEUTERONOMY

Read carefully sections 1 and 2 of Ch. XXXIX, A. The symbols פ״י, פ״ן, ע״ו, ע״ע, and ל״ה are used below.

1. a. וַיֹּאמֶר. A few verbs beginning with א have Holem after the preformative in Impf. Qal.

    b. וּלְמַדְתֶּם. See Ch. XXXII, A, 3.

    c. לַעֲשֹׂתָם. ל״ה verbs lose the ה in many forms. In the Inf., ה is dropped and וֹת— is added.

      Note: The addition of ת in Inf. is characteristic of several classes of verbs; cf. Ch. XXXVI, B, 5, b.

5. a. הַהוּא. Read הַהִיא; see Ch. XI, A, 1, c, (3).

    b. לְהַגִּיד. From נגד; the נ of פ״ן verbs is frequently assimilated and represented by D.F.

    c. עֲלֵיתֶם. In some forms of ל״ה verbs, the ה is replaced by י.

    d. לֵאמֹר. Inf. of אמר; translate "saying."

6. הוֹצֵאתִיךָ. פ״י verbs have וֹ (Holem) instead of י in some voices.

7. a. לֹא־יִהְיֶה. ל״ה verbs end in ֶה— in the Impf. of all voices. For syntax, see note 1, page 168.

    b. פָּנָי. The vowels in a word having a principal accent mark are frequently lengthened.

8. תַּעֲשֶׂה. Qal; the guttural requires Pathah; (Ch. V, D, 2, 3); so in תַעֲבֹד in vs. 13, and often.

9. a. תִּשְׁתַּחֲוֶה. See Ch. XXVIII, D, 2, a; the form is further irregular on account of the guttural and the ל״ה stem.

    b. תָּעָבְדֵם. Ho.; "be made (persuaded) to serve them."

10. מִצְוֹתָו. Read מִצְוֹתַי.

11. תִּשָּׂא. See 5, b above; so also וַיִּתְּנֵם in vs. 19.

12. a. שָׁמוֹר. See Ch. 34, C, 3, b.

   b. צַוֵּךְ. Pi. of a ל"ה verb; the ה is dropped before a suffix.

13. וְעָשִׂיתָ. See 5, c.

14. יָנוּחַ. Impf. Qal of an ע"ו verb; the long vowel under the preformative is characteristic of several forms of these verbs.

15. a. וַיֹּצִאֲךָ. Defectively written for וַיּוֹצִיאֲךָ; see 6.

   b. נְטוּיָה. Cf. 5, c and Ch. XXXV, A, 1, c.

16. a. יַאֲרִיכֻן. See Ch. XXVIII, D, 6.

   b. יִיטַב. Impf. Qal of a פ"י.

21 (24). הֶרְאָנוּ. Hi.; see 12, b.

22 (25). a. תֹּאכְלֶנוּ. See 1, a.

   b. יֹסְפִים. For idiom see Ch. XLVI, C, 6.

   c. וָמַתְנוּ. ע"ו verbs frequently drop the ו, as here in Perf.; נָמוּת is Impf. of the same verb.

23 (26). וַיְחִי. Irregular Impf. Qal of חיה.

25 (28). הֵטִיבוּ. For הֵיטִיבוּ; a פ"י Hi.

26 (29). a. מִי־יִתֵּן. Lit., "Who will give?"—i.e., "O that!"

   b. לְיִרְאָה. See Ch. XXXVI, B, 5, b.

27 (30). לֵךְ. Impf. Qal of הלך; תֵּלְכוּ in vs. 30 is the Impf.

28 (31). a. וְעָשׂוּ. ל"ה verbs drop ה before vowel endings.

   b. לְרִשְׁתָּהּ. Qal Inf. of ירשׁ (with suffix); the י is dropped, and a ת is added (see 1, c, Note).

29 (32). תָּסֻרוּ. For תָּסוּרוּ; see 14.

30 (33). תִּחְיוּן. Cf. 16, a, and 28, a.

CHAPTER III

1. a. וַיִּפֶּן. See note 1, page 173; לְ"ה verbs drop ה in the Jussive—the Impf. נִפְנֶה becoming יִפֶן, then נָפֶן. And וַיַּעַל is similarly from נַעֲלָה.

   b. וַיֵּצֵא. Some פ"י verbs drop the י of the stem in Impf. Qal, and take two Tseres as vowels.

   c. לִקְרָאתֵנוּ. See V, 1, c, Note.

2. נָתַתִּי. From נָתַנְתִּי, by assimilation.

3. a. וַיִּתֵּן. See V, 5, b and note 2, page 203.

   b. נַכֵּהוּ. פ"ן and לְ"ה, with suffix; see V, 12, b.

4. הָיְתָה. 3fs Qal Perf. of היה.

5. הַרְבֵּה. Cf. Ch. XXXIV, C, 3, c.

7. בַּזּוֹנוּ. In ע"ע verbs the double consonant is sometimes represented by D.F.; also, an auxiliary vowel is introduced before the personal endings.

8. וַנִּקַּח. From לקח, which is like a פ"ן (V, 5, b).

9. יִקְרְאוּ. "Used to call."

11. הֲלֹה. Read הֲלֹא.

13. הַהוּא. Rendering uncertain; R. V. translates "the same."

18. וָאֲצַו. Shortened from אֲצַוֶּה (see 1, a).

19. יֵשְׁבוּ. See 1, b.

20. יָנִיחַ (Hi.) and וְשַׁבְתֶּם. See V, 22, c.

21. הָרֹאֹת. Part. of a לְ"ה verb (fourth declension).

24. הַחִלּוֹתָ. See 7.

26. תּוֹסֶף. See V, 6; V, 22, b.

27. עֲלֵה and רְאֵה. Impvs. שָׂא is Impv. of נשא.

28. צַו. Shortened from צַוֵּה (Impv.).

29. וַנֵּשֶׁב. See 1, b and Ch. XXXI, B, 2.

CHAPTER IV

1. a. וּבָאתֶם. See V, 22, c; בָּאִים in vs. 5 is the Part.

   b. וִירִשְׁתֶּם. For יְרִשְׁתֶּם; see note 2, page 18.

2. תֹּסְפוּ. Cf. V, 15, a.

5. צַוֻּנִי. See V, 12, b.

10. הַקְהֵל־. See note 1, page 24.

15. לְנַפְשֹׁתֵיכֶם. "As ye value your lives."

22. מֵת. Cf. 1, a.

26. a. הַעִידֹתִי. Sometimes ע"ו verbs take an auxiliary vowel, like ע"ע verbs (III, 7).

   b. מַהֵר. See Ch. XXXIV, C, 3, c.

27. יָנֻהַג. Cf. Ch. V, D, 1, a.

30. בַּצַּר לְךָ וּמְצָאוּךָ. "In the (time of) distress for you, then shall . . ."; see Ch. XXXI, C, 3 (so also for וַיִּבְחַר in vs. 37).

32. וּלְמִקְצֵה. See note 2, page 20.

34. לָקַחַת. Inf. of לָקַח, formed like a פ"י (V, 28, b); לָדַעַת in vs. 35 is פ"י.

35. הָרְאֵתָ. For הָרְאֵיתָ.

36. הָרְאֵךָ. Cf. V, 21.

38. לָתֶת־. Irregular Qal Inf. of נתן.

39. וַהֲשֵׁבֹתָ. See 26, a.

40. אֲשֶׁר. Indicates purpose; note 1, page 82.

42. a. לָנֻס. Inf. Qal of נוּס.

   b. הָאֵל. For הָאֵלֶּה.

44. שָׁם. See V, 22, c.

45. בְּצֵאתָם. See V, 28, b.

46. הִכָּה. Cf. III, 3, b.

PART FIVE
IRREGULAR VERBS

CHAPTER XXXIX
PE GUTTURAL VERBS (הָטֵל)

A. Types and Treatment of Irregular Verbs

1. Only about one-fifth of the verbs in Hebrew are inflected like קְטַל, —i.e., are *strong* or *regular*. The rest have either gutturals which affect the vowel pointing, or weak consonants which sometimes disappear.

2. There are ten classes of irregular verbs[1]. These are designated by joining the name of the letter causing the irregularity with the name of the letter occupying the corresponding position in פָּעַל; e.g., a word irregular because of an initial נ is called a *Pe Nun*, etc.

Type word	Name of Class	Abbreviation	
עָבַד	Pe Guttural	פ״	Gutt.
יָשַׁב	Pe Yodh	פ״י	
נָפַל	Pe Nun	פ״ן	
גָּאַל	Ayin Guttural	ע״	Gutt.

---

[1] Or, if פ״א and פ״ו are considered separate classes rather than subclasses, twelve. Some verbs belong to two classes and take peculiarities from each; e.g., נָכָה and יָדַע. Some classes, however, cannot be combined; e.g., יָלַל, being פ״י, cannot take ע״ע forms.

קוּם	Ayin Waw	ע"ו
בִּין	Ayin Yodh	ע"י
סָבַב	Ayin Doubled, *or* Double Ayin	ע"ע
שָׁלַח	Lamedh Guttural	ל" Gutt.
מָצָא	Lamedh Aleph	ל"א
גָּלָה	Lamedh He	ל"ה

3. In explaining the general principles of each class of verbs, we use a fictitious verb-root formed by substituting the particular weak letter for the corresponding letter in קָטַל; e.g., for a Pe Guttural root we use חָטַל, and for a Lamedh He, קָטָה. Besides facilitating comparison with the strong verb, this enables the various parallel forms occurring in some classes to be indicated clearly·

4. In skeleton paradigms at the head of each chapter are given the salient forms. Forms that agree fully with the regular verb are enclosed in brackets; the most important deviations from the regular verb are marked with a star—*; forms derived from these leading forms according to regular rules have no mark; but subsidiary forms not regularly derived are marked with a dagger—†.

B. Skeleton Paradigm of Pe Gutturals in Qal

	Q¹	Q²	Q³	Q⁴	Q⁵
Impf. 3ms	*יַחְטֹל	*יַחְטֹל	*יֶחֱטַר	*יֶחְטֹל	*יֶחֱטֹל
3mp	יַחְטְלוּ	יַחְטְלוּ	יֶחְטְלוּ	יֶחְטְלוּ	†יַחַטְלוּ

Impv. 2ms	חֲטֹל	†חֲטַל	חֲטֹל

2mp	†חִטְלוּ	חִטְלוּ
Inf.	(לְ)חֲטֹל	חֲטֹל

+Suf.	†(לְ)חָטְלִי

C. Imperfect Qal

1. There are five possible forms of 3ms, as shown above.

a. The guttural commonly takes a Hateph vowel in place of silent Shewa (see Ch. V, D, 2) as in the forms designated Q¹, Q³, Q⁵; several verbs with initial ה, however, and a few others, have the Silent Shewa, as in the forms designated Q², Q⁴.

b. Because of the affinity of gutturals for the *a* sounds (Ch. V, D, 3), the primitive Pathah (cf. Ch. XXXVII, B) is usually retained under the preformative in *type O* verbs; Segol is used, however, under the א of 1cs (אֶחֱטֹל in Q¹), and thruout the Sing. of the rarer Q⁵ (which occurs chiefly in verbs with initial א). But in statives (*type A*), the preformative has Segol, to avoid so many *a* sounds coming together.

2. When a vowel ending is added, as in forming the Plu., so that the last stem vowel becomes Shewa, a Hateph vowel under the first radical regularly heightens to the corresponding full vowel[1].

3. When suffixes are added, the *type O* verbs undergo the same changes of final vowel as do regular verbs; the *type A* verbs follow the same principles as do regular statives. The first vowels undergo the same changes as when afformatives are added.

D. Other Forms of Qal

1. Since gutturals always take compound Shewa where other consonants have simple Shewa, the 2mp Perf., e.g., has the form חֲטַלְתֶּם, the 3ms with suffix is חֲטָלַנִי, etc.

2. In the 2ms Impv., *type A* verbs regularly have Pathah as final vowel; in the Inf., Holem (Ch. XXXVI, B, 4 and 5). Under the guttural most verbs have Hateph Pathah in both forms, whatever vowel they have in the Impf.[2]

---

*[1] But there are some variations. Thus, several words with compound Shewa in the Sing. take silent Shewa in the Plu.; e.g., יַעֲזֹר, יַחֲרֹד, יַחְרְדוּ; יַעְזְרוּ. Note also the change of actual vowel sound in Q[5]; a similar change occurs in some statives (e.g., יֶחְדַּל, יַחְדְּלוּ) —the guttural asserting its preference for *a* when the final *a* disappears.

*[2] Occasionally, with לְ prefixed to the Inf., the guttural loses its compound Shewa; e.g., לַחְפֹּר.

a. But verbs with initial **א** usually have Hateph Segol; e.g., אֱסֹף׃

b. When endings are added, the Hateph vowel does not heighten to the corresponding full vowel, as apparently the analogy of strong verbs has overcome the usual principles of vowel change; instead of Pathah (or Segol), the Impv. regularly has Hireq, the Inf. Qamets Hatuph[1].

c. אָהֵב is irregular; Impv. אֱהַב, plu. אֶהֱבוּ; Inf., usually אַהֲבָה (see Ch. 36, B, 5, b), also אֱהֹב׃

VOCABULARY

אָהֵב	Q³ or ⁴, love	חָשַׁב	Q² (also Pi.), think, devise, reckon; Ni², be regarded as
אָסַף	Q⁵, collect, gather, assemble	עָבַד	Q¹, serve; Hi¹, cause to work
אָשֵׁם	Q⁴, transgress, be guilty	עָבַר	Q¹, cross over; Hi¹, bring or send over
הָפַךְ	Q¹, turn; Ni², turn back, be changed	עָזַב	Q¹, forsake
הָרַג	Q¹, kill		
חָדַל	Q⁴, cease	עָזַר	Q¹, help
חָפֵץ	Q² or ⁴, delight in (בְּ), desire	עָמַד	Q¹, stand; Hi¹, make stand, set, establish

EXERCISES

1) נַעֲמֹד פֹּה לַעֲזֹר אֶת־כָּל־הָעֲזוּבִים׃ 2) אִם לֹא
יַעַבְדוּ אֹתוֹ וַהֲרָגֵם׃ 3) הַעֲבַרְתֶּם אֲלֵיהֶם וַתַּהַפְכוּם
לְאֹהֲבֵי הָאֱלֹהִים׃ 4) וְהָיָה בְּחָדְלָם לְעָבְדֵנִי וְעָזוֹב אֶעֱזֹב
אֹתָם׃ 5) אֶחְפְּצָה בְמִשְׁכָּנְךָ לְעוֹלָם׃ 6) אַל יַאַסְפוּ בָנַי

---

*[1] But some forms like אָסְפָה (Cohort. Impv.) do occur.

הָהֵם אֶת־כָּל־הָעֵצִים: ‪(7‬ וַיַּעֲבֹר וַיַּעַזְרֵם לַהֲרֹג אֶת־
הָאֲשֵׁמִים: ‪(8‬ חָדַל לַחֲשֹׁב רַע לָמַד לְאַהֲבָה טוֹב:
‪(9‬ וַתַּחְשְׁבְנָה תוֹעֵבוֹת לִפְנֵי יְהֹוָה: ‪(10‬ וַיַּעַבְדֵנוּ וַיֶּחְפַּץ בָּנוּ
וְלֹא עֲזָבָנוּ:

1. Let us turn to Jehovah and delight in Him alone.
2. And he reckoned you as forsakers of your friends.
3. If ye transgress the laws, I will cease to help you. 4. They
will stand to guard you, and ye will go over. 5. Love
those who serve you. 6. Gather ye together all those who
are going over, and kill them. 7. I will never (*say,* not to
eternity) forsake you if ye serve me in faithfulness.

A. Skeleton Paradigm

	Ni¹	Ni²	Hi¹	Hi²	Q⁶ (פ״א)
Perf.	*נֶחְטַל	*נֶחֲטַל	*הֶחֲטִיל	*הֶחְטִיל	
Impf.	*יֵחָטֵל		יַחֲטִיל [וַיַּחְטִיל]		*יֹאטַל
Impv. & Inf.					†אֱטֹל

B. Other Voices

1. In Ni. Perf., and in the Part. derived from it, and thruout Hi., a Hateph vowel is usually used in such verbs as have it in Impf. Qal; while those which have silent Shewa there do here also[1]. The preformative vowel is regularly Segol in Ni. and in Hi. Perf.[2]; but the Impf. Hi. and all allied forms of course have the ordinary Pathah.

2. In Impf. Ni., and in the allied Impv. and Inf., the guttural cannot take D.F. *In all verbs the preceding Hireq is lengthened to Tsere in compensation.*

C. Pe Aleph Verbs (Q⁶)

1. Six verbs beginning with א have a very special form

---

[1] In both Ni. and Hi. the usage of Shewa is sometimes different from that in Qal; e.g., הֶחֱצִיב. יַחְצֹב; נֶהְפַּךְ, יַהֲפֹךְ.

[2] But exceptions occur—especially before ע, or when an afformative is accented; e.g., הֶחֱיִיתָם, וְהַעֲמַדְתָּ, נֶעֶנָה.

in Impf. Qal. Elsewhere they regularly agree with the Pe Gutturals (Ni[1] and Hi[1]); and hence, while they are commonly designated as *Pe Aleph*, they are rather a special subvariety than a separate class[1]. All other verbs with initial א are fully Pe Guttural.[2]

2. *The Impf. Qal has the vowel Holem after the preformative*, the א being quiescent after it.

a. אָחַז is *type E* (see note 2, page 203) — יֹאחֵז; after Waw Consec. the accent is drawn onto the long open penult (Ch. XXXI, B, 2), and the Tsere shortens to Segol.

b. אָבַד, אָכַל, and אָמַר are regularly *type A* (with occasional *type E* forms). After Waw Consec. the accent of course recedes; but this does not affect the form of any of them except אָמַר, which always appears in 3ms as וַיֹּאמֶר.

c. אָבָה and אָפָה, altho having the preformative Holem, in other particulars follow the ל"ה verbs (see further in Chs. XLIII, XLIV).

d. In the first Sing. only one א is written; e.g., אֹמַר, not אֹאמַר.

3. In the Inf. of the one word אָמַר a contraction occurs when ל is prefixed—לֶאֱמֹר becoming לֵאמֹר (translated "saying").

VOCABULARY

אָבַד Q[6], perish; Pi. or Hi[1], destroy

אָחַז Q[6], seize, hold

אזן Hi[1], give ear, hear

אָכַל Q[6], eat, devour; Hi[1], feed

[*1] Occasionally the irregularity of these words extends to Ni. and Hi., and they have there a Holem with the preformative.

[*2] Irregular exceptions occur in אָסַף, אָהֵב, etc.

אמן	Ni¹, be firm, faithful; Hi¹, trust; Qal Pass. Part., the faithful	**חָלַק**	Q¹ or Pi., divide, distribute; Hith., divide among themselves
אָמַר	Q⁶, say; Ni¹, *Pass.*	**חָרַד**	Q³, tremble; Hi¹, terrify
אָסַר	Q⁵, bind; Ni¹, *Pass.*	**חרם**	Hi¹, devote
חָזַק	Q³, be, become strong; Pi., strengthen; Hi¹, make firm, hold fast¹	**חָרַשׁ**	Q¹, plough; Hi¹, be silent, put to silence
		עָרַךְ	Q¹, prepare, set in array

EXERCISES

1) יֹאבְדוּ יַחְדָּו בְּחַטֹּאתֵיהֶם: 2) הֶאֱמִין בֵּאלֹהָיו וַיֹּאכַל
אֶת־לַחְמוֹ בְּשָׁלוֹם: 3) הַאֲזֶן־נָא לִתְפִלָּתִי הָאֱלֹהִים וְאֹמְר־
נָא בְדִבְרֵי־חֵן: 4) וַיַּעֲבִירוּ אֶת־סוּסֵיהֶם אֶל־שָׂדֶם
וַיַּחַרְשׁוּ הַיּוֹם הַהוּא: 5) הַאֲבִידוּ אֶת־בָּתֵּיהֶם וְהִתְחַלְּקוּ
אֶת־נְשֵׁיהֶם: 6) וַיֹּאחֶז אֹתָהּ וַיַּחֲזֶק־בָּהּ לֵאמֹר יַחְשְׁבוּ
דְרָכֶיךָ כְּאָוֶן: 7) נֶהְפַּכְנוּ וַנַּעֲרֹךְ מִלְחָמָה עַל־צָרֵינוּ:
8) וַיֶּאֱסֹר אֶת־הַמַּעֲבָרוֹת וַיַּחֲרֵם אֹתָן: 9) הֶעֱמִידוּ אֶת־
בֵּיתָם עַל־הַצּוּר וְנֶאֱמָן: 10) אַל־תֶּחֱרַדִי כִּי לֹא תֶעָזְבִי
מִכָּל־הָאֱמוּנִים: 11) חִזְקוּ וְהַאֲמִינוּ הַשֹּׁמְרִים בְּחֵיל כְּלֵיכֶם:

1. We will destroy their houses and devote their children
2. And he said to his brothers, "Let us seize their presents."
3. The prophet spoke, saying, "Those who trust in Jeho-

---

¹ Impf. with Waw Consec., וַיְּחֱזַק; cf. Ch. XXXI, B, 2. Other verbs usually retain Tsere.

vah will be helped." 4. He will become strong, and will be regarded as a terror to (*say*, terrifier of) thieves. 5. Give ear, all ye peoples, for the wicked shall surely perish. 6. They were faithful to their charge, and put to silence those who were provoking us. 7. Let them prepare the food, that we may eat.

CHAPTER XLI
AYIN GUTTURAL VERBS (קָחַל, קָרַל).

A. Skeleton Paradigm

	Qal	Pi¹	Pi²	Pi³	Pu¹	Hith¹
Perf. 3ms	[נָקְחַל]	*קָרַל	*קָחַל	*קָחַל	*קֹרַל	*הִתְקָרֵל
3cp	*קָחֲלוּ	קֵרְלוּ	קָחֲלוּ		etc.	etc.
Impf.	*יִקְחַל	*יְקָרֵל	יְקַחֵל		Pu²	Hith²
+Waw		וַיְקָרֵל	וַיְקַחֵל		*קַחַל	*הִתְקַחֵל
Impv.	קְחַל	קָרֵל	קַחֵל		etc.	etc.
Inf.	[וּקְחֹל]					

B. Peculiarities of These Verbs

1. Gutturals have an affinity for *a* sounds:

a. *Verbs with a real guttural are almost always type A in Impf. and Impv. Qal*, even when transitive; but, just as in the case of regular statives, the Inf. usually has Holem. Verbs with ר are usually regular, taking *type O* if transitive.

b. Note the final Pathah in some Piels; cf. Ch. XXVIII, D, 3.

2. Gutturals cannot take simple vocal Shewa: wherever the strong verb has vocal Shewa, the four true gutturals take Hateph Pathah, whether the leading form has

225

Qamets or Tsere; ר usually takes simple Shewa, occasionally Hateph Pathah.

In the Impv. Qal the regular principles of vowel change are followed
(in contrast to the practice with Pe Gutturals); e. g., קְחַל, plu. קַחֲלוּ.

3. Gutturals can never take the D.F. characteristic of
the intensives:

a. The preceding vowel must be lengthened in compensation in all verbs with ר, and in most with א (Pi[1],
Pu[1], Hith[1]).

b. In most of the verbs with ה, ח, or ע, and a few
with א, the guttural has an "implicit dagesh," and the preceding vowel is not lengthened (Pi[2,3], Pu[2], Hith[2]).

VOCABULARY

בָּעַר	Q or Pi[2], burn, set fire to (בְּ); consume	מָאַן	Pi[1], refuse, be unwilling
בָּרַךְ	Pi[1], bless; Hith[1], *Refl.*	מִהַר	Pi[3], hasten
גָּאַל	deliver, redeem	מָעַל	act treacherously
גֵּרֵשׁ	Pi[1], drive out	רִחַם	Pi[3], have mercy, pity; Pu[2], find mercy
טָהֵר	be, become clean, pure; Pi[3], cleanse, purify; pronounce clean; Hith[2], *Reflex.*	רָחַץ	wash
		שָׁחַט	slaughter
		שֵׁרֵת	Pi[1], wait upon, min- ister unto

EXERCISES

1) יְמַהֵר יְהוָֹה גֹּאֲלָם לְרַחֲמָם: 2) אֲשָׁאֲרָה אִתְּךָ
לְשָׁרֲתָךְ: 3) גֵּרְשָׁה אֶת־אֹיְבְךָ בְּטֶרֶם יְשַׁחֵת אֶת־כִּסְאֶךָ:

4) בַּחֲרוּ־נָא לַעֲבֹד יְהוָה וּמַהֲרוּ לְהִטַּהֵר: 5) מֵאֲנָה לְגֹאֵל
אֹתוֹ: 6) צַעֲקִי אֶל־אֱלֹהֵיכֶם פֶּן יְבַעֲרֶכֶם: 7) טַהֲרֵנִי
וַאֲבֹרַךְ: 8) וַיִּרְחַץ אֶת־יָדָיו וַיְשָׁרֶת אֹתָנוּ: 9) נְשַׁחֲטָה אֶת־
הַמֹּעֲלִים וְאֶת־הַמְּמָאֲנִים לְטַהֵר אֶת־לְבוֹתָם: 10) שָׁאֲלוּ
אִם תְּלָחֲמוּ: 11) לֹא יְמָאֲסוּכֶם גֹּאֲלֵי הָעָם: 12) וְהִתְבָּרְכוּ
בְזַרְעֲךָ כֹּל גּוֹיֵי הָאָרֶץ:

1. Bless Jehovah, for ye have been redeemed by Him.
2. He was driven out before he set fire to the village.
3. Will they refuse to pity us as she asked? 4. Cease to act
treacherously, and cleanse yourselves, and ye shall find
mercy. 5. Your heads and your feet shall be washed.
6. And we hastened to slaughter them. 7. Jehovah
will bless your nation if ye be faithful to minister unto
Him.

CHAPTER XLII

LAMEDH GUTTURAL AND LAMEDH ALEPH VERBS
(קְטָא, קָטַח)

A. Skeleton Paradigms

	Qal	Ni.	Pi.	Hi.
Perf.	[קָטַח]	[נִקְטַח]	*קִטַּח	*הִקְטִיחַ
Impf.	*יִקְטַח	*יִקָּטַח	יְקַטַּח	יַקְטִיחַ
Juss.		etc.	etc.	†יַקְטַח
Impv.	קְטַח			הַקְטַח
Inf.	*קְטֹח			הַקְטִיחַ
Part.	*קֹטֵחַ (F. קֹטַחַת)		†מְקַטֵּחַ	מַקְטִיחַ

	Qal		Ni.	Hi.
Perf.				
3ms	*קָטָא	קָטֵא	נִקְטָא	[הִקְטִיא]
2ms	*קָטָאתָ	קָטֵאתָ	†נִקְטֵאתָ	הִקְטֵאתָ
Impf.				
3ms	*יִקְטָא		[יִקָּטֵא]	[יַקְטִיא]
3fp	†תִּקְטֶאנָה		תִּקָּטֶאנָה	תַּקְטֶאנָה

B. Lamedh Guttural Verbs

1. This class includes verbs ending in ח, ע, or הּ (He with Mappiq). Final א and ה (simple) are not guttural, but quiescent, and give rise to special classes.

2. *Qal. Impf. and Impv. are practically always type A*, due to the fondness of gutturals for Pathah; the Inf., however, usually has Holem.

3. When the guttural stands at the end of a word and is preceded by any long vowel except Qamets, it takes a Pathah Furtive; so in the Inf. and Pass. Part. of Qal, in all Hi. forms with Long Hireq, and in the following forms with Tsere—Inf. Absolutes (קָטֹחַ, הַקְטֵחַ, etc.) and Participles in the absolute state (מַקְטֵחַ, etc.).

4. In other forms which ordinarily have Tsere, the prim-itive Pathah is used instead; so in all of Pi. and Hith. except the two forms named in 3, in Ni. Impf. and allied forms, in the Jussive, Impv., and Fem. Plurals in נָה in Hi., and in the Sing. Cst. of Qal and Pi. Part. (e. g., מַקְטֵחַ).

5. A very special peculiarity occurs in the 2fs Perf.: a Pathah is placed under the guttural as a helping vowel, and yet the afformative ת retains the Dagesh and Shewa it regularly has; e. g., Qal, קָטַחְתְּ.

6. When other personal afformatives are added, so that the guttural should have silent Shewa, the forms are perfectly regular—the com-mon preference for a Hateph vowel not manifesting itself; e.g., קָטַחְתָּ. Of course, when a suffix is added which requires vocal Shewa as con-necting vowel, Hateph Pathah is used; e.g., קְטָחֲךָ.

C. Lamedh Aleph Verbs

1. When the א is final the last vowel is always long, for a short vowel does not commonly stand in an open syllable. Hence, in Qal, the Perf. (except of statives in Tsere), and the Impf. and Impv. (which are always *type*

A), have a Qamets where the strong verb has Pathah; so also in various Passive forms.

2. The א is also quiescent before consonantal afformatives. In Qal Perf. the preceding vowel is either Qamets or Tsere, according to the vowel occurring in 3ms; but in all other Perfects Tsere is used, regardless of the vowel in 3ms (of course an afformative ת does *not* take D.L.); the Impf. in all voices has Segol.

3. The Inf. Cst. Qal is sometimes regular; e.g., קְרֹא, "to call"; חֲטֹא. But not infrequently it is formed by adding ת (cf. Ch. 36, B, 5b); e.g., קְרֹאת;מְלֹאת, "to meet" (with suffixes, קְרֹאתוֹ).

*4. Various irregular forms occur. Thus the א may lose a vowel by contraction and become quiescent; e. g., חֹטְאִים for חֹטְאִים מֹצֵאת for מֹצֵאת. Sometimes the Aleph is entirely dropped; e.g., מָצָתִי and הֶחֱטִי. Sometimes there is a partial borrowing from, or confusion with, the forms of the ל"ה verbs; e.g., נִפְלָאת, 3fs Perf.; הִפְלָא for הִתְנַבֵּאת for הִתְנַבֵּית;יְמַלֶּה for יְמַלֵּא;הִפְלִיא.

VOCABULARY

גָּבַה	be high; Hi., exalt	מָלֵא	be full; Pi., fill
צָלַח	prosper, succeed; Hi., give success	מָצָא	find
שָׂבַע	be, become satisfied; Hi., satisfy	פָּלָא	Ni., be wonderful; Hi., make great, wonderful
בָּרָא	create		
חָטָא	Q³, sin; Hi¹, cause to sin	קָרָא	cry out, call to; name
טָמֵא	be, become unclean; Pi., defile, pollute; Ni. or Hith., defile oneself	קָרָא	befall, happen to, meet
		רָפָא	heal, cure

EXERCISES

‏1) וַיְהִי בְּקָרְאתָם הָרַע הַהוּא וַּנִּרְפָּא אֹתָם: 2) וַנִּשְׁכַּח
‏לִבְטֹחַ בֵּאלֹהֵינוּ אֲשֶׁר הִצְלִיחָנוּ: 3) תִּשְׁמַעְנָה הַנָּשִׁים
‏הָהֵנָּה כִּי תִטְמָאנָה: 4) וַיִּקְרָא אֵלֵינוּ לְבִלְתִּי תְקַע אֹהֶל
‏שָׁם: 5) בַּקֵּעַ אֲבַקַּע אֶת־מָגִנֵּיכֶם: 6) נִמְצְאָנִפְלָאוֹת רַבּוֹת
‏בַּהֵיכָל בִּירִיחוֹ: 7) קָרָא אֵלָיו הַמֶּלֶךְ וְהַשְׁמַע אֹתוֹ אֶת־
‏קוֹלֹדֹ: 8) בָּרָאתִי אֶתְכֶם נְאֻם יְהֹוָה וַתֶּחֶטְאוּ וַתִּטַּמָּאוּ:
‏9) הִנֵּה בֹּרַחַת פֶּן תִּבָּלַע: 10) יִצְלַח הַמַּגְבִּיהַ אֶת־הַצְּדָקָה:
‏11) זְבַח אֶל־הָאֱלֹהִים כִּי הִשְׁבִּיעֲךָ וַיְמַלֵּא אֶת־נַפְשְׁךָ טוֹב:

1. And it came to pass when this evil befell me that I forgot God. 2. He has exalted His name and filled His dwelling place with glory. 3. By the word of Jehovah wast thou (f) created, and by His grace hast thou prospered. 4. Ye are unclean, for ye caused him to sin. 5. We found a wonderful old man, and he satisfied our hearts. 6. Send thy servant to sow thy field. 7. He did not make glad my heart when he called me the anointer of kings.

CHAPTER XLIII
LAMEDH HE VERBS (קָטָה)

A. Skeleton Paradigm

Perf.	Qal	Ni.	Pi.	Pu.	Hi.	Ho.	Hith.
3ms	*קָטָה	*נִקְטָה	*קִטָּה	*קָטָּה	*הִקְטָה	*הָקְטָה	*הִתְקַטָּה
3fs	†קָטְתָה						
2ms	†קָטִיתָ	†נִקְטֵיתָ					
3cp	†קָטוּ						

Impf.	Qal	Ni.	Pi.	Pu.	Hi.	Ho.	Hith.
3ms	*יִקְטָה	יִקָּטֶה	יְקַטֶּה	יְקֻטֶּה	יַקְטֶה	יָקְטֶה	יִתְקַטֶּה
3mp	†יִקְטוּ						
3fp	תִּקְטֶינָה						
Juss.	†יִקַט	†יִקָּט	†יְקֵט	†יְקַט	†יֶקֶט	†יִקֵט	†יִתְקַט

B. Perfect and Imperfect

1. These words originally ended in **י** (i.e., קָטַי)[1]. This final consonant, however, has been *entirely lost*, except in a few forms. In the simple forms (i.e., without afformatives), a final **ה** is now written simply as a vowel letter —an orthographic representation of the final vowel, preserving the triliteral appearance of the root (קָטָה for קָטָ).

---

[1] Some few, however, were originally ל"ו; see especially Ch. XLIV, C, 4; but in most forms they have become identical with the ל"י.

2. *The 3ms has the same final vowel in all voices:*

a. All Perfects end in הָ (lengthened from the primitive Pathah; cf. Ch. XXXVII, B).

b. All Imperfects end in הֶ (probably contracted from a primitive יֶ).

3. Before all *vowel afformatives* the final consonant and preceding vowel have been entirely *elided;* e.g., the ground-forms קָטִין and יְקְטִין became קָטוּ and יִקְטוּ[1].

a. The 3fs Perf. is peculiar in that both the primitive afformative ת and the later הָ are added; e.g., Pi. קִטְּתָה.

*b. Sometimes, however, the י is retained, especially at the end of a sentence; e.g., יִשְׁתָּיוּן.

4. Before all *consonantal afformatives* the primitive י is written, but is *quiescent;* the preceding vowel is usually Hireq in the Perf. of the active voices, Tsere in the passive Perfs., Segol in all Impfs.

C. Jussive and Cohortative. Apocopation

1. *The Jussive in all voices is formed by dropping the* הֶ *of the Impf.*[2]; e.g., Ni., יִקָּט from יִקָּטֶה. This process is called *apocopation*, and the resulting forms *apocopated* forms.

a. In three voices this leaves a monosyllabic form

---

[1] We use the term *ground-form* to indicate either an actual primitive form (cf. Ch. XXXVII, B); or a modification thereof, in which standard vowel changes have been made, from which the particular effect of the weak consonant can readily be seen.

*[2] Very occasionally a Jussive in הֶ occurs.

ending in two consonants, which is regularly treated much as were the primitive segolate-noun stems—i.e., a Segol is introduced as helping vowel, and the stem vowel is changed sometimes:

Qal, יָקֵט, apocopated from יִקְטֶה, becomes יִקֶט.

Hi., יַקֵט, apocopated from יַקְטֶה, becomes יַקֶט.

Ho., יָקַט, apocopated from יָקְטֶה, becomes יָקַט.

b. In the intensives the D.F. is not retained in the second radical when this letter becomes final; e.g., Pi. יְקַט (for יְקַטְּ), etc.

2. Of course these apocopated forms are used after Waw Consec.; it produces no further change in them.

3. The cohortative ending הָ— is not used with these verbs; the ordinary Impf. does duty for the cohortative idea also.

D. Suffixes

1. When suffixes are added to any form which has the final ה, this and the preceding vowel are dropped[1]; e.g., קָמָה, קָמַנִי (the Qamets under the first radical of course does not shorten); יְקָטֶה, יְקָטְךָ; etc.

2. The 3ms suffix to the 3ms Perf. is always written in the full form ־הוּ, instead of the contracted וֹ— which is usual with other verbs (cf. fourth declension nouns, which are derived from these verbs).

3. When a suffix is attached to a Jussive form, the Qal or Hi. stem of course does not have the auxiliary Segol, and the D.F. is retained in Pi.; e.g., יְקָטֵם, וַיְקַטְּבֵם.

---

[1] Other forms follow regular rules.

VOCABULARY

אָבָה‎ be willing (פ״א‎)

אָפָה‎ bake (פ״א‎)

בָּכָה‎ weep

גָּלָה‎ disclose; go into captivity; Pi., reveal, uncover; Hi., carry away captive

זָנָה‎ commit fornication

כָּלָה‎ be complete, finished; Pi., complete; destroy

כסה‎ Pi., cover, conceal

מָרָה‎ Q or Hi., rebel (against)

פָּדָה‎ ransom; set free

פָּנָה‎ turn

צוה‎ Pi., command

צָפָה‎ Q or Pi., look about, watch, observe

קָנָה‎ get, obtain

רָבָה‎ be, become many or great; increase; Hi., increase (trans.)

רָעָה‎ feed

EXERCISES

‏1) פָּנְתָה מְתוֹרוֹתִי וַתִּזֶן: 2) וַיִּגַל אֶת־הַמִּזְבֵּחַ וַיְצַו אֶת־‏
‏הַכֹּהֲנִים לִזְבֹּחַ: 3) תֹּאפֶה־לּוֹ רַב־לֶחֶם וְרָצָהוּ: 4) יֶרֶב‏
‏אֶת־מִקְנֵהוּ וַיְּקֶן אֶת־חֵן שָׁרוֹ: 5) הֲנִפְדַּם מֵעֲבוֹדָתָם אַחֲרֵי‏
‏אֲשֶׁר כִּלּוּ אֶת־מְלַאכְתָּם: 6) צִפִּיתִי אֶת־מַעֲשֵׂיהֶם וָאֹבֶה‏
‏לִבְטֹחַ אֶת־אֱמוּנָתָם: 7) נִבְכֶּה־נָּא לִילָדֵינוּ אֲשֶׁר לֹא־נִפְדוּ‏
‏מֵעָנְיָם: 8) וַיִּפֶן וַיְצַף וְלֹא נִרְאֵינוּ: 9) הִתְכַּסֵּיתִי בְּבֶגֶד‏
‏הַצֶּדֶק כַּאֲשֶׁר צִוָּה יְהֹוָה: 10) אִם נִמְרֶה אֶת־פִּי יְהֹוָה וְלֹא‏
‏נִרְצֵהוּ לֹא יַעֲשֵׂנוּ לְעַם גָּדוֹל: 11) רָעַד יְהֹוָה וְלֹא נֶאֱמַנְתָּ‏
‏אֵלָיו וַיִּגֶל אֹתְךָ:‏

1. Didst not thou command that we should obtain this for her? 2. And he increased the number of his servants

and finished the work today. 3. And they were willing to serve him, and did not rebel and weep. 4. May the bread which she has baked be received graciously. 5. And her daughter turned to your queen and said, "Wilt thou feed our people?" 6. If my power increases, I will reveal his iniquities which he has concealed. 7. And his daughter committed fornication, but was set free.

CHAPTER XLIV

LAMEDH HE VERBS. (Continued)

A. Skeleton Paradigm

	Qal	Ni.	Pi.	Hi.	Hith.
Impv.	קְטֵה*	הִקָּטֵה	קַטֵּה	הַקְטֵה	הִתְקַטֵּה
Inf.	קְטוֹת*	הִקָּטוֹת	קַטּוֹת	הַקְטוֹת	הִתְקַטּוֹת
Part.	קָטֶה*	נִקְטֶה	מְקַטֶּה	מַקְטֶה	מִתְקַטֶּה

B. Other Moods

1. All Impvs. (2ms) end in הֶ—; except that the Pi. and Hi. are occasionally *apocopated*, giving קַט and הֶקְט. The inflection is of course like that of the Impf.; e.g., Qal plurals, קְטִינָה ,קְטוּ.

2. The Inf. Abs. usually ends in הֹ—; except that in Pi. and Hi. it commonly has הֵ—.

3. All Inf. Csts. end in וֹת— —the final radical being dropped, and the feminine ת added (cf. Ch. XXXVI, B, 5, b). This ending is unchangeable before suffixes; e.g., קְטֹתְכֶם.

4. All Parts., except Qal Pass., end in הֶ— in Masc. Sing. They are *fourth declension*—i.e., the Masc. Sing. Cst. has Tsere (as in מַקְטֵה), and the ה is dropped before

all endings (e.g., קְטָה‎, קְטִים‎, קְטָף‎)[1]. The Qal Pass. has the primitive י‎, the forms being קָטוּי‎, קְטוּיָה‎ etc.

C. Special Words[2]

1. There are several special types of apocopation:

a. In Qal Juss. of some verbs, the preformative vowel is lengthened to Tsere, especially in the second person (cf. *i* class segolate nouns); e.g., תֵּרֶב‎, from רָבָה‎; also in b, c.

b. Verbs in which the middle radical is a mute (ב‎, ד‎, ט‎, כ‎, ק‎, ה‎, ת‎) frequently retain the monosyllabic form, without introducing a helping vowel; e.g.,

שָׁבָה‎, Qal Juss. יֵשַׁב‎

שָׁתָה‎ and בָּכָה‎, Qal Juss. יֵשְׁתְּ‎ and יֵבְךְ‎

שָׁקָה‎, Hi. Juss. יַשְׁקְ‎

c. Words that are also Ayin Guttural take Pathah instead of Segol as helping vowel; e.g., יֵרַע‎, from רָעָה‎. But רָאָה‎ has יֵרֶא‎ in Qal Juss.[3]; and after Waw consec., a further change occurs in 3ms only, the form being וַיַּרְא‎.

2. Words that are also Pe Guttural (type חָטָה‎):

a. The form of the Qal Impf. may be either יַחֲטָה‎ or

---

2 For verbs also פ"י‎ see Ch. XLVI, C, 3; for those also פ"ן‎ see Ch. XLVIII, A, 2.

3 Distinguish this from Ni. Juss., יֵרָא‎.

יֶחֱטֶה—corresponding, respectively, to the Q[1] and Q[3] of Ch. XXXIX[1].

b. The Jussive of the Q[1] usually has the form יַחַט; e.g., יַעַשׂ from עָשָׂה. This same form of apocopation has been borrowed by some Q[3] verbs; e.g., יַחַל and יַחַן, from חָלָה and חָזָה. But חָרָה (Q[3]) and חָנָה (Q[1]) have יַחַר and יַחַן (the guttural losing all influence over the preceding vowel).

c. It is evident that an Impf. יַחֲטֶה or a Juss. יַחַט may be either Qal or Hi.; in a verb used in both voices, only the context can decide the voice.

3. The two common words הָיָה and חָיָה are specially irregular.

a. The first radical takes Hateph Segol when it has a compound Shewa; e.g., הֱיוֹת, חֱיִיתֶם.

b. When any other letter precedes, the first guttural has silent Shewa; e.g., יֶהְיֶה and יֶחְיֶה; בִּהְיוֹת; וְהָיוּ (Plu. of Impv. הֱיֵה, with וְ)[2].

c. The apocopated forms of Qal are יְהִי and יְחִי—developed from יֶהְי and יֶחְי as was פְּרִי from פְּרִי.

4. שׁחה is used in a *Hithpa'lel* form. In a strong verb this would be הִתְקַטְלֵל; here of course the ת and שׁ are interchanged, the guttural takes compound Shewa, and the

---

*1 A very few words have silent Shewa; e.g., יַהְנֶה, יַעְטֶה.

2 About the only exception to this is Hi. of חיה—הַחֲיָה.

primitive final וֹ is used, giving הִשְׁתַּחֲוָה. The apocopated Impf. is יִשְׁתַּחוּ.

D. Identification Marks

1. Segolate and other apocopated forms in Jussive, and
hence after Waw Consec.

2. וֹת— in Inf. Cst.

3. י before consonantal afformatives; תָה— in 3fs Perf.

4. These are the most numerous of the weak verbs; hence
the student must always be on the alert to recognize the
possibility of the final consonant having been lost from a
form (e.g., before a vowel afformative or a suffix).

VOCABULARY

הָיָה	be, become	עָנָה	Q¹, answer
חָזָה	Q³, see, gaze upon	עָנָה	Q¹, labor; suffer; Pi., oppress, afflict
חָיָה	live	שָׁבָה	take captive
חָלָה	Q³, be, become sick		
חָנָה	Q¹, encamp	שׁחה	Hithpal., bow down, worship
חָרָה	Q³, burn (of anger), be angry	שׁקה	Hi., water, give to drink
עָלָה	Q¹, go up; Hi¹, bring or send up	שָׁתָה	drink

EXERCISES

1) יַשֵּׁק אֶת־עֵנָיו וְיֵרַע אֹתָם׃ 2) וַיְהִי בְּכַסּוֹתִי אֶת־פָּנָיו
וַיִּחַר לָהּ׃ 3) עֲנֵה־נָא אֶת־תְּפִלּוֹתֵינוּ וְעַנֵּה אֶת־צָרֵינוּ וְכֻלָּם

בַּדֶּבֶר׃ (4 בְּעוֹדָם בֹּנִים אֶת־בָּתֵּיהֶם יַחֲנוּ עִמָּנוּ׃ (5 נַעֲלֶה
לְחָצֵר וְנֵרָאֶה לִפְנֵי הַמֶּלֶךְ לַעֲנוֹתוֹ׃ (6 הִשְׁתַּחֲווּ אַרְצָה
וַיֹּאמֶר חֲזוּר־נָא אֶת־עָנְיֵנוּ וְאַל תְּשִׁבֵנוּ מֵאַרְצֵנוּ׃ (7 הֲלֹא
תַעֲנֶינָה בְּדִבְרֵי חֵמָה כִּי יַרְבּוּ כִּי יַרְבּוּ בַעֲלֵיהֶן אֶת־מְלַאכְתָּן׃
(8 יַחֲנוּ כֻלָּם בְּקָצֶה הָעֵמֶק וְיִחְיוּ שָׁם בְּעוֹדָם אֹבִים׃
(9 וַיִּשְׁתּוּ כֻלָּם מִן־הַצּוּר הַהוּא וַיֹּאכְלוּ אֶת־הַלֶּחֶם הַהוּא׃
(10 וַתַּעַל אֶת־הַמַּלְאָךְ לְאָמָה וַיִּרָא אֹתָהּ וַיֹּאמֶר אַיֶּנָּה
חֹלָה׃ (11 כֻּלָּנוּ הָיִינוּ בֹכוֹת עַל־אֲחוֹתֵנוּ וְעַל־כֵּן לֹא צֻוּוּ
אֹתָנוּ לִהְיוֹת בֶּחָג׃

1. And those who took us captive encamped here and
gave us to drink.   2. Let him live here and become a son
to thee, for behold he is weeping.   3. And it came to pass
when I was laboring that he saw me and was angry.
4.   And he took me up to the top of the mountain, and
I gazed on all the country.   5. Do not rebel against Jehovah and bow down before Ba'al.   6. And it came to pass
when they were going up to oppress your brothers that
they were willing to hear your prayer concerning them
and to answer you.   7. And he drank that water and
became sick.

CHAPTER XLV

PE YODH VERBS (יָטַל)

A. Skeleton Paradigm

	Q¹	Q²	Ni	Hi¹	Ho¹
Perf.	[וְיָטַל]	[וְיָמַל]	*נוֹטַל	*הוֹטִיל	*הוּטַל
Impf.	*יֵטַל	*יִיטַל	*יִנָטֵל	יוֹטִיל	יוּטַל
+Waw	וַיֵּטֶל			וַיּוֹטֶל	
Impv.	טֵל יְטַל טַל†	הִנָּטֵל	הוֹטֵל
Inf.	†(לְ)טֶלֶת [וְיָטֹל] טָלֶת	הִנָּטֵל הוֹטִיל
+ Suf.	(לְ)טֶלְתִּי
Part.	[יָטֵל]	נוֹטָל	מוֹטִיל	מוּטָל

B. Character of the Words

1. Most of these verbs originally had Waw as first radical. This does not appear in Qal at all, but does in several other voices.

This chapter treats only such Pe Yodhs as were originally Pe Waw —those which were originally Pe Yodh being treated in the next chapter.

2. Both Yodh and Waw are weak letters, and become quiescent after certain vowel sounds; hence they lose their

consonantal character after most preformatives.   In some
cases, also, they disappear entirely.

C. Qal

1. Several of the commonest words have a *type E* Impf.,
יֵטֵל. Here the י (or ו) of the stem is dropped entirely,
the י which is written being merely preformative.   The
Tsere under the preformative is fixed; but the second
Tsere is tone-long, and the inflection is analogous to that
of an ordinary Ni. Impf.

a. The Impv. is formed from the Impf. according to
the usual principle; the preformative is dropped, leaving
טֵל (Plu. טְלוּ).

b. To form the Inf. Cst., ת is added to the shortened
stem (cf. Ch. *36*, *B*, 5, b), and it is pointed as a segolate
noun — טֶלֶת (for a primitive טְלת).   A prefixed ל is
pointed with Qamets before a simple form (cf. Ch. VIII, *A*, 2,
d), with Shewa before a form with a suffix.

2. A larger number of words have a *type A* Impf., יֵיטֵל,
in which the י of the stem is retained, quiescent in Long
Hireq[1].

a. In forming the Impv., the י is sometimes irregularly
dropped, sometimes retained; e.g., רֵשׁ, also יְרֵה.

b. In the Inf. Cst., יָרֵשׁ has a Q[1] form, רֶשֶׁת.   Most
other verbs are *regular* here; e.g., יְבַשׁ (but also יְבֶשֶׁת).

---

[1] But not infrequently this is written defectively; e.g., יְבַשׁ.

3. In both groups the Inf. Abs. and Part. are quite regular—יָטוֹל and יָטֵל respectively

D. Other Voices

1. In the intensives the י stands at the beginning of a syllable, and hence the forms are perfectly regular[1]. But thruout the other three voices the original Waw reappears.

2. In Ni. Perf. the groundform was נָוְטַל (cf. Ch. XXXVII, B); the Pathah and Waw coalesced, giving נוֹטַל (cf. Ch. XIX, B, 1). Similarly, in all forms of Hi., the Waw appears in Holem—הַוְטִיל having become הוֹטִיל, etc.[2]

3. In Ni. Impf. and allied forms, the ו is fully consonantal, and takes D.F.; e.g , יִנָּטֵל, etc.[3]

4. In all forms of Ho., the ו appears in Shureq; this is the result of a coalescence of the ו and the Qibbuts under the preformative (cf. Ch. XXVIII, D, 4) — הֻוְטַל having become הוּטַל.

E. Effect of Waw Consecutive

When Waw Consec. is used with an Impf. which has a long open penult, the accent is drawn onto the penult,

---

*[1] But sometimes Hith. has the form הִתְוַטֵל. And the Pi. Impf., 3ms, is sometimes contracted; e.g., וַיְבַשֵׁהוּ for וַיְיַבְּשֵׁהוּ.

[2] Such a Holem should always be written fully; but sometimes the etymology has been neglected and it is written defectively, as in Ni. נֹטַל, Hi. יֹטִיל, etc.

*[3] The 1cs always has Hireq under א; e.g., אִוָּסֵר.

and the vowel in the ultima shortened; hence the Q¹ form
becomes וַיִּטַל.[*1] And in Hi. a double change occurs:
Waw Consec. of course requires the Jussive form, which is
יוֹטֵל; and with the moving of the accent, this becomes
וַיּוֹטֵל.

VOCABULARY

יָבֵשׁ Q², be dry, dry up;
Hi¹, make dry, dry up

יָרַד Q¹, go down; Hi¹,
bring down

יכח Hi¹, decide; reprove,
chasten, punish

יָרֵשׁ Q², take possession,
occupy; Hi¹, dispossess

יָלַד Q¹, bear, bring forth;
Ni., be born; Hi¹,
beget

יָשַׁב Q¹, sit, dwell

יָעַץ Q², give counsel; purpose; Ni., take counsel

ישׁע Hi¹, save, deliver; Ni.,
Pass.

יָצָא Q¹, go out; Hi¹, send
or bring out

יתר Hi¹, let remain, leave;
Ni., remain, be left

EXERCISES

1) נוֹלְדוּ יְלָדֵינוּ שָׁם וַיּוֹרִידוּם הֵנָּה: 2) הוֹתֵר פֹּה וְרֵשׁ
אֶת־כַּרְמִי עַד־אֲשֶׁר אוֹצִיא אֶת־אָחִי: 3) תֵּשְׁבוּ בְשָׁלוֹם כִּי
נוֹשַׁעֲכֶם מִמְעַנְּכֶם: 4) וַיֵּרֶד לִשְׂפַת הַנָּהָר וַיִּבַשׁ:
5) נִוָּעֲצָה לְהוֹרִישׁ אֶת־אֹיְבֵינוּ וְאַל נוֹתִירָה אִישׁ בְּעָרֵיהֶם:
6) צְאָה־נָּא עִמִּי וּרְאֵה אֶת־דִרְכְּבִּי: 7) וְהָיָה בְּרִשְׁתְּךָ אֶת־
נַחֲלָתָהּ הַזֹּאת וְהוֹכַחְתָּ: 8) וַיְהִי אַחֲרֵי לִדְתָּהּ לוֹ בַּת
אַחַת וַיּוֹלַד בָּנִים רַבִּים: 9) וַיְהִי בִּיבֹשׁ הַנְּחָלִים וְלֹא נוֹתְרוּ

[*1] And the Q² form occasionally becomes וַיִּטַל.

בַּגֶּגֶב וַתֵּרַדְנָה לַיְאֹר: 10) וַתִּיעֲצוּ אֵלֶיהָ לְבִלְתִּי רַחָמָן
וְלֹא אָבְתָה לוֹכִיחַ אֹתָן: 11) וַיְהִי אַחֲרֵי הוֹלִידוֹ אֶת־בְּנוֹ
הַשְּׁבִיעִי חָמֵשׁ עֶשְׂרֵה שָׁנָה:

1. She was born before we were brought out from Egypt.
2. Go down to that valley, my sons, and dispossess its
inhabitants. 3. And her mother brought her down and
ieft her here to bring forth her first-born. 4. And it came
to pass when he took possession of his inheritance, that
he was delivered from poverty. 5. And it came to pass
as we were taking counsel against his teachers that he sat
(down) with us. 6. And Jehovah dried up all the water
which remained upon the face of the earth. 7. Did ye
reprove them because they did not beget children?

A. Skeleton Paradigm

	Q³	Hi³		Q⁴
Perf.	[וְיָטֵל	*הֵיטִיל		[וְיָטַל
Impf.	*יִיטַל	יֵיטִיל	(+Waw, וַיֵּיטֶל)	*יִטֹל
Impv.	יְטַל	הֵיטֵל		

B. Verbs Originally Pe Yodh (Q³, Hi³)

1. There are a few verbs in which the initial Yodh is the true and original root letter. *It is therefore retained thruout*, being a proper part of the stem.

2. The Qal Impf. is *type A*, with the Yodh quiescent in Long Hireq—coinciding in form with Q². But the Impv. is *regular*, never dropping the Yodh; so also, of course, is the Inf., יְטֹל.

3. All forms of Hi. have Tsere under the preformative, the Yodh being quiescent after it; e.g., הֵיטִיל, etc.[1]

C. Special Words and Idioms

1. Original Pe Waws of the first class which are also Lamedh Guttural have Qal Impf. in *A* instead of in *E*; e.g.,

---

[1] The ground-form was הֵיְטִיל; primitive ־ְי frequently became ־ִי (cf. Ch. XIX, B, 2).

יָדַע, יֵדַע; hence also Impv. דַּע, Inf. דַּעַת (with suffixes, דַּעְתִּי); and Hi. Impf. with Waw, וַיּוֹדַע[1].

2. Verbs which are also ל"א have a long vowel in Impf., and keep it after Waw; e.g., וַיֵּצֵא, יִירָא.

a. יָרֵא retains the י in Impv. Qal, יְרָא; and in Qal Inf. it usually takes the Fem. form in ה, יִרְאָה.

b. In Qal Inf. of יָצָא the vowels coalesce and the א becomes silent—צֵאַת becoming צֵאת.

3. Two common words, יָדָה and יָרָה, have also the weaknesses of ל"ה verbs. Typical forms (Hi.) are: וַיּוֹר; אוֹדְךָ, יוֹדֶה, הוֹדָה[2].

4. הָלַךְ is inflected in almost all forms as tho it were a Pe Yodh (Q[1]); e.g., Qal Impf., יֵלֵךְ; Hi. Perf., הוֹלִיךְ, etc. But Qal Inf. with suffixes is לֶכְתִּי, not לְכְתִּי; also the initial ה is used in Qal Perf. and Inf. Abs., and Hith.

5. יָכֹל is defective. It is used in Qal in the Perf., and in the Inf. יְכֹלֶת (an o class segolate); in Ho. in the Impf.

6. יָסַף has a special idiomatic sense when used with a complementary Inf. (which either may or may not have ל); e.g., הוֹסִיף לִרְנֶּן (lit., He added to shout), may mean "He shouted again," "He continued to shout," or "He shouted yet more (louder)." עוֹד may be added for emphasis.

---

*1 Similar are some verbs with final ר, or a middle guttural; e. g., Qal Impf., יֵקַר; Impv., הַב.

*2 There are also some Qal forms; e.g., Impf., יִירֶה, נִירָם; Inf., יְרוֹת; Impv. Plu., יְדוּ. Less common is the verb יָנָה.

7. יָטַב is used in Hi. with a complementary Inf. (with לְ) to mean "to do a thing well"; e. g., הֵיטִיב לְדַבֵּר, (He 'made good' speaking), "He spoke well"[1].

D. Identification Marks

1. A Waw (consonantal or as a vowel letter) after a preformative letter almost always represents an initial Yodh.

2. "Double Tsere" in Qal Impf.

3. Segolate Infinitives are usually Pe Yodh.

4. When the Yodh appears, tho quiescent, the stem is immediately apparent. (Sometimes, however, the Yodh is omitted, the vowel with the preformative being written defectively).

*E. Verbs Assimilating

1. There are a few Pe Yodhs in which the Yodh is *assimilated*, just as an initial Nun is, and represented by D.F. in the second radical. All Pe Yodhs whose second radical is צ, except יָצָא, are thus inflected; such forms occur occasionally also in a few other verbs. Many of these words also have more regular פ"י forms; e.g., Ho., הוּצַק.

2. In addition to the forms shown in the paradigm (Q⁴), one Qal Impf. in *A* occurs—יֵצַת; also other voices, as Ni. נִצַּת, Hi. הִצִּיק, Ho. הֻצַּג, etc.

---

[1] Occasionally the Inf. Abs. is used after a finite verb form in a similar sense; e.g., דַּבֵּר הֵיטֵב.

VOCABULARY

יָדָה	Hi¹, praise, celebrate	יָסַף	Hi¹, add; increase
יָדַע	Q¹, know; Hi¹, show, make known	יָרֵא	Q², fear; Ni. Part., dreadful; wonderful
יָטַב	Q³, be good; Hi³, do well, do good	יָרָה	Hi¹, throw, shoot; instruct
יָכֹל	be able; *with* לְ, prevail over	יָשַׁר	Q³, be straight, right; Pi., make straight, even
יָלַל	Hi³, wail (עַל, for)		
יָנַק	Q³, suck; Hi³, suckle	הָלַךְ	Hi¹, lead, take away

EXERCISES

1) וַתֵּינֶק אֶת־בֶּן־מוֹשִׁיעָהּ: 2) וַיְהִי בְּלֶכְתּוֹ לְהוֹכִיחָם
וַיּוֹסִפוּ לְהֵילִיל: 3) לֹא תוּכַל לִי כִּי לֹא אִירָא אֹתְךָ:
4) לְכָה־נָא וְאוֹדִיעָה אֹתְךָ אֶת־אֱמוּנַת עֲבָדַי: 5) וַתּוֹצֵא
אֶת־אָבִיהָ וַיֵּיטֶב לְזֶמֶר: 6) אוֹדֶה אֶת־הַמּוֹלִיךְ אֹתִי לְרֵעַי:
7) הֲיְכָלְתֶּם לָלֶכֶת כַּמִּצְוֹת אֲשֶׁר בָּהֶן הוֹרִיתִיכֶם: 8) וַיּוֹסֶף
מְדִינוֹת רַבּוֹת לְמַמְלַכְתּוֹ: 9) וַיְהִי בְּהַוָּשְׁעוֹ בְכֹחִי וַיִּישַׁר
בְּעֵינָיו לְהוֹדוֹתֵנִי: 10) וְהָיָה בְדַעְתְּכֶם אֶת ־ חֻקֵּיהֶם
הַנּוֹרָאִים וְהֵילַלְתֶּם: 11) תִּינְקִי אֶת־חֲלֵב הַגּוֹיִים וְיָדַעַתְּ
כִּי אֲנִי מֹשִׁיעֵךְ בַּת יְרוּשָׁלֵם: 12) וַנָּשֶׁב וְאֵינֶנּוּ מוֹרִים
חֵץ:

1. And I will not be able to show them the dreadful misery of those dispossessed. 2. How will she know that she will go tonight? 3. And he punished them well because they did not make the road straight. 4. And it

came to pass when they knew her sin that she was afraid to go to them. 5. And he again praised us because we prevailed over the king's sons. 6. The mother who suckled thee instructed thee not to be afraid to go out with my army. 7. Take ye away from me those who are wailing about their servitude.

CHAPTER XLVII

PE NUN VERBS (נָטַל)

A. Skeleton Paradigm

	Qal		Ni.	Hi.	Ho.
Perf.		[וְנָטַל]	נָטַל* הִטִּיל*		הֻטַּל*

				Ni.	Hi.	Ho.
Perf.	יִטַּל*		יִטַּל*	יִנָּטֵל	יַטִּיל	etc.
Impv.	[וְנְטֹל]		טַל	etc.	etc.	

Inf.	†(לְ)טֶלֶת וְנְטֹל [וְנְטֹל]	

B. Forms with Nun Assimilated

1. As already explained in connection with the preposition מִן, Nun is a weak letter and easily disappears. *In these verbs the initial נ is regularly assimilated into the following letter whenever it stands at the end of a syllable and consequently has no vowel.*

a. This assimilation occurs in Impf. Qal (יִטַּל for יִנְטֹל), Ni. Perf. and Part. (נִטַּל for נִנְטַל), and all of Hi. and Ho. (הִטִּיל for הִנְטִיל, יַטַּל for יִנְטַל, etc.).

b. *In all such cases the second radical of course has D.F.*

c. Note how similar are the Ni. and Pi. Perfects, actually coinciding in all forms except 3ms; e.g., נִטְּלוּ, נִטַּלְתָּ. The context must indicate the voice.

2. Of the two forms of Qal, *type O* is far more common. *Type A* is used only in the verbs which are also Lamedh Guttural, in נָגַשׁ and נָשַׁק, and in a few less common words.

3. Notice the use of Qibbuts instead of Qamets Hatuph under the preformative in Ho. (Ch. XXVIII, D, 4).

C. Other Forms

1. The נ is *entirely dropped* in certain Qal forms:

a. In Impv. of *all* words with Impf. in *A*; e. g., טַל.

b. In the Inf. Cst. of a few words, which then add ת as Pe Yodhs do; e. g., נָגַשׁ, (לְגֶשֶׁת), (לְגִשְׁתִּי); also three words given in next Chapter.

2. The נ is *retained:*

a. In Qal Impv. of *all* words with Impf. in *O*; e.g., נְטֹל.

b. In Qal Inf. of all words (whether the Impf. is *type A* or *O*), except those mentioned above in 1, b; the נ does not assimilate even after לְ; e.g., לִנְטֹל[1].

c. In all forms where the נ stands at the beginning of a syllable; these verbs are perfectly regular in Qal Perf., Inf. Abs., and Part.; in Ni. Impf. and allied forms; and thruout the intensives.

---

[1] A few words have both forms of Inf.; e.g., נְגֹעַ and גַּעַת; so also נְטֹעַ.

VOCABULARY

נבא Ni., prophesy

נבט Hi., look, gaze; behold; have respect to

נגד Hi., tell, announce, declare

נָגַע touch

נָגַף smite (*esp. with plague*)

נָגַשׁ draw near, approach; Hi., bring near

נדח Hi., thrust out, expel;

Ni., *Pass.*; Part., outcast

נכר Hi., look upon; know

נָסַע pull up; remove (camp)

נָפַל fall; Hi., let fall, throw down

נצל Hi., snatch, deliver; Ni., *Pass.*

נָקַם avenge; Ni., avenge oneself, be avenged

נָשַׁק kiss (+ לְ)

EXERCISES

1) הֲהִנָּבֵא נִבֵּאתֶם כַּאֲשֶׁר הִגִּיד לָכֶם אֱלֹהֵיכֶם: 2) וַיְהִי
בְּגִשְׁתָּם לָנוּ וַיַּכִּירֵנוּ: 3) נִקְם־נָא אֹתִי מִצָּרַי וְאֶנָּצְלָה
מֵחֲמָתוֹ: 4) וַיִּפְּלוּ לְפָנָיו וַיִּשְּׁקוּ לְרַגְלָיו: 5) הַבִּיטוּ עָלָיו
בְּטֶרֶם יַגִּישֻׁהוּ: 6) הֲיַדִּיחַ אֶת־הַנִּגָּפִים: 7) לֹא אֶגָּעֵהוּ אִם
יִסַּע מִמְּגְרָשִׁי: 8) הִנּוֹ מַדִּיחַ אֶת־יֹשְׁבֵי הָעִיר: 9) אַל־נָא
תַפֵּל אֶת־הָאָבֶן הַהִיא עָלָי: 10) וָאֶסַּע מֵהַנֶּגֶב וָאֵלֵךְ לִנְקֹם
אֶת־בְּנִי: 11) הַבֵּט עָלַי וְהַגֵּד אֶת־צִדְקָתִי לְאַחַי: 12) עוֹדֵנִי
נָבָא לִפְנֵי הַנְּשִׂיאִים וַיִּגְּפֵם יְהֹוָה:

1. Hast thou had respect to the appearance of these outcasts? 2. Draw ye near unto me, that I may declare to you the law of Jehovah. 3. And we will prophesy how Jehovah will smite this people and what He will let fall upon them. 4. They refused to approach her and kiss

her.   5. Do not touch her, lest she avenge herself on thee.
6. And it came to pass when he looked upon the valley
that he removed his camp from the hill.   7. And it was
told me that thou didst snatch her from under the falling
rock.

CHAPTER XLVIII

A. Special Words

1. In words which are also Ayin Guttural, the Nun is not usually assimilated, because the guttural will not take D.F. to represent it. Such words are then regular; e.g., נָאַף, Impf. יִנְאַף. But in a few such words assimilation does occur; e.g., the Ni. Perf. of נָחַם is נִחַם—the ח having an "implicit dagesh."[1]

2. Two common words which are also ל"ה require special attention:

נָטָה,   Qal Impf. יִטֶּה;   Jussive יֵט.

          Hi. Impf. יַטֶּה;   Jussive יֵט.

נָכָה,   Hi. Impf. יַכֶּה;   Jussive יַךְ[2].

3. The verb נָתַן has several special irregularities:

a. The *final Nun*, as well as the initial one, is weak, and is assimilated into any consonantal afformative; e.g., נָתַתָּ for נָתַנְתָּ, etc. (This is the only verb in which a final Nun is thus assimilated before any letter except Nun).

b. In Qal Impf. it has a *type E* form יִתֵּן; hence also Impv. תֵּן, Plu. תְּנוּ, etc.

---

*1 נָחַת has Impf. Qal יֵחַת.

2 Less frequent are נָזָה (Qal Juss. יַז), נָשָׂה, etc.

c. The ground-form of the Inf. was תְּנֵת; but instead of this becoming תֶּנֶת, the נ was assimilated into ת and the Hireq lengthened to Tsere (cf. fifth declension nouns), giving תֵת(לְ), with suffixes תִּתִּי(לְ), etc.

4. נָשָׂא, being also ל"א, of course has Qamets in Impf. Qal, יִשָּׂא; also Impv., שָׂא. The Inf. Cst., which adds ת, is irregular in vowel pointing; שְׂאֵת has contracted to שְׂאֵת (but with ל, שְׂאֵת(לְ).

5. לָקַח is inflected like a Pe Nun in Qal, the ל being assimilated into the ק. As it is also Lamedh Guttural, the forms are: Impf. יִקַּח, Plu. יִקְחוּ (cf. Ch. IV, A, 2, b); Impv. קַח; Inf. קַחַת, with suffix קַחְתִּי. The Ni., however, is regular—נִלְקַח.

B. Identification Marks

These verbs are generally very easy to recognize. A verb with only two radicals, the first of which has D.F., is usually Pe Nun. A few forms in the Impv. and Inf., however, are so similar to those of other verbs that it is impossible to discriminate absolutely at sight.

C. Similar Forms of Some Pe Yodh Verbs

Study in this connection Section E of Ch. XLVI.

VOCABULARY

נָאַף commit adultery

נָחַל inherit, get as a possession; Hi., cause to
inherit

נחם Ni., lament, grieve; Pi[3],
comfort

נָטָה stretch; turn away;
Hi., turn away (trans.);
pervert

נָטַע plant

נכה Hi., strike, smite

נָצַב Ni., stand; Hi., set, place

נָצַר keep, guard, watch

נקה Ni., be innocent; go unpunished; Pi., ac-

quit; let go unpunished

נָשָׂא lift up; bear; take away; forgive

נשׂג Hi., attain to, overtake

יָצַק Q[4], pour

יָצַר Q[4], form, fashion, make

EXERCISES.

1) תְּנָה לִי שָׂדֶה אֲשֶׁר־בּוֹ אֶטַּע אֶת־חִטִּי: 2) אִם יִנְאַף
לֹא נִשָּׂא אוֹתוֹ: 3) הֲשִׂיגָם בַּדֶּרֶךְ וַיִּקַּח אֶת־כַּסְפָּם מֵהֶם:
4) הֲלֹא נִחַם אֶת־הַנַּעֲרָה אֲשֶׁר הִכְּתָה: 5) וַיְהִי בְּתִתּוֹ לָהּ
אֶת־הַמַּטֶּה וַתֵּט מִמֶּנּוּ: 6) נֶחֱמוּ מְאֹד כִּי לֹא הִצִּיבוּ אֶת־בֵּיתָם
עַל־הַצּוּר: 7) יִתְּנוּ לִי אֶת־הַיַּיִן וְאֶצְקֵהוּ לְגֵרִי: 8) תִּשְׂאוּ
אֶת־עֲוֹנְכֶם וְלֹא תִנְחֲלוּ אֶת־מִקְנִי: 9) וְהָיָה בְּקַחְתּוֹ אֶת־
קָרְבָּנָיו לַמִּזְבֵּחַ וְנִקָּה: 10) נִצְרוּ אֶת־הַמִּצְוֹת וְנִצַּלְתֶּם:
11) נִצְרָה לָנוּ כֵּלִים וְנַכֶּה אֶת־מַטֵּי הַמִּשְׁפָּט:

1. Did ye stand here to give them gifts? 2. Do not thou turn away the heart of my people, lest they commit adultery and evil overtake them. 3. I will pour oil upon the chariot which he will make. 4. And it came to pass when we took his arrows that he did not grieve. 5. Behold, he is planting his vineyard, which we caused him to inherit, but he will not watch it. 6. Did those who smote us go unpunished? 7. Comfort ye your hearts, for I will forgive your sin.

CHAPTER XLIX

MIDDLE WEAK VERBS: AYIN WAW (קוּל)

A. Skeleton Paradigm

	Qal	Ni.	Hi.	Ho.	Polel
Perf. 3ms	*קָל	*נָקוֹל	*הֵקִיל	*הוּקַל	*קוֹלֵל
2ms	†קַלְתָּ	נְקוּלֹותָ	הֲקִילֹותָ	הוּקַלְתָּ	קוֹלַלְתָּ
3cp	†קָלוּ	נָקֹולוּ	הֵקִילוּ	הוּקְלוּ	קוֹלְלוּ
Impf. 3ms	*יָקוּל	*יִקּוֹל	יָקִיל	יוּקַל	יְקוֹלֵל
3mp	יָקֹוּלוּ	יִקֹּולוּ	יָקִילוּ		יְקוֹלְלוּ
3fp	†תְּקוּלֶינָה	תִּקֹּלְנָה	תָּקֵלְנָה		תְּקוֹלַלְנָה

B. Nature of the Words

1. The term *Middle Weak* is commonly used as a group designation for the closely allied Ayin Waw and Ayin Yodh verbs. The Ayin Waws are far more numerous, and the discussion in this chapter is limited to them; but many of the statements apply equally to Ayin Yodhs.

2. These verbs depart more radically from the strong verb than any others thus far studied. Waw is a very weak letter, and nowhere, in the present forms of these

verbs, has it retained consonantal value[1]. It either coalesced with a vowel sound to form Holem or Shureq (just as in some voices of Pe Yodhs), or was entirely elided. In either case, the stem retains only two consonantal letters, and hence is *monosyllabic* in all forms.

3. In the Qal Perf. the Waw has been elided. Hence these verbs are listed in the lexicon in the Inf. Cst., where the Waw appears (as Shureq).

C. Third Masculine Singular Forms

1. In Qal Perf. the Waw was elided from the ground-form קַוַל, and the two Pathahs combined into Qamets —קַ(ו)ל becoming קָל[2].

2. In Ni. Perf., two steps are to be discerned in the development of the ground-form נַקְוַל into the present form:

a. The Waw and Pathah coalesced into Holem—נַקוֹל.

b. As the ק then became the initial letter of the second syllable, the preformative syllable was left open; so naturally the Pathah was made tone-long, giving נָקוֹל.

---

[1] It is an open question whether these roots really are tri-literal— whether the Waw was at all consonantal, or only a vowel letter; without attempting to settle this theoretical point, we adopt its consonantal character as a working hypothesis in accounting for the forms. (A similar doubt attaches to the tri-literalness of Double Ayins—Ch. LI).

[2] Or, according to another theory, both the Waw and the preceding Pathah were elided, and the final Pathah simply made tone-long.

3. In Hi. Perf. the ground-form was הֻקְוִיל; the Waw was elided, and the preformative vowel lengthened, giving הֵקִיל.

4. In Ho., the first two root letters apparently were transposed, giving הֻוְקַל as a ground-form in the Perf.[1] Coalescence then gave הוּקַל.

5. The ordinary intensives could hardly be used, as they require a D.F. in the middle radical, and it is weak in these verbs. The intensification is therefore accomplished by repeating the last radical instead of doubling the middle one[2]. The respective forms, called *Po'lel*, *Po'lal*, and *Hithpo'lel*, are: קוֹלֵל, קוֹלַל, and הִתְקוֹלֵל (from ground-forms קַוְלֵל, etc.)[3].

6. The principles in the Impf. are very similar to those in the Perf. The Qal יָקוּל is readily derived from the ground-form יַקְוֻל. In Ni., יִקַּוֵל, by coalescence, became יִקּוֹל. And the יָקִיל in Hi. is from יַקְוִיל. The other Impfs. are quite analogous to their respective Perfs.

---

[1] Cf. with this the euphonic transposition occurring in Hith. of verbs whose first radical is a sibilant.

*[2] Another form of reduplication is occasionally used. The weak radical is entirely dropped out, and both strong radicals are repeated. The respective forms are: קִלְקֵל, *Pilpel;* קָלְקַל, *Polpal*; and הִתְקַלְקֵל, *Hithpalpel.*

[3] Sometimes the names *Pi'lel, Pu'lal,* and *Hithpa'lel* are used.

D. Other Persons and Numbers

1. In Qal, Hi., and Ni., *vowel afformatives are not preceded by vocal Shewa*, because the preceding vowels are not tone-long but long by coalescence and hence fixed. Also, *the accent is retained on the stem of the verb;* e.g., קָ֫לוּ, אֶקֹּ֫ילָה, etc. (just as in Hi. of strong verbs).

2. In Qal Perf., and in Ni. and Hi. Impf., consonantal afformatives are attached directly to the stem (the vowels of which are somewhat modified, as shown in the paradigm). But in Qal Impf., and in Ni. and Hi. Perf., there is introduced between the stem and the endings an *auxiliary vowel*—Holem in the Perfs., י֖— in the Impf.[1]

a. This auxiliary vowel always draws the accent from the stem[2]. Therefore the tone-long vowel under the preformative must shorten to Shewa (in Hi. to Hateph Pathah).

b. In Ni. Perf., furthermore, the stem vowel is unaccountably changed from Holem to Shureq.

3. In Ho. and the intensives the various persons are derived from the 3ms by fully regular methods.

---

[1] The auxiliary vowel is sometimes omitted from those forms which regularly have it, and sometimes inserted in forms where the ending is usually directly attached.

[2] The tone is on the syllable containing this vowel, except before תֶּם and תֶּן, which require it themselves.

VOCABULARY

גּוּר sojourn

זוּר turn aside; Part., stranger

כּוּן Hi. (also Po.), set up, establish; appoint; prepare; Ni., *Pass.*

נוּס flee; Hi., put to flight

סוּר turn aside, away; Hi., put away, remove

עוּר Q or Hithpo., awaken; Hi., waken (*trans.*)

פּוּץ Hi., scatter, disperse; Ni., *Pass.*

קוּם rise; Hi., raise up

רוּם be high, lifted up; Hi. (also Po.), lift up

רוּץ run; Hi., make run

שׁוּב turn; return; Hi., turn (*trans.*); bring back

EXERCISES

1) רָצוּ אֱלֹהָרִים פֶּן יָשׁוּבוּ אֹיְבֵיהֶם וּמְצָאוּם: 2) וְנָפֹוצוּ בְּטֶרֶם יָרוּם הַשֶּׁמֶשׁ בַּשָּׁמַיִם: 3) אָרִיץ אֶתְכֶם עַל־דְּרָכִים יְשָׁרִים וַהֲקִימוֹתִי לָכֶם עֹזְרִים: 4) כּוֹנֵן אֶת־גְּבוּרָתוֹ בַּגּוֹיִם: 5) הִתְעוֹרַרְנוּ הַשְׁכֵּם וְנָקוּם וְנָנוּס: 6) עַתָּה תָרֵמְנָה אֶת־קוֹלוֹתֵיכֶן לְהוֹדוֹת אֶת־הָאֱלֹהִים כִּי הֵסִיר אֶת־הַדָּבָר מֵעֲלֵיכֶן: 7) וַיִּכּוֹנוּ עַל הַכִּסֵּא בְּטֶרֶם שַׁבְנוּ: 8) הָעִירוּ אֶת־אַמְּכֶם כִּי הֵנִיסוּ צָרֵינוּ אֶת־אַנְשֵׁי מִלְחַמְתֵּנוּ: 9) הוּשְׁבָה מִדַּרְכָּהּ וְלֹא גָרְה עִמּוֹ: 10) לֹא יוּסַר כְּבוֹדְכֶם אִם תָּסוּרוּ מֵעֲוֹנְכֶם: 11) וּנְפֹוצוֹתָן וְאֵין־דְּרַע לָכֶן אֲשֶׁר אֶל־בֵּיתוֹ תְּזוּרֶינָה:

1. After she wakened them they arose and returned home. 2. They will put our armies to flight, and we will be scattered. 3. Did he turn away from you after he

had been brought back and established in your house? 4. Will these women sojourn with thee after their masters put them away?　5. Wilt thou lift up thy heart to vanity and raise up temples to other gods?　6. We will run quickly and will not turn aside.　7. We set up our altar after we fled to this place.

CHAPTER L

MIDDLE WEAK VERBS (Continued)

AYIN WAW AND AYIN YODH (קוּל, קִיל)

A. Skeleton Paradigm

	Qal		Ni.	Hi.
Impf.	יָקוּל	*יָקִיל		יָקִיל
Juss.	†יָקֹל	יָקֵל		יָקֵל
+Waw	וַיָּקֶל	וַיָּקֶל		וַיָּקֶל
Impv.	קוּל	קִיל	הִקּוֹל	הָקֵל
Inf.	(לָ)קוּל	קִיל		הָקִיל
Part.	†קָל	קָל	נָקוֹל	†מֵקִיל

B. The Moods

1. The Qal Jussive is יָקֹל. Since the penult is long and open, it receives the accent after Waw Consec., and the ultimate vowel shortens to Qamets Hatuph; likewise Hi. has Segol.

2. The other moods are, in general, regularly derived. However, in Hi. Part. the preformative vowel is Tsere (tone-long), not Qamets as in the Impf. In Qal Impv. the 2fp is קֹלֶינָה, instead of קוּלֶינָה (and note the Cohort.

265

(קוֹלָה). In Qal Part., the Qamets is fixed, but does not retain the accent as in the Perf.; e.g., קָלָה, קָלֵי. Note also that a לְ prefixed to Qal Inf. has Qamets; and that the vowels in all the Infs. are unchangeable in inflection.[1]

C. Ayin Yodh Verbs

1. These verbs coincide in form with the Ayin Waws in all voices except Qal; usually also in Qal Perf.[2] and Part.

2. In Qal Impf., and the allied Impv. and Inf., they have Long Hireq where the Ayin Waws have Shureq; e.g., יָקִיל. But some also have parallel forms with Shureq, and lexicons list these sometimes with middle Yodh, sometimes with middle Waw. The three for which a double form is given below usually have the Waw in Inf., the Yodh in Impf. and Impv.

D. Suffixes

Suffixes of course draw the accent from the verb stem. Hence in various forms a long vowel under the preformative must shorten to Shewa; e.g., יְקוֹלֵנִי, הֲקִילוּנִי .

E. Special Words

1. The several statives belonging to this class of verbs are so lacking in uniformity that general rules can scarcely be stated. The most common are the following:

---

*[1] The Hi. Inf. Abs. sometimes has the form הָקֵיל or הָקִיל, as well as הָקֵל.

[2] Occasionally, however, the Yodh appears there; e.g., בִּין has בִּינוֹתִי as well as בַּנְתָ (cf. note 1, page 262).

a. מוּת has Qal Perf. מֵת, מֵתָה, מֵתָ, מַתָּה (cf. Ch. 28, D, 5), etc.; Part. מֵת; Impf. as in קוּל. In Hi. Perf. it does not have the auxiliary vowel; e. g., הֵמַתִּי, הֵמִית, הֲמַתֶּם.

b. בּוֹשׁ has Holem instead of Shureq thruout Qal:

	Perf.	Impf.	Impv.	
3ms	בּוֹשׁ	יֵבוֹשׁ		Inf. בּוֹשׁ
2ms	בֹּשְׁתָּ		בּוֹשׁ	Part. בּוֹשׁ
3mp	בּוֹשׁוּ	יֵבוֹשׁוּ		
2fp	בָּשְׁתֶּן	בָּשְׁתֶּן	תֵּבֹשְׁנָה	בֹּשְׁנָה	Hi., הֵבִישׁ, etc.[1]

c. בּוֹא is like קוּל in Qal Perf.; in Impf., Impv., and Inf., it has Holem (יָבוֹא, בּוֹא, etc.). Because it is also ל״א, the final vowel does not shorten after Waw Consec.; e.g., Hi., וַיָּבֵא.

d. אוֹר has Holem thruout Qal; Perf., אוֹר, אוֹרוּ; Impf. יָאוֹר, etc. The Ni. Impf. is יֵאוֹר, on account of the initial guttural.

2. Words that are also Lamedh Guttural take final Pathah after Waw Consec.; e. g., וַיָּנַח for either וַיָּנַח or וַיִּנַח. So also do some with final ר, especially סוּר.

3. נוּחַ has a secondary form of Hi. in which the first radical receives D.F. This is an Aramaic form, similar to a subclass of Double Ayins (see further in Ch. LII)[2].

---

*[1] Forms הוֹבִישׁ, etc., also occur, as tho from יָבֵשׁ.

*[2] Other similar forms occur rarely; e.g., in לוּן, סוּת, לוּט, and מוּל.

4. שׁוּב is used in a special idiom, to mean "to do again"; e.g., וַיָּשָׁב וַיָּקָם, (*lit.*, And he returned and arose), "And he arose again."

5. A few verbs, especially those which are also לְ"ה, have a fully consonantal Waw; it then causes no irregularities.

*6. A few Piels are in use, in which Yodh has been substituted for Waw; e.g., קִיֵּם, from קוּם.

*7. In the forms of Hi. Perf. which require Shewa under the preformative, a verb which is also Pe Guttural takes instead a full Pathah; e.g., הֶעִידֹתָ. (The same thing occurs in Pe Guttural Double Ayins).

F. Identification Marks

1. Long vowel under the preformative

a. As a corollary from this, the occurrence of Shewa there before suffixes and some afformatives.

b. The only occurrences outside the monosyllabic roots are יֵטֵל and יַעֲטֵל (which are self-evident), and יָקֹט (Ch. XLIV, C, 1, a).

2. Recessive accent; i. e., on the penult in various forms which are accented on the ultima in strong verbs.

3. Helping vowels before personal afformatives.

4. Unusual forms of the intensives.

5. Waw (or Yodh) appearing in a vowel sound between two strong consonants.

VOCABULARY

אוֹר be light, shine; Hi., illumine

בּוֹא come; Hi., bring

בּוֹשׁ be ashamed; Hi., put to shame

בִּין perceive, discern; Hi., explain

חוּל‎ or חִיל‎, writhe in pain, tremble   רִיב‎ strive, contend

לוּן‎ or לִין‎, pass the night, lodge   שִׂים‎ or שׂוּם‎, set, place, put, lay

מוּת‎ die; Hi., kill

נוּחַ‎ rest; Hi., הֵנִיחַ‎, give   שִׁיר‎ sing

rest; Hi., הִנִּיחַ‎, set down   שִׁית‎ set, put, place

EXERCISES

1) וַיְהִי בַּהֲבִינָם אֵלָיו כִּי חָלָה וַיָּקָם וַיָּרָץ אֵלֶיהָ מַהֵר: 2) וַתָּשֶׁת אֶת־יָדָהּ עַל־רֹאשׁוֹ וַתְּעִירֵהוּ: 3) הַמֵּמִיתִים בַּחֶרֶב מֹות יָמוּתוּ בַּחֶרֶב: 4) וַיְהִי בְּהָאִיר הַשֶּׁמֶשׁ אֶת־דַּרְכּוֹ וַיָּסַר אֶת־מָגִנּוֹ: 5) הֲבִיאֵנִי אֶל־הַהֵיכָל וְאָשִׁירָה שָׁם: 6) הָבִישָׁה אֶת־אֹיְבֵיךָ הָאֱלֹהִים וְאַל תָּנַח לָהֶם מֵחֲמַס הַנִּקְמִים: 7) יֵשֵׁב וְיָבֹא לִי וְיָלֶן בְּבֵיתִי: 8) וַיָּשֶׂם אֶת־בֵּיתוֹ עַל־הַיָּם בָּטוּחַ בְּהִכּוֹנוֹ עַל־צוּר: 9) וְהָיָה בְּרִיבְךָ עִם הַזָּר הַזֶּה וּבְנָתְךָ אֶת־כֹּחוֹ: 10) אוֹר־נָא עָלֵינוּ הַשֶּׁמֶשׁ וַהֲנִיסֹותָ אֶת־חָשְׁכֵּנוּ: 11) הִנִּיחַ אֶת־שְׁלָמָיו לִפְנֵי הַכֹּהֵן וַיֹּאמֶר הִנְנִי מֵבִיא אֶת־בִּרְכָתִי:

1. They brought the dead men and placed them here.
2. And it came to pass when she perceived that it was not light that she returned to her bed (עֶרֶשׂ) and rested.
3. Do not thou sing in a loud (*say*, great) voice, for behold she is writhing in pain.   4. We were ashamed to return,

and she explained the thing to the men who came. 5. And he lifted up his weapons and strove with the strangers. 6. Do not flee from before me, for I have come to give you rest and not to kill you. 7. And he turned aside from his path and lodged with me.

CHAPTER LI

DOUBLE AYIN VERBS (קטט)

A. Skeleton Paradigm

Perf.	Qal		Ni.	Hi[1]	Ho[1]	Poel
3ms	קַט*	וְקָטַט|	נָקַט*	הֵקַט*	הוּקַט*	קוֹטֵט*
2ms	קַטּוֹתָ†		נְקַטּוֹתָ	הֲקִטּוֹתָ	הוּקַטּוֹתָ	
3cp	קַטּוּ† וְקָטְטוּ		נָקַטּוּ	הֵקַטּוּ		

Impf.	Q[1]	Q[2]				
3ms	יָקֹט*	יֵקַט*	יִקַט	יָקֵט	יוּקַט	
3mp	יָקֹטּוּ†	יֵקַטּוּ		יָקֵטּוּ		
3fp	תְּקֻטֶּ֫ינָה†		תִּקַּטֶּינָה	תְּקַטֶּינָה		

B. Nature of the Words

1. It is obvious that the weakness of these verbs lies in
the fact that the last two radicals of the stem are the same.
In practically all inflectional forms this consonant is written only once—the vowel which should stand between the
last two radicals being removed, and the one letter being
assimilated into the other. In forms with endings the
double letter is of course represented by D.F. (e.g., קַטְטוּ
became קַטּטוּ and then קַטּוּ); but in the simple forms the
D.F. is omitted (e.g., קַט for קַטּ; cf. Ch. IV, A, 2, a).

2. In many forms these words are similar to the Middle Weak verbs, since, like them, they appear with only two radicals. The Middle Weak and Double Ayin verbs are therefore often classed together as the *monosyllabic* or *biliteral* roots, in distinction from all other verbs.

C. Third Masculine Singular Forms

1. In all forms in which the regular verb has no vowel between the first two radicals, the vowel belonging between the last two radicals has been transposed to that place; e.g., נְקַטֵט, the ground-form of Ni. Perf., became נֵקַטְט, and then נֵקַט—for the vowel under the preformative, coming to stand in an open syllable, became tone-long (just as in the Ayin Waws).

a. Likewise, in Qal Impf., the ground-forms יַקְטֵט and יִקְטַט became יָקֵט and יַקֵּט. And in Ho., the ground-forms הָקְטַט and יָקְטַט became הוּקַט and יוּקַט.

b. In Hi. Perf. the ground-form הִקְטֵט of course became הִקַט; and then, by a very special irregularity of these verbs, the second vowel was lengthened to Tsere instead of to the characteristic Long Hireq of Hi., giving הֵקֵט. The ground-form of the Impf., יַקְטֵט, smilarily became יָקֵט.

2. In Ni. Impf., which already has a vowel between the first two radicals, the vowel between the last two is simply dropped—יָקַטֵט becoming יָקַטְט, then יָקַט. The Qal Perf. is sometimes similarly contracted (cf. B, 1, above); but usually the full regular form קָטַט is used.

3. The regular intensives are sometimes used. But quite frequent also are the following special forms, similar to those used by the Ayin Waws: קוֹטֵט (here called *Po'el*), קוֹטַט (*Po'al*), and הִתְקוֹטֵט (*Hith-po'el*)[1]. All these forms are of course conjugated regularly, and hence are disregarded in D.

D. Other Persons and Numbers

1. Forms with vowel afformatives in Qal Perf. are usually regular. But occasionally there, and always elsewhere, the double final consonant is indicated by a D.F. in the letter. Note that the preceding vowel of course does not become Shewa, and that *the accent stays on the stem of the verb.*

2. *All* consonantal afformatives are preceded by an auxiliary vowel—וֹ—in all Perfs., ־ֶי in all Impfs.; of course the last radical has D. F. This vowel, just as in the Ayin Waws, draws the accent from the stem of the verb. Then—

a. In all forms in which the preformative had a tone-long vowel, it must shorten to Shewa; e.g., נְקַטּוֹת.

b. A long vowel in the ultima must shorten before the D.F. (cf. fifth declension nouns, many of which are derived from verbs of this class); the Holem in Qal Impf. (Q[1]) becomes Qibbuts, the Tsere in Hi. becomes Hireq; e.g., הֲקַטּוֹת, תְּקַטֶּינָה.

---

*[1] Occasionally also these verbs have a *Pilpel*, etc.

VOCABULARY

אָרַר Q¹, curse

הלל Pi., praise; Hith., boast

חלל Pi., profane, defile; Hi¹, begin

חָתַת Q², be dismayed; Hi¹, terrify, confound

מָדַד Q¹, measure

מָרַר Q², be bitter; Hi¹, embitter

פלל Hith., supplicate, pray, intercede

צָרַר Q², be pressed, distressed; Hi¹, straiten, distress

קָלַל Q², be insignificant; Ni., be light; Hi¹, make light

שָׁדַד Q¹, oppress, spoil, destroy; Pu. or Ho., *Pass.*

EXERCISES

1) וַיֵּקַלּוּ בְעֵינָיו וַיּוֹשָׁדוּ מִמֶּנּוּ: 2) וַיָּחַתּוּ אֹתָנוּ כִּי הֵחֵלּוּ
לַהֲמִיתָן: 3) וְהִתְפַּלַּלְנוּ לָאֱלֹהִים אֲשֶׁר־בּוֹ נָמַדּוּ יָמֵינוּ:
4) וְצַר בְּבִינוֹ כִּי נָקַל זְהָבוֹ: 5) אִם תַּחַת בִּרְאוֹתְךָ כִּי
קַלּוֹת בְּעֵינֵיהֶם: 6) אִם לֹא תִמְדֶּינָה אֶת־הַחֹטִים בְּמִדַּת
צֶדֶק יֵאַר מַרְאֲכֶן: 7) אָצֵר אֶת־עִירְכֶם כִּי שַׁדּוֹתֶם אֶת־
עֲבָדַי: 8) אָרְרוּ אֶת־יוֹם הִוָּלְדָם כִּי מָרָה מְאֹד נַפְשָׁם:
9) וְהֵמַר אֹתָם אִם יְחַלֵּל אֶת־הֵיכָלָם: 10) הַלְלוּךְ כִּי
פָדִיתָ אֶת־אֲחִיוֹתָיִךְ: 11) לֹא הֲקִלּוֹתִי אֶת־הַשֶּׁקֶל וָאֲשֶׁר
אֶת־הָעָם:

1. He did not boast in the length of his sword after it had been measured. 2. She will curse you to your face, for she will be bitter against you. 3. I will make light the work of your wives; therefore let them not be dis-

mayed.   4. Will they profane my temple, or will they spoil
it?   5. And those women began to perceive that they
were insignificant in our eyes.   6. We were distressed (*say*,
it was distressed to us) and prayed to God.   7. Let their
servitude be light, lest we embitter them.

CHAPTER LII

DOUBLE AYIN VERBS (Continued)

A. Skeleton Paradigm

	Q¹	Ni.	Hi¹		Q³	Hi³	Ho³
Impf.				Impf.			
+Waw	וַיָּקָט		וַיִּקֵט	3ms	יִקֹּט*	יֵקַט*	יֻקַט*
Impv.	קֹט	הִקַּט	הָקֵט	3mp	יִקְּטוּ	יֵקַטּוּ†	
Inf.	(לְ)קֹט			3fp	תְּקֹטֶינָה	יֵקַטְנָה	
Part.	[קוֹטֵט]	נָקֹט	†מְקֵט				

B. The Moods

1. The Jussive is always like the simple Impf. But after Waw Consec. with Qal or Hi., the accent of course is on the penult, and the ultima is shortened.

2. The Impvs. are all regularly derived from the Impfs., and are conjugated according to the same principles; e.g., Qal Plurals, קֹטּוּ, קֹטֶינָה. The same is true of most of the Infs.; e.g., Qal קֹט, with suffixes קָטִּי, etc.[1]

3. Of the Parts., note that Qal has a full regular form; and that Hi. has Tsere under the preformative, instead of Qamets.

4. There are only rare occurrences of the Q² forms in the moods, and they show various individual peculiarities.

---

[1] When a simple Inf. or Impv. is joined by Maqqeph to the following word, the Holem shortens to Qamets Hatuph; e.g., קָט־.

C. Aramaic Forms (Q³, Hi³)

1. Several verbs are partly declined according to an entirely different principle, following forms that occur in the kindred Aramaic dialect. The characteristic is the *insertion of D.F. in the first radical*, making them resemble Pe Nuns; e.g., Qal Impf. יִקֹּט, plu. יִקֹּטוּ (*not* יִקֹּטוּ)[1]; stative, יֵקַּט.

2. These forms are limited to the Impf. of Qal, Hi., and Ho. The Impv. and Inf. of Qal follow the Q¹ forms; e.g., דִּמֹּן, Impv. Plu. of דְּמָם; תֹּם, Inf. of תָּמַם (with suff., תֻּמִּי).

D. Suffixes

When suffixes are added to ordinary forms, exactly the same changes are effected as when afformatives are attached; i.e., the last radical takes D.F., the preceding vowel shortens if it be long, and a tone-long vowel under the preformative becomes Shewa; e.g., יָקֹט, יְקָטֵהוּ; הֲקָטַנִי, הֲקֵט. But of course the Aramaic forms follow the same principles as do regular verbs.

E. Special Words

1. Words with a guttural or ר as doubled radical:

a. Forms that commonly have Tsere sometimes have

---

[1] This may be the result of an assimilation in the reverse direction from that which usually occurs, the ט in יְקַטֵּט being assimilated into the ק. Since the second radical has thus gone into combination with the first, the last radical cannot be doubled when endings are added. The Hi. Plu. יָקֵטוּ is an exception to Ch. XXVIII, B, 1.

Pathah instead, sometimes have Tsere followed by Pathah Furtive; e.g., Hi. Perf. הֻמַר, הֻרַע or הֻרֵע; Impf. יָרַע, with Waw וַיָּרַע, etc.

b. These letters cannot of course take D.F. to represent the doubled letter. If the form ordinarily has a short vowel, this is lengthened in compensation; e.g., 3fs Perf. מָרָה, for מַרְרָה; מְרֵעִים, Plu. of Hi. Part. מֵרַע. But if the form already has a long vowel, nothing further can be done; e.g., אוֹרוּ, Impv. Plu.

2. In חָנַן a Holem, when it shortens, becomes Qamets Hatuph instead of Qibbuts; e.g., חָנֵּנִי; so also sometimes in various other words.

3. שָׁמַם follows the Q³ form in the Sing., the Q¹ in the Plu. (a few stative forms also occur in it).

*4. A few words have borrowed occasional forms from the Ayin Waws; e.g., רָנַן has Qal Impf. יָרֻון as well as יָרָן; the Inf. of בָּרַר is לָבוּר; and Hi. Impf. of שָׁמַם is יָשִׁים.

F. Identification Marks

1. These verbs are so similar to the Ayin Waws that they have many marks in common. *The first four points given in Ch. L, F apply equally to the Double Ayin verbs, being generic marks of the monosyllabic roots.* In some cases there is no further mark to differentiate between the two classes; in other cases either the fifth point there given or one of the following points will indicate the class.

2. Special marks of Double Ayin verbs:

a. The D.F. in the second radical before endings.

b. The use of Tsere thruout Hiphil.

c. Occasionally D.F. in the first radical.

VOCABULARY

בָּזַז Q[1], plunder, seize as prey

בָּלַל Q[1], anoint

דָּמַם Q[3], be silent

חָנַן Q[1], be gracious to (*with Accus.*); Ho., be shown favor; Hith., make entreaty

מָסַס Ni., melt, faint

סָבַב Q[1] or [3], turn; surround; Hi[3], turn (*trans.*), cause to turn; Po., go about

רָנַן Q[1] or Pi., shout for joy, rejoice

רָעַע Q[2], be evil; Hi[1], do evil

שָׁמַם Q[1] and [3] or Hithpo., be astonished

תָּמַם Q[3], or Hi[3], be finished, ended, consumed; finish, complete

EXERCISES

1) יַתֵּם לְהָרַע לָנוּ וְהֵסֵב אֶת־דַּרְכּוֹ עוֹד בֵּיתָה:

2) נָקַלָּה אֶת־מַעֲשָׂם וְיָרֹנּוּ: 3) יַד אֶת־כָּל־עָרֵיהֶם וַיִּבְזֹ֑ז:

4) וַיָּסָב אֶת־בָּתֵּינוּ לְשָׁדֵּנוּ: 5) אָשֹׁם אִם יֵרַע כָּמוֹךָ:

6) וַיַּקְרֵב אֶת־מִנְחַת מַצּוֹת בְּלוּלֹת בַּשֶּׁמֶן וַיִּתֹּם זִבְחוֹ:

7) דְּמֵינָה וְאַל תְּרֻנֶּנָּה: 8) הָרֵעֹהוּ וַיָּחָן אֹתָם: 9) הַהַחֲתֹנוּ

אֶת־הַיְלָדִים בְּסוֹבְבֵנוּ בֶּחָצֵר: (see Ch. L, E, 7) 10) וַיְהִי

בְּאָרְכֶם אֹתָם וַיִּשְׁתּוֹמְמוּ וַיִּדְמוּ: 11) וַתָּחֶל אִשְׁתְּךָ לָרֹן עַל

הַנִּדָּחוֹת: 12) הִנּוּ מֵחַת אֶת־עַמּוֹ וַיָּמַר אֹתָם:

1. And they surrounded our friends to do them evil. 2. And it came to pass when we were gracious to him that he was astonished and shouted for joy. 3. And the governor plundered his vineyard and distressed him, and he

was silent. 4. And the deeds of your prince were evil, and he confounded the people. 5. Finish plundering their houses, and let them not be shown favor. 6. And the king turned his face against me, and my heart melted within me. 7. And ye will be distressed and will begin to make entreaty.

CHAPTER LIII

REVIEW OF IRREGULAR VERBS .

A. Further Remarks on Identification

1. The identification marks as given in the several preceding chapters are of course to locate a verb within its proper class. In most cases the tense or mood and voice can then be determined according to the principles given in Ch. 37 for regular verbs—altho much allowance must often be made for the disturbing effect of gutturals and weak consonants.

    a. Special Jussive forms should be firmly fixed; they occur (outside of Hi.) only in Qal of Middle Weak verbs and in all voices of ל״ה.

    b. Note carefully also that Waw Consec., which always requires the Jussive form, furthermore causes recessive accent and shortening of the ultimate vowel of that form in both Qal and Hi. of פ״י, Middle Weak, and ע״ע verbs, and in some guttural verb forms (in addition, of course, to Ni.).

2. There is sometimes a rather fine distinction between the forms of certain classes of verbs. In the following cases, especially, the beginner may be confused—altho usually other marks may be found to distinguish the forms:

a. The D.F. in the second radical of Double Ayins, and the occasional Shewa under preformative in both these and the Middle Weaks, may seem to indicate a Pi. (especially of a ל"ה).

b. In some cases an apocopated ל"ה (i.e. with ultimate Segol) may not readily be distinguished from the shortened Jussives mentioned above in 1, b. However, in most cases the ל"ה verb has a short vowel under the preformative, while the other forms have a long vowel there.

c. A Yodh before a consonantal afformative may be either a helping vowel for one of the monosyllabic roots, or the primitive final Yodh of a ל"ה.

d. The forms קָטֹוּ (from קָטְה) and קָ֫לֹוּ (from קוּל) are distinguished only by the place of the accent.

3. Sometimes the identification marks will not indicate the class absolutely, since some forms are identical in several classes. So it is occasionally necessary to investigate several possibilities. Some cases are:

a. A D.F. in the first radical, while proper to פ"ן, also occurs sometimes in פ"י and ע"ע; seldom, also, in ע"ו.

b. A segolate Inf. is usually פ"י, sometimes פ"ן.

c. Shureq after the preformative of Ho. occurs in פ"י, Middle Weak, and ע"ע verbs.

d. Monosyllabic Impvs. occur in both פ"י and פ"ו verbs (and occasionally in ל"ה).

4. The acquisition of a thoro knowledge of the most

common verbs will enable one to recognize at sight the
majority of the roots encountered; e.g., the two strong
radicals of בּוֹא, חָיָה, יָלַד, יָסַף, יָצָא, מוּת, נֶגֶד, נָכָה,
שִׂים, רוּם, צָוָה, עָשָׂה, עָנָה, נָשָׂא, etc., should be immediately recognized. Also, three common and specially
irregular verbs should be thoroly fixed—הָלַךְ, לָקַח, and
נָתַן·

5. There are many sets of words in which the two strong radicals
are the same; some of them are easily confused—tho many are quite
distinct in form.

a. The more common ones are:

רָאָה, יָרֵא	בּוֹשׁ, יָבֵשׁ
יָשַׁב, שׁוּב, שָׁבָה	בָּנָה, בִּין
רָבָה, רִיב, ⟨רָבַב⟩	חָלַל, חָלָה, חוּל
רוּץ, רָצָה	חָנָה, חָנַן
רָעָה, רָעַע, ⟨רוּעַ⟩	יָטַב, טוֹב
שָׁתָה, שִׁית	יָכֹל, כָּלָה, ⟨כּוּל⟩

b. Others are:

שִׁיר, יָשַׁר	אָרַר, אוֹר
מוּל, מָלַל	בָּזַז, בָּזָה
מָרָה, מָרַר	דָּמַם, דָּמָה
נוּס, נָסָה	גָּלָה, גִּיל, גָּלַל
נָצַב, יָצַב	זוּר, זָרָה, זָרַר
שָׁקָה, נָשַׁק	יָנַק, נָקָה
סוּר, יָסַר	יָצַר, נָצַר, צָרַר, צוּר·
עָלָה, עָלַל	יָרַשׁ. רוּשׁ

6. The student is reminded that not infrequently a Long Hireq or a Holem, on which he may be depending as an identification mark of a tense or voice, or even of a root, may be written defectively; and he must therefore be alert to recognize by sound the missing vowel letter. (So also occasionally even a Shureq).

B. Frequency of Occurrence

The following table, compiled from the word lists collected by Harper, indicates the relative importance of the various classes of verbs. A word with two weaknesses is counted twice. The first row gives the number of words occurring more than 100 times in the O.T.; the second row, those occurring from 10 to 100 times.

Regular	Guttural	Pe Nun	Pe Yodh	Middle Weak	Double Ayin	Lamedh He	Total
31	52	11	14	13	3	21	123
86	257	39	27	47	43	64	488

EXERCISES

Locate fully, and translate, the following forms:

15 מָעֲקָה	8 שֵׂה	1 וַיָּנָס
16 הָשֵׁב	9 שָׁמָה	2 יָדַע
17 שְׁחַתּוּם	10 מַכָּה	3 הוֹרִיתִיךָ
18 וַיֵּרֶד	11 גֵּרְשׁוּם	4 הָחֵלּוּ
19 הִצִּילָנוּ	12 וַיִּגֶל	5 וַתַּהַר
20 מֵהָרְתָּו	13 יֵרָא	6 נָכוֹן
21 יוֹשִׁעוּ	14 לְכָה	7 הֵעָזְבוּ

64 וַיֵּשֶׁב	43 יֵעָשֶׂה	22 לָחֹן
65 יְמָרְרוּ	44 תֵּבֹשׁוּ	23 וַיֵּךְ
66 וַיִּשָּׁק	45 בְּלֶכְתְּךָ	24 וַיָּרֶץ
67 מוֹכִיחַ	46 נָדָח	25 תְּחַיּוּם
68 וַיֵּסַר	47 יַעֲבֹדוּ	26 נִגְפְּכֶם
69 בָּנוּ	48 עַנֹּתוֹ	27 תְּבִאֵהוּ
70 יֵרַע	49 תֵּאוֹר	28 שַׁלַּח
71 וַיַּעַן	50 נֵצֵאָה	29 יָקַּח
72 וִישִׁיתֶךָ	51 מְבַעֵר	30 יַסֵּב
73 הִטֵּיתִי	52 הַשְׁתִיתָן	31 נִבְנְתָה
74 וַיֶּחֱזַק	53 גֵּרַתֶּם	32 לָרֶשֶׁת
75 יֻגַּד	54 הֵינִקֻהוּ	33 תְּרִימֵהוּ
76 וַיֵּצְאוּ	55 תִּירֶאןָ	34 אֶתֵּן
77 מְרֵעִים	56 הָפְדֵּה	35 וַתִּקְנֶנָּה
78 הַמְרֹתִי	57 יָרְצוּ	36 תְּחָתֶּינָה
79 הֻתַּמֶּם	58 יְקַלֶּךְ	37 תְּכַלֶּינָה
80 תִּטְּעִי	59 וַיֵּיטַב	38 וַיֵּרֶב
81 הוֹדָה	60 הֲמִתֶּן	39 נוֹסָף
82 וַתַּחַר	61 בֹּכֶה	40 לָנוּ
83 יְמָדֵם	62 הַאֵלֵךְ	41 הַמְרָחָם
84 נֹאפָה	63 קַחְתָּהּ	42 מִשְׁתֹּמֵם

חַגּוֹת 101	אוֹבִילֵן 93	הַפִּיצוֹתָ 85
בְּהֲלָה 102	מְצֹרַעַת 94	הָפְנֹתָם 86
הוּכַחַתְּ 103	הָרֶף 95	וַיָּנַח 87
פָּרְשְׁכֶם 104	וַיָּגֶל 96	מְעִירִים 88
תֹּאבוּ 105	נְשַׁנִּי 97	לָשֵׂאת 89
הָשַׁע 106	הִשָּׁנֹת 98	וַיִּשְׁתַּחוּ 90
הַחֲלָם 107	נִשְׁבְּתָה 99	טַהֲרוּ 91
מַשַּׂגְתָּן 108	הַטֵּף 100	תִּקְחוּ 92

PART SIX
APPENDIX

CHAPTER LIV
FURTHER NOTES ON ORTHOGRAPHY

A. Accent Marks

1. The following is a list of the accent marks as used in *prose*, arranged in the order of their separative strength[1]. Those marked *i* are always written on the initial letter of the word, and those marked *f* on the final letter; all others are written on the first letter of the tone syllable.

a. The disjunctive accents.

— Silliq[2]	— Tiphḥa	— Geresh *or* Teres
—Athnaḥ[2]	— Rebhia	—Gerashim
— Segolta *f*	— Zarqa *f*	— Pazer
— Shalsheleth	— Pashta *f*	— Qarne Phara
— Zaqeph Gadhol	— Yethibh *i*	— Telisha Gedhola *i*
— Zaqeph Qaton	— Tebhir	⌐ Legarmeh Pesiq

b. The conjunctive accents.

— Munaḥ	— Merekha	—Qadhma *or* Azla
— Mahpakh *or*	— Merekha Kephula	— Telisha Qetannah *f*
Mehuppakh	—Darga	— Yeraḥ ben Yomo

---

1 Such an arrangement can be only approximate, for the punctuation depends partly on the length of the verse; in a short verse the lesser disjunctives have a conjunctive power, while in a long verse a conjunctive may be equivalent to a lighter disjunctive.

2 Every verse has Silluq, and all but the shortest have Athnah.

289

2. In *poetry*, $\overset{>}{\underset{\jmath}{-}}$, Merekha Mehuppakh, is a disjunctive superior to Athnah; $\underset{\mathsf{c}}{-}$, Tarḥa, is a conjunctive; and other minor variations from the prose system occur.

3. The secondary accent is usually marked by Metheg, $\underset{\mathsf{i}}{-}$; but on words *in pause* (see B, below), $\underset{\mathsf{c}}{-}$, Meaila, is sometimes used. The secondary accent is used—

    a. To emphasize a long vowel separated by one or more vowels from the tone syllable; e.g., הֹולַדְתִּיכֶם, כְּבְדוּ.

    b. To emphasize a short vowel before a Hateph vowel; e.g., לַהֲרֹג.

    c. Occasionally, to place a slight stress on a word joined to another by Maqqeph; e.g., זֶה־לְּךָ .

B. Pause Forms

The words at the end of a sentence and at the principal pause within it (i.e., at Silluq and Athnah), and sometimes one at a lesser pause (e.g., at a Zaqeph), were pronounced slowly to give them greater emphasis. These words are said to be *in pause;* and their forms, lengthened for the more prolonged pronunciation, are called *pause forms.* Changes are effected both in the vowels and in the accent, the principal ones being:

1. A short vowel under the accent is lengthened; e.g., noun and verb forms such as דְּבַשׁ, מַיִם, נִקְטַל, and קָטַלְתָּ become דְּבָשׁ, מָיִם, נִקְטָל, and קָטָלְתָּ . Also—

    a. In *a* class segolates the first Segol becomes Qamets; e.g., דָּרֶךְ for דֶּרֶךְ . (There are, however, a few exceptions, as in מֶלֶךְ and קֶדֶם).

    b. Lamedh guttural verbs take Tsere wherever the regular verb does; e.g., יְשַׁלֵּחַ instead of יְשַׁלַּח; and words like דבר (Ch. XXVIII, D, 3) also take Tsere (דְּבֵר instead of דְּבַר).

2. A pretonic Shewa usually becomes a full vowel and is accented:

a. Before the suffix דְ to either nouns or verbs, Segol is used; e.g., קְטָלְךָ ,דְּבָרְךָ. But with the prepositions בְּ, אֶת, ל, עִם, etc., the forms are לָךְ, עִמְּךָ, etc.

b. In the inflectional forms of verbs the full vowel that was dropped before a vowel afformative returns; and, if it was short, it is lengthened; e.g., קָטְלָה becomes קָטְלוּ; also קֹטְלוּ, Plu. of קֹטֵל, becomes קֹטְלוּ.

c. The nouns חֲלִי ,אֲרִי ,פְּרִי, etc., become פֶּרִי ,אָרִי ,חֹלִי, etc.

d. The Jussives יְהִי and יְחִי become יֶהִי and יֶחִי (probably by false analogy to the foregoing nouns).

e. לְ and וֹ sometimes take Qamets (Ch. VIII, A, 2, d, and note).

3. The displacement of accent by Waw Consec. does not occur; e. g., וַיֵּשֶׁב instead of וַיֵּשֶׁב; וְקָטַלְתָּ instead of וְקָטַלְתָּ.

4. On certain words the tone is shifted from the ultima to the penult, and the vowels lengthened; e.g., אָתָּה instead of אַתָּה (so also עַתָּה); אָנִי instead of אֲנִי; אָנֹכִי instead of אָנֹכִי.

C. Recessive Accent

When a word is followed by a monosyllable, or by a word accented on the first syllable, its accent is commonly shifted to the penult in order to avoid having two accented syllables together, and the ultimate vowel is then shortened; e.g., אֻלַּד בּוֹ (Job 3:3), for אֻלַּד בּוֹ. Such shortening is also common when a word is joined by Maqqeph to the following word; e.g., הַשָּׁמָר־לָךְ (cf. note 1, page 24).

D. Massoretic Notes

1. The Massoretes placed numerous footnotes to the text of the O.T. These are usually in unpointed Hebrew, and many abbreviations are used (the mark ′ or ″ is used after a letter to indicate that it is

an abbreviation)[1]. The mark * or ° is written above a word to call attention to the footnote.

2. Instead of venturing direct emendations in many passages in which the accepted text seemed corrupt, the Massoretes put in footnotes what they considered the true reading. The word in the text is designated as the *Kethibh* (i.e., what is *written*), and the substituted word as the *Qere* (i.e., what it is to be *called* or read); e.g., in Is. 65:4, וּפָרֵק has a note וּמרק קרי, and in Dt. 21:7 שָׁפְכָה has a note שפכוק'—i.e., וּמְרַק and שָׁפְכוּ are to be read. The vowels which are to be used with the Qere are always attached to the word in the text (the Kethibh).

a. It is also to be noted that certain words are always pronounced differently than they are written. No footnote is used on these, but the vowels pronounced are written with the consonants in the text and the reader supplies the proper consonants mentally; these are designated as *Perpetual Qeres*. Examples: the Divine name (note 5, page 30)[2]; יְרוּשָׁלַם, of which the Kethibh is understood to be יְרוּשְׁלָם, the Qere being יְרוּשָׁלַיִם; יִשָּׁשְׂכָר, the Qere being יִשָּׂכָר; and הוּא for הִיא thruout the Pentateuch.

3. Peculiarities in the punctuation are especially noted; e.g., קמץ בז"ק means "Qamets with Zaqeph Qaton"—calling attention to a pause form with lengthened vowel at [this lesser disjunctive; הב' בצרי means "The Beth with Tsere"—another unusual pause form. Other names of letters and marks will be easily identified if carefully examined (בדגש הד' being "The Daleth with Dagesh," etc.).

---

[1] In interpreting notes, it is to be remembered that to the forms given below a Fem. or Plu. ending may be added.

[2] In case the actual word אֲדֹנָי immediately precedes the tetragrammaton, the latter is pointed יֱהוִֹה and read אֱלֹהִים; e.g., 2 Sam. 7:18.

4. Various slight peculiarities of the orthography are also noted (they probably felt these had some cryptic significance which they would preserve, even tho not understanding it); e.g.—

ב׳ רבתי	—"Beth large" (Gen. 1:1).
א׳ זעירא	—"Aleph small" (Lev. 1:1).
נ׳ תלוי	—"Nun suspended" (above the line; Jg. 18:30).
נ׳ הפוך	—"Nun inverted" (Num. 10:35).
נקוד על ו׳	—"Point over Waw ' (Gen. 19:33); also written

ניקוד.

5. Of the other notes, the following are the most important.

בנ״א—"In other MSS."; followed by the alternative reading (frequently the only difference is in the accentual marks). Specific MSS. are often designated by ב with the proper letters.

הפטרה or הפטרת—"The end"—used in designating the pericope sections of the prophets.

יתיר—"Superfluous"; preceded or followed by a letter which is to be eliminated from the text (a sort of substitute for a Qere note). So also חסר—"Omitted"—indicates a letter which should be inserted.

מלרע (Milra)—"Below"; indicates that the word is accented on the ultima, altho regularly accented on the penult. מלעיל (Milel)— "Above"—is the opposite, noting an accented penult in a word usually oxytone.

סימן—"Sign, symbol."

ס and פ; used to indicate sections in the Pentateuch.

קדש—"Holy"—and חול—"Profane"—showing whether a divine name indicates Deity or not (e.g., Gen. 18:3; 19:2).

E. Vocal and Silent Shewa

1. Altho a Shewa after a long vowel is usually vocal (Ch. V, C, 2, d), it is silent if the vowel is *accented* (cf. Ch. II, E, 2, a); e.g., in certain

pause forms (such as אֲנַחְנוּ), and in some verb forms (such as קְטָֽנְתְּ,
תִּקְטֹֽלְנָה, and קְטָֽלְנָה). Likewise, a short vowel, if *accented*, can be
be followed by vocal Shewa; e.g., לַֽיְלָה.

2. Vocal Shewa follows an *unaccented short vowel* in the following
cases:

   a. When two Shewas would come together, and the first is replaced by a full short vowel:

   (1) In Cst. Plurals of first and second declension nouns; e.g.,
   מַלְכֵי, לִבְבוֹת. And with heavy suffixes to the same;
   e.g., דַּרְכֵיהֶם, שִׂפְתֵיכֶם.

   (2) In some polysyllabic nouns in Cst. or with suffixes; e.g.,
   בִּרְכָתִי (but contrast מִשְׁפַּחְתִּי).

   (3) With second Sing. and Plu. suffixes to Sing. nouns of the
   third declension and to middle guttural segolates; e.g.,
   נַעַרְכֶם, שָׁפְטְךָ. Also, the same with various verb forms;
   e.g., קְטַלְכֶם, יָקְטָלְךָ. (Cf. also b, below).

   (4) When בּ, כּ, ל, or He Interrogative is prefixed to a word
   beginning with Shewa—*except* an Inf. with ל; e.g., בִּגְבוּל,
   לִזְכֹּר; הַכְתַבְתֶּם.

   (5) In Qal Impv. forms; e.g., כָּרְתָה, כִּרְתוּ.

   (6) In Impf. Qal, Perf. Ni., and Ho. of Pe Guttural verbs;
   e.g., נֶעֶבְדָה, יַעֲמְדוּ.

   b. In various cases where a vowel shortens before כֶם and כֶן; e.g.,
קְטַלְכֶם, שָׂרְכֶם, דְּבַרְכֶם, אֶתְכֶם.

   c. When a letter which should have D.F. drops it over vocal
Shewa; e.g., הַיְאֹר, יִשְׂאוּ.

   d. In various forms in which a guttural has D.F. implicit; e.g.,
שַׁחֲתוּ.

e. In various cases where a guttural has a Hateph vowel instead of a silent Shewa; e.g., יַעֲבִיד, as compared with יַסְתִּיר.

3. A Shewa used as described above in 2 is often called a *Medial Shewa*, and the preceding syllable a *half-open* syllable—by which it is meant that the Shewa is only partially vocal, and the consonant carrying it partly goes with the preceding syllable and thus partly closes it; e.g., יַלְדֵי is intermediate between "yal-dēy" and "ya-ləd͡hēy." But there is scarcely adequate justification for such meticulous distinctions—at least for burdening beginners with them; hence the terms have been avoided in the earlier chapters[1].

---

[1] It would be equally defensible (perhaps more so) to call a consonant carrying a half-vowel a *half-syllable*, and to multiply similar technicalities.

CHAPTER LV
FURTHER SYNTAX OF NOUNS AND PRONOUNS

A. Special Pronoun Uses

1. The separate personal pronouns are sometimes used absolutely to emphasize a preceding affixed pronoun; e.g., יָלֹקוּ הַכְּלָבִים אֶת־דָּמְךָ גַּם־אָתָּה (1 Ki. 21:19), "The dogs shall lick thy blood, even thine"; בָּרֲכֵנִי גַם־אָנִי (Gen. 27:34), "Bless me, even me also."

2. The pronoun suffixes are sometimes reflexive or intensive; e.g., in Isa. 3:9, לָהֶם means "unto themselves"; and in Isa. 49:26, בְּשָׂרָם means "their own flesh."

3. זֶה is often used as a sort of enclitic; e.g., מִי זֶה (Job 38:2), "Who then"? And זֶה . . . זֶה may be used correlatively, meaning "this . . . that," or "one . . . another."

4. מִי and מַה are sometimes used as indefinite pronouns, "whoever, whatever"; e.g. Jg. 7:3; 1 Sam. 20:4; Ex. 24:14.

B. Nouns Used for Pronouns

1. The word most commonly used thus is אִישׁ.

   a. It may be indefinite; e.g., אִם־יוּכַל אִישׁ לִמְנוֹת (Gen. 13:16), "If any one is able to number . . ."

   b. It frequently means "each, every"; e.g., וַיִּפְתְּחוּ אִישׁ אַמְתַּחְתּוֹ (Gen. 44:11), "And each one opened his sack." It is especially common in a reciprocal sense with a following רֵעֵהוּ (note the form of the suffix); e.g., וַיֹּאמְרוּ אִישׁ אֶל־רֵעֵהוּ (Gen. 11:3), "And they said to one another (lit., each one to his neighbor)"; it is similarly used also with אָחִיו.

   c. With a negative it means "no one"; e.g., אִישׁ מִמֶּנּוּ אֶת־קִבְרוֹ לֹא־יִכְלֶה (Gen. 23:6), "No one of us will withhold his sepulchre."

2. Other words are similarly used: e.g., אִשָּׁה for "each" in referring to females, לֹא כֹל for "none," לֹא דָבָר for "nothing," etc.

3. The word נֶפֶשׁ is sometimes used in a reflexive sense; e.g., נַפְשׁוֹ, "himself."

C. Special Uses of the Plural

The Plural of nouns is used in a number of idiomatic expressions, especially those involving abstract ideas.

1. The Plural of spatial extension: an extended surface is regarded as made up of a great number of small points, which are integrated into one whole; such is the conception underlying the use of such plurals as שָׁמַיִם, מַיִם, and פָּנִים ("heaven, water, face").

2. The Plural of abstract quality: similarly, the combination of individual characteristics or actions makes up a generic concept; e.g., בְּחוּרִים, "youth"; חֲנָטִים, "embalming."

3. The Plural of majesty: the honor implied in some names is intensified by making them plural; e.g., the Divine Names, and אֲדֹנָיהֶם (Gen. 40:1), "their lord."

D. Paragogic Letters[1]

1. The syllable ‑ָה is sometimes added to a noun without having the locative sense mentioned in Ch. XVI, E, 3; e.g., in הַמָּוְתָה, "death," and in the poetic double feminine termination ‑ָתָה (as in יְשׁוּעָתָה for יְשׁוּעָה)[2].

2. The syllable ‑י is sometimes added to a construct; e.g., מְלֵאֲתִי מִשְׁפָּט (Isa. 1:21), "full of justice"; also in אֲבִי and in many proper names such as מַלְכִּי־צֶדֶק, "Melchizedek." More rarely the syllable ‑וֹ is similarly used; e.g., חַיְתוֹ אֶרֶץ (for . . . חַיַּת; Gen. 1:24), "the beast of the earth."

---

1 These are remnants of old case endings.

2 Somewhat different is the not infrequent addition of ה (as a vowel letter) to various endings; e.g., לְכָה for לְךָ.

CHAPTER LVI
VERB AND SENTENCE SYNTAX

A. The Perfect Tense (Completed Action)

1. *Used for simple action:*

    a. At a certain point of time, which may be—

        (1) Usually in the past (Greek Aorist); e.g., הָרַגְתָּ אֶת־הַמִּצְרִי (Ex. 2:14), "You killed the Egyptian."

        (2) Sometimes in the present (something regarded as definitely accomplished); e.g., כֹּה אָמַר יְהוָֹה (Ex. 4:22), "Thus saith Jehovah"; הִשְׁתַּחֲוֵיתִי (2 Sam. 16:4), "I do obeisance."

        (3) Occasionally in the future (chiefly of divine promise or prophetic assurance, but also of something "as good as done" on account of personal determination); e.g., לָכֵן גָּלָה עַמִּי (Isa. 5:13), "Therefore my people shall go into captivity"; לָקַחְתִּי בְחָזְקָה (1 Sam. 2:16), "I will take it by force."

    b. Before a certain time, which may be—

        (1) In the past (the pluperfect use); e.g., לֹא עָשׂוּ כַּאֲשֶׁר דִּבֶּר הַמֶּלֶךְ (Ex. 1:17), "They did not do as the king had commanded."

        (2) In the present (an indefinite perfect); e.g., מִי שָׂמְךָ שַׂר עָלֵינוּ (Ex. 2:14), "Who has made you a prince over us?"

        (3) In the future (a future perfect use); e.g., וְעָלִינוּ כִּי נְתָנָם יְהֹוָה בְּיָדֵנוּ (1 Sam. 14:10), "And we will go up, for Jehovah will have delivered them into our hand."

    c. Timeless—the result of experience, stated as a universal

truth; translated by the present; e.g., יָדַע שׁוֹר קֹנֵהוּ (Isa. 1:3), "An ox knoweth his master."

    2. *Used for action involving continuity or condition*[1]:

    a. A course of action completed in the past; e.g., שָׁלֹשׁ שָׁנִים מָלַךְ (1 Ki. 15: 2), "He reigned three years"; פָּרוּ וַיִּרְבּוּ (Ex. 1:7), "They were fruitful and multiplied."

    b. A past condition existing for a limited period only; e.g., לֹא יָכְלָה הַצְּפִינוֹ (Ex. 2:3), "She was not able to hide him."

    c. Action resulting in a state; e.g., שָׁתוּ עָלָי (Ps. 3:7), "They have set themselves against me;" רָאִיתִי אֶת־עֳנִי עַמִּי (Ex. 3:7), "I have seen the affliction of my people"; נוֹדַע הַדָּבָר (Ex. 2:14), "The thing is known (i.e., has become known)". In the first two cases the past action is the predominant idea, with resulting state (of alienation, and knowledge) implied; in the third, the resulting state is emphasized.

B. The Imperfect Tense (Uncompleted Action)

    1. The *incipient* Impf. (representing an action as just beginning or about to begin):

    a. In the past; e.g., מִן־אֲרָם יַנְחֵנִי (Num. 23: 7), "From Aram he brot me (i.e., started guiding me)." This is especially used after the particles אָז and טֶרֶם; e.g., אָז יָשִׁיר מֹשֶׁה (Ex. 15:1), "Then did Moses (begin to) sing"; טֶרֶם יִגָּלֶה אֵלָיו דְּבַר־יְהֹוָה (1 Sam. 3:7), "The word of Jehovah was not yet revealed unto him."

    b. In the present (especially of an attempted action); e.g., לָמָּה תַפְרִיעוּ אֶת־הָעָם מִמַּעֲשָׂיו (Ex. 5:4), "Why do ye (try to) set loose the people from their work?"

---

[1] Some of these uses approach very closely to the Impf.; the dividing line cannot always be drawn sharply. In fact, there is a considerable subjective element; and in "borderline cases" the writer may follow his discretion or predilection or special viewpoint.

c. Most commonly, in the future; e.g., מָה אֹמַר אֲלֵהֶם (Ex. 3:13), "What shall I say to them?"

(1) The futurity may also be from some indicated past time; e.g., וַתֵּתַצַּב לְדֵעָה מַה־יֵּעָשֶׂה לוֹ (Ex. 2:4), "And she stationed herself to know what would be done to him."

(2) The use after Waw Consecutive is included here.

2. The *progressive* Impf. (i.e., of action or state in process):

a. In the past; e.g., כַּאֲשֶׁר יְעַנּוּ אֹתוֹ כֵּן יִרְבֶּה (Ex. 1:12), "The more they afflicted them, the more they multiplied"[1].

b. In the present; e.g., לָמָה תַעֲשֶׂה כֹה לַעֲבָדֶיךָ (Ex. 5: 15), "Why dost thou deal thus with thy servants?" A special application is in descriptions of character in subordinate clauses not introduced by a relative; e.g., יֵצֵא יְשׁוּעָתָהּ כְּלַפִּיד יִבְעָר (Isa. 62:1), "Her salvation shall go forth as a lamp that burneth."

c. In the future; e.g., כִּי תַעֲבֹד אֶת־הָאֲדָמָה לֹא־תֹסֵף תֵּת־ כֹּחָהּ לָךְ (Gen. 4:12), "When you till the ground, it shall no longer yield its strength to you."

3. The *frequentative* Impf. (i.e., of repeated or customary action):

a. In the past; e.g., וּמֹשֶׁה יִקַּח אֶת־הָאֹהֶל וְנָטָה־לוֹ (Ex. 33:7), "Now Moses used to take the tent and pitch it"; בְּתוֹעֵבֹת יַכְעִיסֻהוּ (Dt. 32:16), "With abominations they kept provoking Him"; אִם־כֹּה יֹאמַר וְיָלְדוּ (= יֵלְדוּ) כָל־הַצֹּאן נְקֻדִים (Gen. 31:8), "If he would say thus, then all the flock would bear speckled."

b. In the present; e.g., עֹרֶף יִפְנוּ (Josh. 7:12), "They turn their backs"; כַּאֲשֶׁר תַּעֲשֶׂינָה הַדְּבֹרִים (Dt. 1:44), "Just as bees do"[2].

---

[1] Note the different viewpoint from that of the Perf. in A, 2, a above; there the process as a whole, completed, is thought of; here, the process in the actual course of accomplishment.

[2] Cf. the parallel use of the Perf. for a general truth in A, 1, c above;

c. In the future; e.g., כָּל־הַבֵּן הַיִּלּוֹד הַיְאֹרָה תַּשְׁלִיכֻהוּ (Ex. 1:22), "Every son ye shall cast into the river."

4. The *modal Impf.* (expressing "subjunctive" ideas, etc.):

a. The potential Impf. (indicating ability, possibility, contingency, permission, etc.; cf. also conditional sentences below in C); e.g., יָדַעְתִּי כִּי יְדַבֵּר (Ex. 4:14), "I know that he can speak"; קְחוּ תֶבֶן מֵאֲשֶׁר תִּמְצָאוּ (Ex. 5:11), "Get straw wherever you can find it"; כָּל־מֹצְאִי יַהַרְגֵנִי (Gen. 4:14), "Every one that finds me may kill me"; מִכֹּל עֵץ תֹּאכַל (Gen. 2:16), "From every tree thou mayest eat."

b. The imperative Impf.

(1) In commands and prohibitions (mostly divine); e.g., נָע וָנָד תִּהְיֶה (Gen. 4:12), "A fugitive and a wanderer shalt thou be"; לֹא תִּנְאָף (Ex. 20:14), "Thou shalt not commit adultery."

(2) In statements of obligation and necessity; e.g., אָשֵׁב עִם־הַמֶּלֶךְ (1 Sam. 20:5), "I ought to sit with the king."

c. In clauses of Purpose; e.g., לְמַעַן יַאֲמִינוּ (Ex. 4:5), "In order that they may believe."

C. Conditional Sentences

1. The clauses may be connected in one of three ways:

a. The most primitive (and least frequent) is full and simple coördination by Waw Consec. (indicating logical sequence); e.g., וְעָזַב אֶת־אָבִיו וָמֵת (Gen. 44:22), "And if (the lad) leave his father, he will die"[1].

b. More frequent is the full subordination of the protasis to the

---

there the truth is regarded as the result of past experience—here, as something likely to happen at any time.

[1] Weak Waw is sometimes similarly used; e.g., in Job 12:15.

apodasis, as in Western languages; e.g., לֹא אֶעֱשֶׂה אִם־אֶמְצָא שָׁם שְׁלֹשִׁים (Gen. 18:30), "I will not do it if I find there thirty."

c. The form most characteristic of O. T. Hebrew is a sort of intermediate, or mixture of those two conceptions: the protasis is introduced by a subordinating conjunction (usually אִם, sometimes הֵן or כִּי), and the apodasis by the coördinating Waw Consec.; e.g., אִם יִפְקְדֵנִי וְאָמַרְתָּ (1 Sam. 20:6), "If he shall miss me, then shalt thou say."

2. The use of tenses in simple conditions.

a. In most simple conditions, whether particular or general, the apodasis is in the future, and therefore takes the Impf., or Waw Consec. with the Perf., or a voluntative; nominal sentences of course occur also.

> (1) Sometimes the Perf. is used for vividness or to express absolute certainty. And occasionally the Perf. occurs in a mixed condition; e.g., אִם תָּשׁוּב לֹא־דִבֶּר יְהוָה בִּי (1 Ki. 22:28), "If thou return, Jehovah hath not spoken by me."
>
> (2) Sometimes the apodasis is introduced by Weak Waw, or by כִּי עַתָּה.

b. The protasis has the Impf. in—

> (1) Future more vivid; e.g., אֶת־שְׁנֵי בָנַי תָּמִית אִם־לֹא אֲבִיאֶנּוּ (Gen. 42:37), "If I do not bring him, thou shalt (or, mayest) kill my two sons."
>
> (2) Future less vivid; e.g., אִם־תַּחֲנֶה עָלַי מַחֲנֶה לֹא־יִירָא לִבִּי (Ps. 27:3), "If a host should encamp against me, my heart would not fear."

c. The protasis has the Perf. (representing a probable fact as actually accomplished at some point of time) in—

> (1) Future most vivid; e.g., אִם מָכַר לֹא־יִגָּאֵל (Lev. 27:20),

"If he shall have sold it, it shall not be redeemed."

(2) General conditions — future, present, or past; e.g., כִּי
הִזְהַרְתָּ רָשָׁע וְלֹא שָׁב יָמוּת (Eze. 33:9), "If thou shalt
warn the wicked and he turn not, he shall die"; אִם חָטָאתִי
וּשְׁמַרְתָּנִי (Job 10: 14), "If I sin, thou watchest me";
אִם־אָמַרְתִּי מָטָה רַגְלִי חַסְדְּךָ יִסְעָדֵנִי (Ps. 94:18), "If
I would say, 'My foot slippeth,' thy loving-kindness
would uphold me" (with a past frequentative Impf.
in apodasis).

d. The protasis may be stated by a participle, an infinitive, or
a voluntative.

e. It is evident that there is no such sharp discrimination of conditional forms as in Greek.   The context must be considered carefully,
and the translation is often far from certain.

3. "Unreal" conditions (i.e., contrary to fact) are introduced by
the particle לוּ (negative, לוּלֵי or לוּלֵא); they usually have the Perf.
in both protasis and apodasis (representing a completed action, whether
real or postulated)—altho frequentative or other special Impfs. may
occur; e.g., לוּ הַחֲיִתֶם אוֹתָם לֹא הָרַגְתִּי אֶתְכֶם (Jg. 8:19), "If ye had
saved them alive, I should not have killed you."

D. Special Uses of Waw

1. Waw Consec. is sometimes used to add specific details to a general statement, or to add contemporaneous or explanatory material.
It may also occasionally be used with a verb which retains its own
proper tense meaning—especially in stating simultaneous events and
in poetic writing.

2. Sometimes verbs occurring in "parallelistic" statements keep
their own proper tense and are joined by Weak Waw instead of taking
Waw Consecutive.

a. This is most common in cases in which the verbs are strictly coördinate, being either simultaneous, synonymous, or contrasted; see, e.g., Isa. 40:12; 41:11; Prov. 14:25.

　b. Also, the second member of a double question may be thus introduced; e.g., Job 15:8.

　3. Sometimes clauses expressing cause, purpose, result, etc., are introduced by Weak Waw; e.g., וְגֵר לֹא תִלְחָץ וְאַתֶּם יְדַעְתֶּם אֶת־נֶפֶשׁ הַגֵּר (Ex. 23:9), "And a sojourner thou shalt not oppress, for thou knowest the heart of a sojourner"; אַל־נָא נֵלֵךְ כֻּלָּנוּ וְלֹא נִכְבַּד עָלֶיךָ (2 Sam. 13:25), "Let us not all go, so that we be not burdensome unto thee"; לֹא אִישׁ אֵל וִיכַזֵּב (Num. 23:19), "God is not a man, that he should lie."

　4. Occasionally a Weak Waw is used where there is no adequate explanation except simple laxity of syntax.

PARADIGMS

(A) THE STRONG VERB

Perf.	Qal	Niph'al	Pi'el	Pu'al	Hiph'il	Hoph'al	Hithpa'el	Qal Stative
3ms	קָטַל	נִקְטַל	קִטֵּל	קֻטַּל	הִקְטִיל	הָקְטַל	הִתְקַטֵּל	כָּבֵד, קָטֹן
3fs	קָטְלָה	נִקְטְלָה	קִטְּלָה	קֻטְּלָה	הִקְטִילָה	הָקְטְלָה	הִתְקַטְּלָה	כָּבְדָה, קָטְנָה
2ms	קָטַלְתָּ	נִקְטַלְתָּ	קִטַּלְתָּ	קֻטַּלְתָּ	הִקְטַלְתָּ	הָקְטַלְתָּ	הִתְקַטַּלְתָּ	כָּבֵדְתָּ
2fs	קָטַלְתְּ	נִקְטַלְתְּ	קִטַּלְתְּ	קֻטַּלְתְּ	הִקְטַלְתְּ	הָקְטַלְתְּ	הִתְקַטַּלְתְּ	כָּבֵדְתְּ
1cs	קָטַלְתִּי	נִקְטַלְתִּי	קִטַּלְתִּי	קֻטַּלְתִּי	הִקְטַלְתִּי	הָקְטַלְתִּי	הִתְקַטַּלְתִּי	כָּבֵדְתִּי
3cp	קָטְלוּ	נִקְטְלוּ	קִטְּלוּ	קֻטְּלוּ	הִקְטִילוּ	הָקְטְלוּ	הִתְקַטְּלוּ	כָּבְדוּ
2mp	קְטַלְתֶּם	נִקְטַלְתֶּם	קִטַּלְתֶּם	קֻטַּלְתֶּם	הִקְטַלְתֶּם	הָקְטַלְתֶּם	הִתְקַטַּלְתֶּם	כְּבֵדְתֶּם
2fp	קְטַלְתֶּן	נִקְטַלְתֶּן	קִטַּלְתֶּן	קֻטַּלְתֶּן	הִקְטַלְתֶּן	הָקְטַלְתֶּן	הִתְקַטַּלְתֶּן	כְּבֵדְתֶּן
1cp	קָטַלְנוּ	נִקְטַלְנוּ	קִטַּלְנוּ	קֻטַּלְנוּ	הִקְטַלְנוּ	הָקְטַלְנוּ	הִתְקַטַּלְנוּ	כָּבֵדְנוּ

Impf.	Qal	Niph'al	Pi'el	Pu'al	Hiph'il	Hoph'al	Hithpa'el	Qal Stative
3ms	יִקְטֹל	יִקָּטֵל	יְקַטֵּל	יְקֻטַּל	יַקְטִיל	יָקְטַל	יִתְקַטֵּל	יִכְבַּד
3fs	תִּקְטֹל	תִּקָּטֵל	תְּקַטֵּל	תְּקֻטַּל	תַּקְטִיל	תָּקְטַל	תִּתְקַטֵּל	תִּכְבַּד
2ms	תִּקְטֹל	תִּקָּטֵל	תְּקַטֵּל	תְּקֻטַּל	תַּקְטִיל	תָּקְטַל	תִּתְקַטֵּל	תִּכְבַּד
2fs	תִּקְטְלִי	תִּקָּטְלִי	תְּקַטְּלִי	תְּקֻטְּלִי	תַּקְטִילִי	תָּקְטְלִי	תִּתְקַטְּלִי	תִּכְבְּדִי
1cs	אֶקְטֹל	אֶקָּטֵל	אֲקַטֵּל	אֲקֻטַּל	אַקְטִיל	אָקְטַל	אֶתְקַטֵּל	אֶכְבַּד

	קָטַל						
3mp							
3fp							
2mp							
2fp							
1cp							
+ Waw							
Impv. 2ms							
2fs							
2mp							
2fp							
Coh.							
Inf. Abs.							
Cst.							
+ Suf.							
Part.							

(B) SUFFIXES TO QAL OF קָטַל

Suff.	Perfect 3ms קָטַל	3fs קָטְלָה	2ms קָטַלְתָּ	2fs קָטַלְתְּ	3cp קָטְלוּ	Imperfect 3ms יִקְטֹל	3mp יִקְטְלוּ	Impv. 2ms קְטֹל
1cs	קְטָלַנִי	קְטָלַתְנִי	קְטַלְתַּנִי	קְטַלְתִּינִי	קְטָלוּנִי	יִקְטְלֵנִי	יִקְטְלוּנִי	קָטְלֵנִי
2rns	קְטָלְךָ	קְטָלַתְךָ			קְטָלוּךָ	יִקְטָלְךָ	יִקְטְלוּךָ	
2fs	קְטָלֵךְ	קְטָלָתֶךְ			קְטָלוּךְ	יִקְטְלֵךְ	יִקְטְלוּךְ	
3ms	קְטָלָהוּ	קְטָלַתְהוּ	קְטַלְתָּהוּ	קְטַלְתִּיהוּ	קְטָלוּהוּ	יִקְטְלֵהוּ, יִקְטְלֶנּוּ	יִקְטְלוּהוּ	קָטְלֵהוּ
3fs	קְטָלָהּ	קְטָלַתָּה	קְטַלְתָּהּ	קְטַלְתִּיהָ	קְטָלוּהָ	יִקְטְלֶהָ, יִקְטְלֶנָּה	יִקְטְלוּהָ	קָטְלֶהָ
1cp	קְטָלָנוּ	קְטָלַתְנוּ	קְטַלְתָּנוּ	קְטַלְתִּינוּ	קְטָלוּנוּ	יִקְטְלֵנוּ	יִקְטְלוּנוּ	קָטְלֵנוּ
2mp	קְטַלְכֶם				קְטָלוּכֶם	יִקְטָלְכֶם	יִקְטְלוּכֶם	
2fp	קְטַלְכֶן							
3mp	קְטָלָם	קְטָלָתַם	קְטַלְתָּם		קְטָלוּם	יִקְטְלֵם	יִקְטְלוּם	קָטְלֵם
3fp	קְטָלָן	קְטָלָתַן	קְטַלְתָּן		קְטָלוּן	יִקְטְלֵן		קָטְלֵן

(C) OTHER VERBAL SUFFIXES

Suff.	Pi'el 3ms Perf. קִטֵּל	Stative 3ms Perf. אָהֵב	Guttural Qal 3ms Impf. יֹאכַל	Double Ayin Hi¹ 3ms Perf. הֵסֵב	Qal 3ms Perf. קָטַל	Lamedh He Qal 3mp Perf. גָּלוּ	Qal 3ms Perf. גָּלָה	Hi. 3ms Perf. הִגְלָה
1cs	קִטְּלַנִי	אֲהֵבַנִי	יֹאכְלֵנִי	הֲסִבַּנִי	קְטָלַנִי	גְּלוּנִי	גְּלָנִי	הִגְלַנִי
2ms	קִטֶּלְךָ	אֲהֵבְךָ	יֹאכָלְךָ	הֲסִבְּךָ	קְטָלְךָ	גְּלוּךָ	גְּלְךָ	הִגְלְךָ
3ms	קִטְּלוֹ	אֲהֵבוֹ	יֹאכְלֵהוּ	הֲסִבּוֹ	קְטָלוֹ	גְּלוּהוּ	גְּלָהוּ	הִגְלָהוּ
1cp	קִטְּלָנוּ	אֲהֵבָנוּ	יֹאכְלֵנוּ	הֲסִבָּנוּ	קְטָלָנוּ	גְּלוּנוּ	גְּלָנוּ	הִגְלָנוּ
2mp	קִטֶּלְכֶם	אֲהֵבְכֶם	יֹאכָלְכֶם	הֲסִבְּכֶם	קְטַלְכֶם	גְּלוּכֶם	גְּלָכֶם	הִגְלָכֶם

	Pi'el 3ms Impf. יְקַטֵּל	Stative 2ms Impv.	Guttural 2mp Impv.	Double Ayin Qal (Q¹) 3ms Impf. יָסֹב	Qal 3fs Perf. קָטְלָה	Lamedh He 3ms Impf. יִגְלֶה	Pi. 2ms Impv. גַּלֵּה
1cs	יְקַטְּלֵנִי		אִכְלוּנִי	יְסֻבֵּנִי	קְטָלַתְנִי	יִגְלֵנִי	גַּלֵּנִי
2ms	יְקַטֶּלְךָ			יְסֻבְּךָ	קְטָלַתְךָ	יִגְלְךָ	
3ms	יְקַטְּלֶנּוּ		אִכְלוּהוּ	יְסֻבֶּנּוּ	קְטָלַתְהוּ	יִגְלֵהוּ	
3mp	יְקַטְּלֵם		אִכְלוּם	יְסֻבֵּם	קְטָלָתַם		

309

	(D) PE GUTTURAL VERB				(E) AYIN GUTTURAL VERB				
Perf.	Qal (Qˡ)	Niph'al	Hiph'il	Hoph'al	Qal	Pi¹	Pu¹	Pi³	Hith²
3ms									
3fs									
2ms¹									
2fs									
1cs									
3cp									
2mp									
2fp									
1cp									
Impf.									
3ms									
3fs									
2ms									
2fs									
1cs									

3mp	יַעֲבְדוּ	יַעֲבְדוּ	יַעֲבִידוּ	יַעֲבְדוּ	יְגֹאֲלוּ	יִגָּאֲלוּ	יְגֹאֲלוּ	יִטַּהֲרוּ	יִטַּהֲרוּ
3fp	תַּעֲבֹדְנָה	תַּעֲבַדְנָה	תַּעֲבֵדְנָה	תַּעֲבַדְנָה	תִּגְאַלְנָה	תִּגָּאַלְנָה	תִּגֹאַלְנָה	תִּטַּהֵרְנָה	תִּטַּהַרְנָה
2mp	תַּעֲבְדוּ	תַּעֲבְדוּ	תַּעֲבִידוּ	תַּעֲבְדוּ	תִּגְאֲלוּ	תִּגָּאֲלוּ	תִּגֹאֲלוּ	תִּטַּהֲרוּ	תִּטַּהֲרוּ
2fp	תַּעֲבֹדְנָה	תַּעֲבַדְנָה	תַּעֲבֵדְנָה	תַּעֲבַדְנָה	תִּגְאַלְנָה	תִּגָּאַלְנָה	תִּגֹאַלְנָה	תִּטַּהֵרְנָה	תִּטַּהַרְנָה
1cp	נַעֲבֹד	נַעֲבֵד	נַעֲבִיד	נַעֲבֵד	נִגְאַל	נִגָּאֵל	נִגֹאַל	נְטַהֵר	נְטַהַר
+Waw						וַיִּגָּאֵל			וַיִּטַּהֵר
Impv.									
2ms	עֲבֹד	הַעֲבֵד	הָעֳבַד		גְּאַל	גָּאֵל		טַהֵר	הִטַּהֵר
2fs	עִבְדִי	הַעֲבִידִי	הָעָבְדִי		גַּאֲלִי	גָּאֲלִי		טַהֲרִי	הִטַּהֲרִי
2mp	עִבְדוּ	הַעֲבִידוּ	הָעָבְדוּ		גַּאֲלוּ	גָּאֲלוּ		טַהֲרוּ	הִטַּהֲרוּ
2fp	עֲבֹדְנָה	הַעֲבֵדְנָה	הָעֲבַדְנָה		גְּאַלְנָה	גָּאַלְנָה		טַהֵרְנָה	הִטַּהֵרְנָה
Coh.	עָבְדָה	הַעֲבִידָה	הָעָבְדָה						
Inf.									
Abs.	עָבוֹד	נַעֲבֹד	הַעֲבֵד	הָעֲבֵד	גָּאוֹל	גָּאֹל		טַהֵר	
Cst.	עֲבֹד	הֵעָבֵד	הַעֲבִי	הָעֲבֵד	גָּאֹל	גָּאֵל		טַהֵר	הִטַּהֵר
+Suf.	עָבְדִי								
Part.	עֹבֵד	נֶעֱבָד	מַעֲבִיד	מָעֳבָד	גֹּאֵל	נִגְאָל	מְגֹאָל	מְטַהֵר	מְטַהֵר
	עָבוּד				נָגֹאוּל				

(F) PE ALEPH VERB   (G) LAMEDH GUTTURAL VERB

	Qal (Q⁶)		Qal	Niph'al	Pi'el	Hiph'il	Hithpa'el
Perf.	אָכַל		שָׁלַח	נִשְׁלַח	שִׁלַּח	הִשְׁלִיחַ	הִשְׁתַּלַּח
3ms			שָׁלַח	נִשְׁלַח	שִׁלַּח	הִשְׁלִיחַ	הִשְׁתַּלַּח
3fs			שָׁלְחָה	נִשְׁלְחָה	שִׁלְּחָה	הִשְׁלִיחָה	הִשְׁתַּלְּחָה
2ms			שָׁלַחְתָּ	נִשְׁלַחְתָּ	שִׁלַּחְתָּ	הִשְׁלַחְתָּ	הִשְׁתַּלַּחְתָּ
2fs			שָׁלַחַתְּ	נִשְׁלַחַתְּ	שִׁלַּחַתְּ	הִשְׁלַחַתְּ	הִשְׁתַּלַּחַתְּ
1cs			שָׁלַחְתִּי	etc.	etc.	הִשְׁלַחְתִּי	etc.
3cp			שָׁלְחוּ			הִשְׁלִיחוּ	
2mp			שְׁלַחְתֶּם			הִשְׁלַחְתֶּם	
2fp			שְׁלַחְתֶּן			הִשְׁלַחְתֶּן	
1cp			שָׁלַחְנוּ			הִשְׁלַחְנוּ	
Impf.	יֹאכַל		יִשְׁלַח	יִשָּׁלַח	יְשַׁלַּח	יַשְׁלִיחַ	יִשְׁתַּלַּח
3ms	יֹאכַל		יִשְׁלַח	יִשָּׁלַח	יְשַׁלַּח	יַשְׁלִיחַ	יִשְׁתַּלַּח
3fs	תֹּאכַל		תִּשְׁלַח	תִּשָּׁלַח	תְּשַׁלַּח	תַּשְׁלִיחַ	etc.
2ms	תֹּאכַל		תִּשְׁלַח	תִּשָּׁלַח	תְּשַׁלַּח	תַּשְׁלִיחַ	
2fs	תֹּאכְלִי		תִּשְׁלְחִי	תִּשָּׁלְחִי	תְּשַׁלְּחִי	תַּשְׁלִיחִי	
1cs	אֹכַל		אֶשְׁלַח	אֶשָּׁלַח	אֲשַׁלַּח	אַשְׁלִיחַ	

3mp	יַאֲבִ֫ילוּ	תַּשְׁלִ֫יכוּ	תַּשְׁלֵ֫כוּ	יַשְׁלִ֫יכוּ	יֻשְׁלְכ֫וּ
3fp	תַּאֲבֵ֫לְנָה	תַּשְׁלֵ֫כְנָה	תַּשְׁלַ֫כְנָה	תַּשְׁלֵ֫כְנָה	תֻּשְׁלַ֫כְנָה
2mp	תַּאֲבִ֫ילוּ	תַּשְׁלִ֫יכוּ	תַּשְׁלֵ֫כוּ	תַּשְׁלִ֫יכוּ	תֻּשְׁלְכ֫וּ
2fp	תַּאֲבֵ֫לְנָה	תַּשְׁלֵ֫כְנָה	תַּשְׁלַ֫כְנָה	תַּשְׁלֵ֫כְנָה	תֻּשְׁלַ֫כְנָה
1cp	נַאֲבִיל	נַשְׁלִיךְ	נַשְׁלֵךְ	נַשְׁלֵךְ	נֻשְׁלַךְ
Juss.				יַשְׁלֵךְ	
Impv.					
2ms	אַבֵ֫ל	הַשְׁלֵךְ	הַשְׁלֵךְ	הַשְׁלֵךְ	הָשְׁלַ֫שְׁכָה
2fs	הַ֫אֲבִ֫ילִי	הַשְׁלִ֫יכִי	הַשְׁלִ֫יכִי	הַשְׁלִ֫יכִי	etc.
2mp	הַ֫אֲבִ֫ילוּ	הַשְׁלִ֫יכוּ	הַשְׁלִ֫יכוּ	הַשְׁלִ֫יכוּ	
2fp	הָ֫אֲבֵ֫לְנָה	הַשְׁלֵ֫כְנָה	הַשְׁלֵ֫כְנָה	הַשְׁלֵ֫כְנָה	
Coh.	נַ֫אֲבֵ֫לָה			הַשְׁלֵ֫כָה	
Inf.					
Abs.	הַאֲבֵל	הַשְׁלֵךְ	הַשְׁלֵךְ		
Cst.	הַ֫אֲבֵל	הַשְׁלִיךְ	הַשְׁלֵךְ	הַשְׁלִיךְ	הָשְׁלֵךְ
+Suf.	הַ֫אֲבִילִי	הַשְׁלִיכִי			
Part.	מַאֲבֵל	מַשְׁלֵךְ	מַשְׁלִיךְ	מַשְׁלִיךְ	מֻשְׁלָךְ

313

(J) AYIN YODH VERB

ORIGINAL PE YODH

(H) PE YODH VERB

ORIGINAL PE WAW

	Qal	Hi³	Q³	Hoph'al	Hi¹	Niph'al	Qal	Q¹	Q²
Perf.									
3ms									
3fs									
2ms									
2fs									
1cs				etc.					
3cp									
2mp									
2fp									
1cp									
Impf.									
3ms									
3fs				etc.					
2ms									
2fs									
1cs									

3mp	יֵשְׁבוּ	יִירְשׁוּ	יִוָּשְׁבוּ	יוֹשִׁיבוּ		יִיטְבוּ	יֵיטִיבוּ	יָבִינוּ
3fp	תֵּשַׁבְנָה	תִּירַשְׁנָה	תִּוָּשַׁבְנָה	תּוֹשֵׁבְנָה		תִּיטַבְנָה	תֵּיטֵבְנָה	תְּבִינֶינָה
2mp	תֵּשְׁבוּ	תִּירְשׁוּ	תִּוָּשְׁבוּ	תּוֹשִׁיבוּ		תִּיטְבוּ	תֵּיטִיבוּ	תָּבִינוּ
2fp	תֵּשַׁבְנָה	תִּירַשְׁנָה	תִּוָּשַׁבְנָה	תּוֹשֵׁבְנָה		תִּיטַבְנָה	תֵּיטֵבְנָה	תְּבִינֶינָה
1cp	נֵשֵׁב	נִירַשׁ	נִוָּשֵׁב	נוֹשִׁיב		נִיטַב	נֵיטִיב	נָבִין
Juss.				יוֹשֵׁב			יֵיטֵב	יָבֵן
+Waw	וַיֵּשֶׁב			וַיּוֹשֶׁב			וַיֵּיטֶב	וַיָּבֶן
Impv. 2ms	שֵׁב	רַשׁ	הִוָּשֵׁב	הוֹשֵׁב		יְטַב	הֵיטֵב	בִּין
2fs	שְׁבִי	רְשִׁי	הִוָּשְׁבִי	הוֹשִׁיבִי		יִטְבִי	הֵיטִיבִי	בִּינִי
2mp	שְׁבוּ	רְשׁוּ	הִוָּשְׁבוּ	הוֹשִׁיבוּ		יִטְבוּ	הֵיטִיבוּ	בִּינוּ
2fp	שֵׁבְנָה	רַשְׁנָה	הִוָּשַׁבְנָה	הוֹשֵׁבְנָה		יְטַבְנָה	הֵיטֵבְנָה	
Inf. Abs.	יָשׁוֹב	יָרוֹשׁ		הוֹשֵׁב		יָטוֹב	הֵיטֵב	בּוֹן
Cst.	(לָ)שֶׁבֶת	(לָ)רֶשֶׁת	הִוָּשֵׁב	הוֹשִׁיב	הוּשַׁב	יְטֹב	הֵיטִיב	בִּין
+Suf.	(לְ)שִׁבְתִּי	(לְ)רִשְׁתִּי						בִּינִי
Part.	יֹשֵׁב	יֹרֵשׁ	נוֹשָׁב	מוֹשִׁיב	מוּשָׁב	יֹטֵב	מֵיטִיב	בָּן
	יָשׁוּב					יָטוּב		בּוֹן

(K) AYIN WAW VERB

Perf.	Qal	Niph'al	Hiph'il	Hoph'al
3ms	קָם	נָקוֹם	הֵקִים	הוּקַם
3fs	קָ֫מָה	נָק֫וֹמָה	הֵק֫ימָה	ה֫וּקְמָה
2ms	קַ֫מְתָּ	נְקוּמ֫וֹתָ	הֲקִימ֫וֹתָ	הוּקַ֫מְתָּ
2fs	קַמְתְּ	נְקוּמוֹת	הֲקִימוֹת	הוּקַמְתְּ
1cs	קַ֫מְתִּי	נְקוּמ֫וֹתִי	הֲקִימ֫וֹתִי	ה֫וּקַ֫מְתִּי
3cp	קָ֫מוּ	נָק֫וֹמוּ	הֵק֫ימוּ	ה֫וּקְמוּ
2mp	קַמְתֶּם	נְקוּמוֹתֶם	הֲקִימוֹתֶם	הוּקַמְתֶּם
2fp	קַמְתֶּן	נְקוּמוֹתֶן	הֲקִימוֹתֶן	הוּקַמְתֶּן
1cp	קַ֫מְנוּ	נְקוּמ֫וֹנוּ	הֲקִימ֫וֹנוּ	הוּקַ֫מְנוּ
Impf.				
3ms	יָקוּם	יִקּוֹם	יָקִים	יוּקַם
3fs	תָּקוּם	תִּקּוֹם	תָּקִים	תּוּקַם
2ms	תָּקוּם	תִּקּוֹם	תָּקִים	תּוּקַם
2fs	תָּק֫וּמִי	תִּקּ֫וֹמִי	תָּק֫ימִי	תּוּקְמִי
1cs	אָקוּם	אֶקּוֹם	אָקִים	אוּקַם

(L) PE NUN VERB

Perf.	Qal	Niph'al	Hiph'il	Hoph'al
3ms	נָתַן	נִגַּשׁ	הִגִּישׁ	הֻגַּשׁ
3fs	נָ֫תְנָה	נִגְּשָׁה	הִגִּ֫ישָׁה	הֻגְּשָׁה
2ms	נָתַ֫תָּ	נִגַּ֫שְׁתָּ	הִגַּ֫שְׁתָּ	הֻגַּ֫שְׁתָּ
2fs	נָתַתְּ	נִגַּשְׁתְּ	הִגַּשְׁתְּ	הֻגַּשְׁתְּ
1cs	נָתַ֫תִּי	נִגַּ֫שְׁתִּי	הִגַּ֫שְׁתִּי	הֻגַּ֫שְׁתִּי
3cp	נָ֫תְנוּ	נִגְּשׁוּ	הִגִּ֫ישׁוּ	הֻגְּשׁוּ
2mp	נְתַתֶּם	נִגַּשְׁתֶּם	הִגַּשְׁתֶּם	הֻגַּשְׁתֶּם
2fp	נְתַתֶּן	נִגַּשְׁתֶּן	הִגַּשְׁתֶּן	הֻגַּשְׁתֶּן
1cp	נָתַ֫נּוּ	נִגַּ֫שְׁנוּ	הִגַּ֫שְׁנוּ	הֻגַּ֫שְׁנוּ

	Qal Q¹	Qal Q²	Niph'al	Hiph'il	Hoph'al
Impf.					
3ms	יִפֹּל	יִגַּשׁ	יִנָּגֵשׁ	יַגִּישׁ	יֻגַּשׁ
3fs	תִּפֹּל	תִּגַּשׁ	תִּנָּגֵשׁ	תַּגִּישׁ	תֻּגַּשׁ
2ms	תִּפֹּל	תִּגַּשׁ	etc.	תַּגִּישׁ	etc.
2fs	תִּפְּלִי	תִּגְּשִׁי		תַּגִּ֫ישִׁי	
1cs	אֶפֹּל	אֶגַּשׁ		אַגִּישׁ	

	Qal	Niphal	Hiphil	Hophal	Polel	Polal	Hithpolel
3mp	יָקֻ֫מוּ	יִקֹּ֫מוּ	יָקִ֫ימוּ	יוּקְמוּ	יְקוֹמְמוּ	יְקוֹמְמוּ	יִתְקוֹמְמוּ
3fp	תְּקוּמֶ֫ינָה	תִּקֹּמְנָה	תָּקֵ֫מְנָה	תּוּקַמְנָה	תְּקוֹמֵ֫מְנָה	תְּקוֹמַ֫מְנָה	תִּתְקוֹמֵ֫מְנָה
2mp	תָּקֻ֫מוּ	תִּקֹּ֫מוּ	תָּקִ֫ימוּ	תּוּקְמוּ	תְּקוֹמְמוּ	תְּקוֹמְמוּ	תִּתְקוֹמְמוּ
2fp	תְּקוּמֶ֫ינָה	תִּקֹּמְנָה	תָּקֵ֫מְנָה	תּוּקַמְנָה	תְּקוֹמֵ֫מְנָה	תְּקוֹמַ֫מְנָה	תִּתְקוֹמֵ֫מְנָה
1cp	נָקוּם	נִקּוֹם	נָקִים	נוּקַם	נְקוֹמֵם		נִתְקוֹמֵם
Juss.	יָקֹם		יָקֵם				
+ Waw	וַיָּ֫קָם		וַיָּ֫קֶם				
Impv.							
2ms	קוּם	הִקּוֹם	הָקֵם		קוֹמֵם	etc.	הִתְקוֹמֵם
2fs	ק֫וּמִי	הִקּֽוֹמִי	הָקִ֫ימִי		קוֹמְמִי		הִתְקוֹמְמִי
2mp	ק֫וּמוּ	הִקּֽוֹמוּ	הָקִ֫ימוּ		קוֹמְמוּ		הִתְקוֹמְמוּ
2fp	קֹ֫מְנָה	הִקּוֹמֵ֫נָה	הָקֵ֫מְנָה		קוֹמֵ֫מְנָה		הִתְקוֹמֵ֫מְנָה
Coh.	ק֫וּמָה						
Inf.							
Abs.	קוֹם	הִקּוֹם	הָקֵם	הוּקֵם	קוֹמֵם		הִתְקוֹמֵם
Cst.	קוּם	הִקּוֹם	הָקִים	הוּקַם	קוֹמֵם		הִתְקוֹמֵם
+Suf.	ק֫וּמִי	הִקּֽוֹמִי	הֲקִימִי				
Part.	קָם	נָקוֹם	מֵקִים	מוּקָם	מְקוֹמֵם	מְקוֹמָם	מִתְקוֹמֵם
	קָם						

317

M) DOUBLE AYIN VERB

Aramaic Forms

	Qal	Hiph'il	Hoph'al

Perf.	Qal	Niph'al	Po'el	Po'al	Hiph'il	Hoph'al		Qal (Q³)	Hiph'il (Hi³)	Hoph'al (Ho³)
3ms	סָבַב, סַב	נָסַב	סוֹבֵב	סוֹבַב	הֵסֵב	הוּסַב		סַב	הֵסֵב	הֻסַב
3fs	סָבְבָה, סַבָּה	נָסַבָּה	סוֹבְבָה	סוֹבְבָה	הֵסֵבָּה	הוּסַבָּה		etc.		etc.
2ms	סַבּוֹתָ	נְסַבּוֹתָ	סוֹבַבְתָּ		הֲסִבּוֹתָ	הוּסַבְתָּ				
2fs	סַבּוֹת	נְסַבּוֹת	סוֹבַבְתְּ	etc.	הֲסִבּוֹת	הוּסַבְתְּ				
1cs	סַבּוֹתִי	נְסַבּוֹתִי	סוֹבַבְתִּי		הֲסִבּוֹתִי	הוּסַבּוֹתִי				
3cp	סָבְבוּ, סַבּוּ	נָסַבּוּ	סוֹבְבוּ		הֵסֵבּוּ	הוּסַבּוּ				
2mp	סַבּוֹתֶם	נְסַבּוֹתֶם	סוֹבַבְתֶּם		הֲסִבּוֹתֶם	הוּסַבּוֹתֶם				
2fp	סַבּוֹתֶן	נְסַבּוֹתֶן	סוֹבַבְתֶּן		הֲסִבּוֹתֶן	הוּסַבּוֹתֶן				
1cp	סַבּוֹנוּ	נְסַבּוֹנוּ	סוֹבַבְנוּ		הֲסִבּוֹנוּ	הוּסַבּוֹנוּ				

Impf.	Q¹	Q²(Stative)	Niph'al	Po'el	Po'al	Hiph'il	Hoph'al		Qal (Q³)	Hiph'il (Hi³)	Hoph'al (Ho³)
3ms	יָסֹב	יֵקַל	יִסַּב	יְסוֹבֵב	יְסוֹבַב	יָסֵב	יוּסַב		יִסַּב	הֵסֵב	הֻסַב
3fs	תָּסֹב	תֵּקַל	תִּסַּב	תְּסוֹבֵב	etc.	תָּסֵב	תּוּסַב		תִּסַּב	etc.	etc.
2ms	תָּסֹב	תֵּקַל	תִּסַּב	תְּסוֹבֵב		תָּסֵב	תּוּסַב		תִּסַּב		
2fs	תָּסֹבִּי	תֵּקַלִּי	תִּסַּבִּי	תְּסוֹבְבִי		תָּסֵבִּי	תּוּסַבִּי				
1cs	אָסֹב	אֵקַל	אֶסַּב	אֲסוֹבֵב		אָסֵב	אוּסַב		אֶסַּב		

3mp	יִסֹּב		יָסֹבּוּ	יִסַּבּוּ	יִסֹּב			
3fp	תִּסֹּב							
2mp			תָּסֹבּוּ	תִּסַּבּוּ	תִּסֹּב			
2fp								
1cp			נָסֹב	נִסַּב	נִסֹּב			
+Waw					וַיָּ֫סָב			

Impv. 2ms	סֹב		הָסֵב					
2fs	סֹ֫בִּי		הָסֵ֫בִּי					
2mp	סֹ֫בּוּ		הָסֵ֫בּוּ					
2fp	סֻבֶּ֫ינָה		הֲסִבֶּ֫ינָה					

Inf. Abs.	סָבוֹב		הָסֵב					
Cst.	סֹב (לָ)		הָסֵב					
Part.	סֹבֵב		מֵסֵב					

319

(N) LAMEDH HE VERB

Perf.	Qal	Niph'al	Pi'el	Pu'al	Hiph'il	Hoph'al	Hithpa'el
3ms	גָּלָה	נִגְלָה	גִּלָּה	גֻּלָּה	הִגְלָה	הָגְלָה	הִתְגַּלָּה
3fs	גָּלְתָה	נִגְלְתָה	גִּלְּתָה	גֻּלְּתָה	הִגְלְתָה	הָגְלְתָה	הִתְגַּלְּתָה
2ms	גָּלִיתָ	נִגְלֵיתָ	גִּלִּיתָ	גֻּלֵּיתָ	הִגְלֵיתָ	הָגְלֵיתָ	הִתְגַּלֵּיתָ
2fs	גָּלִית	נִגְלֵית	גִּלִּית	גֻּלֵּית	הִגְלֵית (־תְּ)	הָגְלֵית	הִתְגַּלֵּית (־תְּ) etc.
1cs	גָּלִיתִי	נִגְלֵיתִי	גִּלִּיתִי	גֻּלֵּיתִי	הִגְלֵיתִי (־תִי)	הָגְלֵיתִי	הִתְגַּלֵּיתִי
3cp	גָּלוּ	נִגְלוּ	גִּלּוּ (־לֵּי)	גֻּלּוּ	הִגְלוּ	הָגְלוּ	הִתְגַּלּוּ
2mp	גְּלִיתֶם	נִגְלֵיתֶם	גִּלִּיתֶם	גֻּלֵּיתֶם	הִגְלֵיתֶם (־תֶּם)	הָגְלֵיתֶם	הִתְגַּלִּיתֶם
2fp	גְּלִיתֶן	נִגְלֵיתֶן	גִּלִּיתֶן	גֻּלֵּיתֶן	הִגְלֵיתֶן (־תֶּן)	הָגְלֵיתֶן	הִתְגַּלִּיתֶן
1cp	גָּלִינוּ	נִגְלֵינוּ	גִּלִּינוּ	גֻּלֵּינוּ	הִגְלֵינוּ	הָגְלֵינוּ	הִתְגַּלֵּינוּ
Impf.							
3ms	יִגְלֶה	יִגָּלֶה	יְגַלֶּה	יְגֻלֶּה	יַגְלֶה	יָגְלֶה	יִתְגַּלֶּה
3fs	תִּגְלֶה	תִּגָּלֶה	תְּגַלֶּה	תְּגֻלֶּה	תַּגְלֶה	תָּגְלֶה	תִּתְגַּלֶּה
2ms	תִּגְלֶה	תִּגָּלֶה	תְּגַלֶּה	תְּגֻלֶּה	תַּגְלֶה	תָּגְלֶה	תִּתְגַּלֶּה
2fs	תִּגְלִי	תִּגָּלִי	תְּגַלִּי	תְּגֻלִּי	תַּגְלִי	תָּגְלִי	תִּתְגַּלִּי
1cs	אֶגְלֶה	אֶגָּלֶה	אֲגַלֶּה	אֲגֻלֶּה	אַגְלֶה	אָגְלֶה	אֶתְגַּלֶּה

3mp	יִגְלוּ	יִגָּלוּ	יְגַלּוּ	יְגֻלּוּ	יַגְלוּ	יָגְלוּ	יִתְגַּלּוּ
3fp	תִּגְלֶינָה	תִּגָּלֶינָה	תְּגַלֶּינָה	תְּגֻלֶּינָה	תַּגְלֶינָה	תָּגְלֶינָה	תִּתְגַּלֶּינָה
2mp	תִּגְלוּ	תִּגָּלוּ	תְּגַלּוּ	תְּגֻלּוּ	תַּגְלוּ	תָּגְלוּ	תִּתְגַּלּוּ
2fp	תִּגְלֶינָה	תִּגָּלֶינָה	תְּגַלֶּינָה	תְּגֻלֶּינָה	תַּגְלֶינָה	תָּגְלֶינָה	תִּתְגַּלֶּינָה
1cp	נִגְלֶה	נִגָּלֶה	נְגַלֶּה	נְגֻלֶּה	נַגְלֶה	נָגְלֶה	נִתְגַּלֶּה
Juss.	יִ֫גֶל	יִגָּל	יְגַל	יְגֻל	יֶ֫גֶל	יָ֫גֶל	יִתְגַּל
Impv.							
2ms	גְּלֵה	הִגָּלֵה	גַּלֵּה, גַּל		הַגְלֵה, הֶ֫גֶל		הִתְגַּלֵּה
2fs	גְּלִי	הִגָּלִי	גַּלִּי		הַגְלִי		הִתְגַּלִּי
2mp	גְּלוּ	הִגָּלוּ	גַּלּוּ		הַגְלוּ		הִתְגַּלּוּ
2fp	גְּלֶינָה	הִגָּלֶינָה	גַּלֶּינָה		הַגְלֶינָה		הִתְגַּלֶּינָה
Inf. Abs.	גָּלֹה	נִגְלֹה	גַּלֹּה, גַּלֵּה		הַגְלֵה	הָגְלֵה	
Cst.	גְּלוֹת	הִגָּלוֹת	גַּלּוֹת	גֻּלּוֹת	הַגְלוֹת	הָגְלוֹת	הִתְגַּלּוֹת
Part.	גֹּלֶה גָּלוּי	נִגְלֶה	מְגַלֶּה	מְגֻלֶּה	מַגְלֶה	מָגְלֶה	מִתְגַּלֶּה

Perf.	Qal	Niph'al	Pi'el	Pu'al	Hiph'il
3ms	מָצָא	נִמְצָא	מִלֵּא	מֻלָּא	הִמְצִיא
3fs	מָצְאָה	נִמְצְאָה	מִלְּאָה	מֻלְּאָה	הִמְצִיאָה
2ms	מָצָאתָ	נִמְצֵאתָ	מִלֵּאתָ	מֻלֵּאתָ	הִמְצֵאתָ
2fs	מָצָאת	נִמְצֵאת	מִלֵּאת	etc.	הִמְצֵאת
1cs	מָצָאתִי	נִמְצֵאתִי	מִלֵּאתִי		הִמְצֵאתִי
3cp	מָצְאוּ	נִמְצְאוּ	מִלְּאוּ		הִמְצִיאוּ
2mp	מְצָאתֶם	נִמְצֵאתֶם	מִלֵּאתֶם		הִמְצֵאתֶם
2fp	מְצָאתֶן	נִמְצֵאתֶן	מִלֵּאתֶן		הִמְצֵאתֶן
1cp	מָצָאנוּ	נִמְצֵאנוּ	מִלֵּאנוּ		הִמְצֵאנוּ

Impf.					
3ms	יִמְצָא	יִמָּצֵא	יְמַלֵּא	יְמֻלָּא	יַמְצִיא
3fs	תִּמְצָא	תִּמָּצֵא	etc.	etc.	תַּמְצִיא
2ms	תִּמְצָא	תִּמָּצֵא			תַּמְצִיא
2fs	תִּמְצְאִי	תִּמָּצְאִי			תַּמְצִיאִי
1cs	אֶמְצָא	אֶמָּצֵא			אַמְצִיא
3mp	יִמְצְאוּ	יִמָּצְאוּ			יַמְצִיאוּ
3fp	תִּמְצֶאנָה	תִּמָּצֶאנָה			תַּמְצֶאנָה
2mp	תִּמְצְאוּ	תִּמָּצְאוּ			תַּמְצִיאוּ
2fp	תִּמְצֶאנָה	תִּמָּצֶאנָה			תַּמְצֶאנָה
1cp	נִמְצָא	נִמָּצֵא			נַמְצִיא

Impv.					
2ms	מְצָא	הִמָּצֵא	מַלֵּא		הַמְצֵא
2fs	מִצְאִי	הִמָּצְאִי	etc.		הַמְצִיאִי
2mp	מִצְאוּ	הִמָּצְאוּ			הַמְצִיאוּ
2fp	מְצֶאנָה	הִמָּצֶאנָה			הַמְצֶאנָה

Inf.					
Abs.	מָצוֹא	נִמְצֹא	מַלֹּא		הַמְצֵא
Cst.	מְצֹא	הִמָּצֵא	מַלֵּא		הַמְצִיא

| Part. | מֹצֵא, מָצוּא | נִמְצָא | מְמַלֵּא | מְמֻלָּא | מַמְצִיא |

VOCABULARIES

HEBREW-ENGLISH VOCABULARY[1]

א

אָב father (*Irr*)

אָבַד Q[6], perish; Pi. (*in* —)
or Hi[1], destroy

אָבָה Q[6], be willing

אֶבְיוֹן 34, poor, needy

אֶבֶן 9, (f) stone (*Irr*)

אָדוֹן 9, master, lord

אָדָם 24, man; mankind

אֲדָמָה ground

אֲדֹנָי Lord (30, 50)

אֶדְרָעִי Edrei

אָהַב Q[3, 4], love (219)

אֹהֶל tent, tabernacle

אוֹ 9, or

אָוָה Hith., desire for oneself

אָוֶן nothingness, vanity,
wickedness

אוֹר be light, shine; Hi., illu-
minate (267)

אוֹר 15, light

אוֹת 28, (f) sign

אָז 26, then

אָזַן Hi[1], give ear, hear

אֹזֶן (f) ear

אָח brother (*Irr*)

אֶחָד one (44)

אָחוֹת sister (*Irr*)

אָחַז Q[6], seize, hold

---

1 The vocabulary in which a word is first given is indicated by the
chapter numeral after the word (except those in Chs. 17-22, and 39-
52, which are self-evident). Fifth declension words are marked (5).
Feminines with segolate forms are marked (2). All nouns listed in
Ch. 22 are marked (*Irr*). Regular stative verbs are marked (A).
For other words specially discussed, page references are given, making
a complete Hebrew index. All words in Dt. 3–5 are included.

אַחֵר 10, other, another; second (*Irr*)

אַחַר, אַחֲרֵי 9, after, behind (137)

אַחֲרֵי־אֲשֶׁר 14, after

אַחֲרֵי־כֵן 10, afterwards

אַחֲרִית final end

אַחַת *fem. of* אֶחָד

אֹיֵב enemy (118)

אַיֵּה 26, where?

אֵיךְ 26, how?

אַיִל ram

אֵין (אַיִן) nothing; not (135, 199)

אִישׁ 7, man; husband (*Irr*)

אַךְ 26, surely; only; wholly

אָכַל Q⁶, eat, devour; Pi., consume; Hi¹, feed

אָכְלָה *or* אֹכֶל 34, food

אֵל God

אֶל 8, unto (77)

אַל not (168)

אֵלֶּה these (61)

אֱלֹהִים 8, God (50, 56)

אֶלֶף thousand

אֵם mother (5)

אִם 9, if; whether; *sign of question* (54)

אַמָּה 23, cubit

אָמָה handmaid (*Irr*)

אֱמוּנָה 35, faithfulness

אָמַן Ni¹, be firm, faithful; Hi¹, trust; Qal Pass. Part., the faithful

אָמַץ Pi., strengthen, encourage

אָמַר 9, Q⁶, say; Ni¹, *Pass.* (222)

אֱמֹרִי Amorite

אֱמֶת 28, (f) truth

אֲנַחְנוּ we

אָנֹכִי, אֲנִי I

אָנַף Hith., be angry

אָסַף Q⁵, collect, gather, assemble

אָסַר 13, Q⁵, bind; Ni¹, *Pass.*

אַף nose; anger (5)

אָפָה Q⁶, bake

אַרְבָּעָה, אַרְבַּע four

אַרְגֹּב Argob

אָרוֹן 16, ark

אֶרֶז 33, cedar

אֲרִי lion (*Irr*)

אֹרֶךְ 34, length

אָרַךְ Hi[1], prolong; be made long

אַרְנֹן Arnon

אֶרֶץ 8, (f) earth, land, country (44)

אָרַר Q[1], curse

אֵשׁ (1) fire

אֲשֵׁדָה ravine

אִשָּׁה 9, woman; wife (*Irr*)

אָשֵׁם Q[4], transgress; be guilty

אָשָׁם 33, guilt-offering

אֲשֶׁר who, which, what (80)

אֵת 8, with (76)

אֵת, אֶת־ *sign of accusative* (45; 78)

אַתָּ, אַתָּה thou

אַתֶּן, אַתֶּם ye

ב

בְּ in, on; among; with (49, 76; 153)

בֶּגֶד (i) garment

בַּד 24, separation; *with* מִן, besides; לְבַדִּי, by myself

בָּדַל 31, Hi., separate, select, choose out; Ni., *Pass.*

בְּהֵמָה 12, cattle; beast (112)

בּוֹא come; Hi., bring (267)

בּוֹשׁ be ashamed; Hi., put to shame (267)

בָּזַז Q[1], plunder, seize as prey, spoil

בָּחַר 35, choose, desire, delight in

בָּטַח 36, trust, be confident

בֵּין 24, between (138)

בִּין perceive, discern; Hi., explain

בִּינָה understanding, intelligence

בַּיִת 9, house (*Irr*)

בָּכָה weep (238)

בְּכוֹר 12, first-born

בָּלַל Q[1], anoint

בָּלַע 12, Q. *or* Pi., swallow, consume, destroy

בְּלִי, בִּלְתִּי not (192)

בָּמָה 32, high place (— fixed)

בֵּן 8, son (Irr)

בָּנָה 9, build

בַּעֲבוּר 25, for the sake of, on account of

בַּעַל master

בָּעַר Q. or Pi2, burn, set fire to (בְּ); consume

בָּצַר 31, cut off, fortify

בֶּצֶר Bezer

בָּקַע 12, cleave; Pi., rend, tear in pieces

בָּקָר 23, cattle

בֹּקֶר morning

בָּקַשׁ 28, Pi., seek, search, inquire of (158)

בָּרָא create

בַּרְזֶל iron

בָּרַח 31, flee

בְּרִיחַ bar, bolt

בְּרִית 10, (f) covenant

בָּרַךְ Pi1, bless

בְּרָכָה 8, blessing; gift

בָּשָׂר 25, flesh

בָּשָׁן Bashan

בַּת 7, daughter (Irr)

ג

גָּאַל redeem, deliver

גָּבַהּ be high; Hi., exalt

גָּבֹהַּ high; tall

גְּבוּל 11, territory; boundary

גִּבּוֹר 15, mighty man, hero; warrior

גְּבוּרָה 14, strength, might

גִּבְעָה hill (2)

גָּדוֹל 10, great, large

גָּדִי Gadites

גָּדַל 36, (A) be, become great; grow up; Hi., make great

גֹּדֶל greatness

גּוֹי 11, nation

גּוֹלָן Golan

גּוּר sojourn

גַּיְא valley (Irr)

גָּלָה disclose; go into captivity; Pi., reveal,

uncover; Hi., carry
away captive

גִּלְעָד Gilead

גַּם 30, also; even

גָּמָל 9, camel (5)

גָּנַב 31, steal

גֵּר 12, stranger, sojourner

גָּרַע take away, detract

גָּרַשׁ Pi¹, drive out

גְּשׁוּרִי Geshurites

ד

דָּבֵק 34, (A) cleave, adhere
(to, בּ or לְ)

דָּבַר 27, Pi., speak; Ni. or
Hith., converse with
(159)

דְּבָר 11, word; thing

דֶּבֶר 29, plague

דָּגָה fish

דּוֹר 12, generation

דֶּלֶת (f) gate

דָּם 12, blood

דְּמוּת (f) likeness

דָּמַם Q³, be silent

דַּעַת 28, (f) knowledge

דֶּרֶךְ 15, way, path; journey

דָּרַשׁ 29, seek, ask, require

ה

ה Article (43)
Cohortative (164, 168)
Feminine ending (60, 93)
Interrogative (53)
Locative (95)
Paragogic (297)
Pronoun suffix (70)
Vocative (44)
Voice preformative (152)

הוּא he; that (61, 66)

הִיא she; that (61, 66)

הָיָה be, become; come to
pass, happen (174,
198, 239, 291)

הֵיכָל 7, temple, palace

הָלַךְ 8, go, walk; Hi., lead,
take away (248)

הָלַל Pi., praise; Hith., boast

הֵן, הֵנָּה, הֵם, הֵמָּה, tney;
those (61, 66)

הֵן, הִנֵּה behold! (136)

הֵנָּה 30, hither

הָפַךְ Q¹, turn; Ni², turn back; be changed

הַר 7, mountain (44; 5)

הָרַג Q¹, kill

ו

וְ and; but (50, 55, 171, 178)

ז

זֹאת this (61)

זָבַח 32, sacrifice

זֶבַח (i) sacrifice

זֶה this (61)

זָהָב 11, gold

זוּב flow

זוּלָתִי except, aside from

זוּר turn aside; Part., stranger

זָכַר 7, remember; Hi., bring to remembrance, c o m m e m o r a t e; mention

זָכָר 31, male

זָמַר 33, Pi., sing

זָנָה commit fornication

זָעַק 32, cry out, exclaim

זָקֵן 36, (A) be, become old

זָקֵן old; old man, elder

זְרוֹעַ 25, (f) arm; might, power

זָרַע 31, sow

זֶרַע 24, seed

ח

חֶבֶל region, district

חַג 25, feast, festival (5)

חָדַל Q⁴, cease

חָדָשׁ 35, new

חֹדֶשׁ 16, new moon; month

חַוָּה town, village

חוֹמָה 11, wall

חוּץ 16, outside; street (*Irr*; 51)

חָזָה Q³, see, gaze upon

חֹזֶה seer

חָזַק Q³, be, become strong; Pi., strengthen; Hi¹, make firm, hold fast; seize (223)

חָזָק 10, strong

חָטָא Q³, sin; Hi¹, cause to sin

חַטָּאת 25, (f) sin (2; Plu., חַטָּאוֹת; 111)

חִטָּה 33, wheat (Irr)

חַי alive, living; Abstract Plu., life (123; 5)

חָיָה live; Pi. or Hi., give life to, revive, preserve alive (239, 291)

חַיִל strength, might

חִיל writhe in pain, tremble

חִיצוֹן 10, outer

חָכָם 10, wise

חָכְמָה 24, wisdom

חֵלֶב 34, fat

חָלָה Q³, be, become sick

חֲלוֹם 9, dream (Irr)

חָלוּץ armed

חָלִילָה God forbid (192)

חָלַל Pi., profane, defile; Hi¹, begin

חָלַק Q¹ or Pi., divide, distribute

חֵלֶק portion, share (110)

חָמַד take delight in, covet

חֵמָה 33, heat; anger, wrath

חֲמוֹר 12, ass

חָמָס 35, violence, wrong, oppression

חֲמִשָּׁה, חָמֵשׁ five

חֵן grace, favor (5)

חָנָה Q¹, encamp

חָנַן Q¹, be gracious to; Hith., entreat (278)

חֶסֶד 15, goodwill, kindness, mercy

חָפֵץ Q²,⁴, delight in, desire

חֵץ arrow (5)

חֲצִי 16, half

חָצֵר 16, court; village

חֻקָּה, חֹק statute (123;5)

חֹרֵב Horeb

חֶרֶב 13, (f) sword

חָרַד Q³, tremble; Hi¹, terrify

חָרָה Q³, burn (of anger); be angry

חָרַם Hi¹, devote

חֶרְמוֹן Hermon

חֶרְפָּה 30, reproach (2)

חָרַשׁ Q¹, plough; Hi¹, be silent; put to silence

חָשַׁב Q² or Pi., think, reckon, devise; Ni², be regarded as

חֶשְׁבּוֹן Heshbon

חֹשֶׁךְ 28, darkness

חֹתֵן father-in-law

חָתַת Q², be dismayed; Hi¹, terrify, confound

ט

טָהוֹר 35, clean

טָהֵר be, become clean, pure; Pi³, cleanse, purify; pronounce clean; Hith.², purify oneself

טוֹב 10, good

טָמֵא be, become unclean; Pi., defile, pollute; Ni. or Hith., defile oneself

טַף children

טֶרֶם, or בְּטֶרֶם 26, before (148)

׳

יָאִיר Jair

יְאֹר 10, river (esp. the Nile)

יַבֹּק Jabbok

יָבֵשׁ Q², be dry; dry up; Hi¹, make dry, dry up

יָד 12, (f) hand (99)

יָדָה Hi¹, praise; celebrate (248)

יָדַע Q¹, know; Hi¹, show, make known (248)

יְהֹוָה 8, Jehovah (30, 50, 292)

יְהוֹשׁוּעַ Joshua

יוֹבֵל 25, jubilee

יוֹם 16, day (Irr)

יַחְדָּו 26, together

יָטַב Q³, be good; be well; Hi³, do good, do well (249)

יַיִן 24, wine

יָכַח Hi¹, decide; reprove, chasten, punish

יָכֹל be able; with לְ, prevail over (248)

יָלַד Q¹, bear, bring forth; Ni., be born; Hi¹, beget

יֶלֶד 15, child

יָלַל Hi³, wail (עַל, for)

יָם sea (5)

יָמִין 24, (f) right hand

יָנַק Q³, suck; Hi³, suckle

יָסַף Hi¹, add, increase (248)

יָסַר Pi., admonish

יָעַץ Q², give counsel; purpose; Ni., take coun-
sel

יַעַר 32, forest

יָפֶה fair, beautiful

יָצָא 13, Q¹, go out; Hi¹,
bring, lead, or send
out (248)

יָצַק Q⁴, pour

יָצַר Q⁴, form, fashion, make

יָרֵא 34, Q², fear, be afraid;
Ni. Part., dreadful,
fearful (192; 248)

יָרַד Q¹, go down; Hi¹, bring
down

יַרְדֵן Jordan

יָרָה Hi¹, throw, shoot;
instruct (248)

יְרוּשָׁלֵם 8, Jerusalem (292)

יָרֵחַ moon

יְרִיחוֹ 9, Jericho

יְרִיעָה 12, curtain

יָרַשׁ Q² or Hi¹, take possession, occupy, dis-
possess (243)

יְרֻשָּׁה possession

יִשְׂרָאֵל 9, Israel

יֵשׁ there is (135)

יָשַׁב 8, Q¹, sit, dwell, inhabit

יֹשֵׁב inhabitant

יְשׁוּעָה deliverance

יָשֵׁן Ni., be old

יָשַׁע Hi¹, save, deliver; Ni.,
Pass.

יָשַׁר Q³, be straight, right;
Pi., make straight,
even

יָשָׁר straight, right, upright

יָתַר Hi¹, let remain, leave;
Ni., be left, remain

יֶתֶר (i) remnant

כ

כְּ like; according to (49, 76)

כַּאֲשֶׁר 14, as; when

כָּבֵד 36, (A) be heavy; Ni.,
be honored; Pi., hon-
or; Hi., make heavy

כָּבֵד heavy; hard

כָּבוֹד 25, glory, honor, majesty

כָּבַס 35, Pi., wash, cleanse;
Q. Part., fuller (159)

כֶּבֶשׂ 23, he-lamb, young
ram

כֹּה 11, thus (*refers ahead*)

כֹּהֵן priest

כּוֹכָב star

כּוּן Hi. *or* Po., set up, appoint, establish; Ni.,
Pass.

כּוּר furnace

כֹּחַ 28, strength

כִּי that; for; when; if; but
(56)

כִּי אִם but (56)

כֹּל 15, all; whole; every;
with לֹא, none; (62,
89, 123; 5)

כֶּלֶב 9, dog

כָּלָה be complete, finished;
Pi., complete, finish,
destroy

כְּלִי vessel, weapon, implement, utensil (*Irr*)

כֵּן 11, thus (*refers back*)

כָּנָף (f) wing (101)

כִּנֶּרֶת Chinnereth

כִּסֵּא throne (*Irr;* 118)

כָּסָה Pi., cover, conceal

כְּסִיל 31, fool

כֶּסֶף 13, silver

כָּעַס 33, Hi., provoke

כַּף (f) palm (5)

כָּפַר 29, Pi., cover; atone
for, expiate; forgive
(159)

כְּרוּב 12, cherub

כֶּרֶם 9, vineyard

כָּרַת 13, cut, cut off (78)

כָּשַׁל 35, be weak; totter,
stumble

כָּתַב 30, write

כָּתֵף (f) shoulder (113)

ל

לְ to; for (49; 76; 153; 189)

לֹא not (56; 168, 192, 199)

לֵב (5) *or* לֵבָב 24, heart
(*Irr*)

לַבָּה flame

לְבָנוֹן Lebanon

לָבַשׁ 33, Q. (A) *or* Hi., put on

לוּחַ tablet, table

לוּן pass the night; lodge

לָחַם 29, Ni., fight (בְּ, against)

לֶחֶם bread

לַיְלָה 16, (m) night (95; *Irr*)

לָכַד 31, take, capture

לָכֵן 26, therefore

לָמַד 33, (A) learn; Pi., teach

לָמָה why? (54)

לְמַעַן 26, in order that; because of (148)

לָקַח 11, take (257)

לָשׁוֹן tongue

מ

מְאֹד 10, very

מֵאָה hundred

מֵאָז 34, since

מָאֵן Pi¹, refuse, be unwilling

מָאַס 34, reject, refuse, despise

מִגְדָּל 12, tower

מָגֵן shield (5; — *fixed*)

מִגְרָשׁ 28, pasture

מִדְבָּר desert

מָדַד Q¹, measure

מִדָּה measure

מְדִינָה 12, province

מָה, מַה what? how! (54)

מָהַר Pi³, hasten

מוּל in front of, opposite

מוּסָר 32, chastisement; admonition

מוֹעֵד set time; assembly

מוֹפֵת miracle

מוֹקֵשׁ snare

מוֹרָא wonderful deed

מוּת die; Ni., kill (267)

מָוֶת death

מִזְבֵּחַ altar (*Irr; Cst. in* —)

מִזְמוֹר 33, song, psalm

מִזְרָח rising (of sun); east

מַחֲנֶה camp; army

מַחֲשֶׁבֶת counsel, purpose, plan

מַטֶּה rod; tribe (*Irr*)

מִי who? (53)

מַיִם water (*Irr*)

מִישׁר plain

מָכִיר Machir

מָכַר 33, sell

מָלֵא be full; Pi., fill

מַלְאָךְ 9, angel; messenger

מְלָאכָה work, labor, business (2)

מֶלַח salt

מִלְחָמָה 14, war (2; 90, 112)

מָלַט 27, Pi., deliver; Ni., be delivered, escape

מָלַךְ 11, 27, be, become king; rule(עַל, over); Hi., make king, crown

מֶלֶךְ 7, king

מַלְכָּה queen (2)

מַמְלָכָה kingdom (2)

מִן from (50; 62; 76; 153; 192)

מִנְחָה 16, meal-offering (2)

מְנַצֵּח 33, precentor, chief musician

מְנַשִּׁי Manassites

מַסָּה trial

מָסַס Ni., melt, faint

מִסְפָּר 23, number

מְעַט 15, little, few; fewness (89, 113)

מַעֲכָתִי Maachathites

מָעַל act treacherously

מַעַל 16, above; up

מַעֲשֶׂה work, deed

מַעֲשֵׂר tithe (*Irr; Cst. in* —)

מָצָא find

מַצָּה 25, unleavened

מִצְוָה 16, command (95)

מִצְרַיִם Egypt; Egyptians

מִקְדָּשׁ 31, sanctuary

מָקוֹם 14, place (*Irr*)

מִקְנֶה wealth, cattle

מַרְאָה sight; appearance

מָרָה Q. *or* Hi., rebel

מָרַר Q², be bitter; Hi¹, embitter (278)

מֹשֶׁה Moses

מָשַׁח 33, anoint

מָשִׁיחַ anointed one; Messiah

מָשַׁךְ 33, pull, draw, drag

מִשְׁכָּן 12, dwelling-place

מָשַׁל 30, rule, have dominion (בְּ, over)

מִשָּׁם 14, thence

מִשְׁמֶרֶת (f) custody; charge

מִשְׁפָּחָה 12, family, clan (2)

מִשְׁפָּט judgment; justice

מַת, Plu. מְתִים males, men;

מְתֵי מִסְפָּר few men

נ

נָא prithee (164, 168)

נְאֻם 15, oracle

נָאַף Q. *or* Pi., commit adultery

נָבָא Ni., prophesy

נָבוֹן discreet, intelligent

נָבַט Hi., look, behold; have respect to

נָבִיא 7, prophet

נֶגֶב the South

נָגַד Hi., tell, announce, declare

נָגַע strike, smite; touch

נָגַף smite

נָגַשׁ (A) draw near, approach; Hi., bring near (253)

נָדַח Hi., thrust out, expel; Ni., *Pass.;* be seduced

נֶדֶר 28, vow

נָהַג Q. *or* Pi., lead, drive

נָהָר stream, river

נוּחַ rest; Hi., הֵנִיחַ, set down; הִנִּיחַ, give rest to (267)

נוּם flee; Hi., put to flight

נָחַל get as a possession, inherit; Hi., cause to inherit

נַחַל brook; torrent

נַחֲלָה 29, possession (2)

נָחַם Ni., lament, grieve; Pi[3], comfort (256)

נְחֹשֶׁת 24, (f) brass; copper

נָטָה stretch; turn away; Hi., turn away, pervert (256)

נָטַע plant

נָכָה Hi., smite, strike (256)

נָכַר Hi., look upon; know

נָסָה Pi., try

נָסַע pull up; remove (camp)

נַעַר lad, attendant, servant

נַעֲרָה maiden, maidservant (2)

נָפַל fall; Hi., let fall, throw down

נֶפֶשׁ 15, (f) soul; life

נָצַב Ni., stand; Hi., set, place

נָצַל Hi., snatch, deliver, preserve; Ni., *Pass.*

נָצַר keep, guard, watch

נְקֵבָה female

נָקָה Pi., acquit, let go unpunished; Ni., be innocent

נָקַם avenge; Ni., avenge oneself, be avenged

נָשָׂא lift up; bear; take away; forgive (257)

נָשַׂג Hi., attain to; overtake

נָשִׂיא 23, prince

נָשַׁל put off

נָשַׁק (A) kiss (*with* לְ; 253)

נָתַן 8, give; *with Accus. and Inf.*, permit (256)

ס

סָבַב Q[1,3], turn; surround; Hi[1,3], turn, cause to turn

סָבִיב 25, circuit; *Adv. Accus. with* לְ, around, about

סָגַר 31, shut, close; Hi., deliver over

סוּס 10, horse

סוּר turn aside, away; Hi., put away, remove (267)

סִיחֹן Sihon

סַלְכָה Salchah

סֶמֶל likeness, image

סָפַר 27, count; Pi., recount, declare, narrate

3, congregation	קָרָה Q. or Ni., meet
voice; sound (*Irr*)	קָרוֹב 10, near
se, rise up; Hi., raise p	קִרְיָה city, town
	קֶרֶן 14, (f) horn
(A) be small; Hi., ake small	קָרַע 32, rend, tear
	קָשֶׁה hard; stubborn
Pi., burn incense	קֶשֶׁת 31, (f) bow
be insignificant; i., be light; Hi¹, ke light	**ר**
s	רָאָה 7, see, look; Ni., be seen, appear; Hi., show (238)
tain	
	רְאוּבֵנִי Reubenites
xtremity	רָאמֹת Ramoth
st	רֹאשׁ 10, head, top (*Irr*)
o, harvest	רִאשׁוֹן 10, first
happen, meet	רֵאשִׁית 30, (f) beginning; first-fruits
call to; name	רֹב abundance, multitude, greatness (5)
draw near, ap-; Hi., bring ffer	רַב great; much, many; enough! (5)
	רְבָבָה myriad; ten thousand
dst	רָבָה be, become many, great; increase; Hi., make great, in-crease; *Inf. Abs.*,

סֵפֶר book	עוֹלָה 16, burnt-offering
סָתַר 28, Hi., hide, conceal; Ni. or Hith., be hid, hide oneself	עוֹלָם 25, eternity
	עָוֹן iniquity (*Irr*)
ע	עוֹף fly
עָבַד 13, Q¹, serve; Hi¹, cause to work	עוּר awake; be awake; Hi., waken
עֶבֶד 10, servant; *Abstract Plu.*, bondage	עִוֵּר blind (118)
עֲבוֹדָה 14, servitude	עָזַב Q¹, forsake
עָבַר Q¹, cross over; Hi¹, bring, send over; Hith., be wroth	עָזַר Q¹, help
	עַיִן (f) eye
עֵבֶר 30, region beyond; אֶל־עֵבֶר or בְּעֵבֶר, beyond, across	עִיר 16, (f) city (*Irr*)
	עַל 7, upon; by, near; con-cerning; against (77)
עֵד 12, witness	עַל־כֵּן 26, therefore
עַד 9, as far as; until	עָלָה Q¹, go up; Hi¹, bring, send up
עַד־אֲשֶׁר 26, until	עַם 8, people (5; 44)
עַד־מָתַי 26, how long?	עִם 7, with (76)
עֵדָה congregation; ordi-nance	עָמַד 14, Q¹, stand; Hi¹, make stand, set, es-tablish
עוֹג Og	עִמָּד with
עוּד Hi., call as witness (בְּ, against)	עַמּוּד 24, column, pillar
עוֹד still; yet; again (136, 199)	עַמּוֹן Ammon

עֵמֶק valley

עָנָה Q¹, answer; speak

עָנָה Q¹, labor, suffer; Pi., oppress, afflict

עֳנִי 9, affliction, misery, poverty

עָנָן cloud

עָפָר 25, dust (*Irr*)

עֵץ tree

עָצוּם mighty, powerful

עֶצֶם (f) bone

עֶרֶב 28, evening

עֲרָבָה 16, desert (Arabah)

עָרַךְ Q¹, prepare, set in array

עֲרֹעֵר Aroer

עֲרָפֶל thick clouds, darkness

עֶרֶשׂ bed, couch

עָשָׂה 14, Q¹, do, make

עֶשְׂרֵה, עָשָׂר ten

עֵת (f) time (5; *Irr*)

עַתָּה 12, now

פ

פָּדָה set free, ransom

פֹּה 9, here

פֶּה mouth (*Irr*)

פּוּץ Q. *or* Hi., scatter, disperse; Ni., *Pass*.

פֶּחָה governor (*Irr*)

פָּלָא Ni., be wonderful; Part., a wonder; Hi., make great, wonderful

פָּלַל Hith., supplicate, pray, intercede

פֶּן 26, lest (148)

פָּנָה turn

פָּנֶה *used only in Plu.*, פָּנִים, face; לִפְנֵי before, in front of (137)

פִּסְגָּה Pisgah

פֶּסֶל carved image

פְּעוֹר Peor

פָּעַל 14, do

פַּעַם 23, (f) time (*Irr*)

פָּקַד 27, visit; charge; look upon; Hi., appoint, set over, make overseer

פַּר bullock (5)

פְּרָזִי rustic; עָרֵי פְרָזִי country towns

פְּרִי fruit

פָּרַשׂ 30, spread, spread ... scatter

פָּרָשׁ 29, horseman (*fi... fixed*)

פֶּשַׁע 16, (i) transgr... trespass

פֶּתַח (i) door

צ

צֹאן 12, flock

צָבָא 25, host (*Irr...*)

צַדִּיק 10, just, ri...

צָדַק 28, (A) b... eous; ... make ri... tify; ... oneself

צֶדֶק (i) right...

צְדָקָה righte...

צָוָה Pi., co...

צוּר 12, ro...

צִידוֹנִים S...

קָהָל 2...

קוֹל 9,

קוּם ari... u...

קָטַל kil...

קָטֹן 36, ... n...

קָטַר 34,

קָלַל Q², N... ma...

קִנְא jealou...

קָנָה get, o...

קָנֶה reed

קָצֶה end, e...

קָצִיר harve...

קָצַר 31, rea...

קָרָא befall, (230)

קָרָא cry out...

קָרַב 27, (A) ... proach... near, ...

קָרֵב 15, (i) mi...

קָרְבָּן 33, gift

much, many, greatly (238)

רַבָּה Rabbah

רְבַע a fourth-generation descendant

רָגַל 34, walk; Pi., spy out

רֶגֶל (f) foot

רָדַף 29, pursue

רוּחַ 15, (f) spirit; breath

רוּחַ Hi., smell

רוּם be high, lifted up; Po. or Hi., lift up

רוּץ run; Hi., make run

רֹחַב 34, breadth

רַחוּם merciful, compassionate

רָחַם Pi[3], have mercy, pity; Pu[2], find mercy

רָחַץ wash

רָחַק 28, be distant; Hi., remove

רִיב strive, contend

רִיב 13, contention, controversy

רֵיחַ 34, smell, odor

רָכַב 36, (A) ride

רֶכֶב 29, (i) chariot

רָם 10, high, tall

רָמַשׂ creep, crawl

רָנַן Q[1] or Pi., shout for joy, rejoice

רֵעַ 12, friend, neighbor

רַע evil, bad (5)

רָעָב 29, famine

רָעָה feed (238)

רֹעֶה shepherd \

רָעַע Q[2], be evil, bad; Hi[1], do evil (278)

רָפָא heal, cure

רְפָאִים Rephaim, giants

רָפָה Hi., forsake

רָצָה 9, delight in, be gracious to, receive graciously

רָצוֹן delight, pleasure; לְרָצוֹן acceptable, delightful

רָצַח slay, murder

רַק 23, only; surely

רָשָׁע evil

ש

שָׂבַע be, become satisfied; Hi., satisfy

שָׂדֶה field (*Irr*)

שֶׂה sheep; goat (*Irr*)

שִׂים *see* שׂוּם

שָׂחַק 35, laugh (לְ, at)

שִׂיאָן Sion

שִׂים set, put, place, lay

שָׂכַל 28, Hi., be wise, act wisely; make wise

שְׂמֹאל left hand

שָׂמַח 34, rejoice, be glad; Pi., rejoice, make glad

שִׂמְחָה 16, joy, festivity (2)

שִׂמְלָה garment (2)

שָׂנֵא 36, hate

שְׂנִיר Senir

שָׂפָה lip; edge

שַׂר 15, prince (5)

שָׂרִיד survivor

שִׂרְיוֹן Sirion

שָׂרַף 29, burn

ש

שְׁאוֹל 13, Sheol

שָׁאַל 9, ask (לְ, about)

שָׁאַר 29, Hi., leave, let remain; Ni., be left, remain

שָׁבָה take captive (238)

שְׁבוּת 24, (f) captivity; captives (*coll.*)

שֵׁבֶט rod; tribe

שְׁבִיעִי seventh

שָׁבַע 31, Ni., swear (בְּ, by; לְ, to); Hi., adjure, bind with an oath

שִׁבְעָה, שֶׁבַע seven

שָׁבַר 30, break

שָׁבַת 31, rest, cease; Hi., give rest to

שַׁבָּת (f) rest; Sabbath (5)

שָׁדַד Q¹, do violence, oppress; spoil, destroy

שָׁוְא emptiness; iniquity; falsehood

שׁוּב turn, return (268); Hi., turn, bring back; שׁוּב אֶל־לֵב, recall to mind, lay to heart

שׁוֹפָר trumpet (*Irr*)

שׁוֹר 34, ox (*Plu.,* שְׁוָרִים; 111)

שָׁחָה Hith., bow down, worship (239)

שָׁחַט slaughter

שָׁחַת 33, Hi. *or* Pi², overthrow, destroy; pervert one's way, become corrupt

שִׁיר sing

שִׁיר 33, song, hymn

שִׁית set, put, place

שָׁכַב 36, (A) lie, lie down

שָׁכַח 11, forget

שָׁכֹל 36, (A) be bereaved; Pi., bereave

שָׁכַם 32, Hi., rise early

שָׁכֵן 35, lie down; dwell

שָׁלוֹם 13, peace

שָׁלַח 13, send, send away; stretch out

שֻׁלְחָן 10, table

שָׁלַךְ 27, Hi., cast, throw

שָׁלָל plunder, booty

שָׁלֵם 28, (A) be whole; be at peace; Pi., make whole; perform; recompense; Hi., make peace (159)

שֶׁלֶם 33, peace-offering

שְׁלֹשָׁה, שָׁלֹשׁ three

שִׁלֵשׁ a third-generation descendant

שִׁלְשֹׁם three days ago;

מִתְּמֹל שִׁלְשֹׁם,

from time past,

formerly

שָׁם 14, there

שֵׁם name (*Irr;* 118)

שָׁמַד 33, Hi., cut off, destroy, lay waste; Ni., *Pass.*

שָׁמָּה 16, thither

שָׁמַיִם 10, heaven

שָׁמֵם Q¹,³ *or* Hithpo., be astonished (278)

שֶׁמֶן oil

שְׁמֹנָה, שְׁמֹנֶה eight

שָׁמַע 7, hear; *with* לְ, hearken; Hi., cause to hear

שָׁמַר 27, keep, watch, guard; Ni. *or* Hith., beware, take heed, refrain

שֶׁמֶשׁ (i) sun

שָׁנָה 23, year (*Irr;* 131)

שְׁנַיִם two

שַׁעַר 10, gate

שָׁפַט 32, judge

שֹׁפֵט judge

שָׁפַךְ 29, pour out

שָׁקָה Hi., water, give drink (238)

שֶׁקֶל 23, (i) shekel

שֶׁקֶר 24, (i) lie, falsehood, deceit

שָׁרַת Pi¹, wait upon, minister unto

שֵׁשׁ ,שִׁשָּׁה six

שָׁתָה drink (238)

שְׁתַיִם *fem. of* שְׁנַיִם

ת

תַּבְנִית image, form, likeness

תְּהִלָּה 31, praise

תָּוֶךְ midst

תּוֹעֵבָה abomination

תּוֹרָה 13, law

תַּחַת under, beneath; at the foot of; instead of; תַּחַת כִּי, because (137)

תֵּימָן south

תְּמוֹל yesterday

תְּמוּנָה form; image, likeness

תָּמִיד 35, perpetuity; *Adv. Acc.*, continually

תָּמִים 10, perfect, upright

תָּמַם Q³ *or* Hi³, finish, complete; be finished, consumed

תִּפְאֶרֶת beauty; splendor

תְּפִלָּה 31, prayer

תָּפַשׂ 12, seize; hold

תָּקַע 30, strike, drive; pitch; blow

תִּשְׁעָה, תֵּשַׁע nine

ENGLISH-HEBREW VOCABULARY

A

abomination תּוֹעֵבָה

about עַל; לְ; סָבִיב

according to כְּ

account of, on בַּעֲבוּר

adjure שׁבע, Hi.

admonition מוּסָר

adversary צַר (5)

affliction עֳנִי

after אַחֲרֵי (137);

אַחֲרֵי־אֲשֶׁר

against עַל

all כֹּל (5)

alone—*see* בַּד

also גַּם

altar מִזְבֵּחַ (*Irr*; 117)

among בְּ

ancient זָקֵן

and וְ

anger אַף (5); חֵמָה

anoint משח

appearance מַרְאֶה

army מַחֲנֶה

arrow חֵץ (5)

as כַּאֲשֶׁר

ask שׁאל (about, לְ)

atone for כפר, Pi. (159)

attendant נַעַר

B

bad רַע (5)

beautiful יָפֶה

because כִּי

before בְּטֶרֶם (137); לִפְנֵי

begin חלל, Hi[1]

behind אַחֲרֵי (137)

behold! הִנֵּה (136)

347

bind אָסַר, Q⁵

blood דָּם

bone עֶצֶם (f)

book סֵפֶר

boundary גְּבוּל

bread לֶחֶם

break שׁבר

bring near קרב, Hi.

brother אָח (Irr)

build בנה

bullock פָּר (5)

burn בּער ;שׂרף, Q or Pi²

burnt-offering עוֹלָה

but כִּי אִם ;וְ (56)

by לְ ,בְּ ;עַל (153)

C

camel גָּמָל (5)

camp מַחֲנֶה

captives שְׁבוּת (f)

captive, take שׁבה, Hi.; גלה

capture לכד

cast שׁלך, Hi.

cease חדל ;שבת, Q⁴

charge פקד

charge מִשְׁמֶרֶת

chariot רֶכֶב (i)

child יֶלֶד

choose בדל ;בחר, Hi.

city עִיר (Irr)

clan מִשְׁפָּחָה (2)

collect אסף, Q⁵; קבץ

come near נגש (A);קרב (253)

command מִצְוָה (95)

conceal סתר, Hi.

concerning עַל

confound חתת, Hi¹

congregation עֵדָה ;קָהָל

controversy רִיב

counsel מַחֲשֶׁבֶת

country אֶרֶץ (f; 44)

court חָצֵר

covenant בְּרִית (f); make,

כרת

crown מֶלֶךְ, Hi.

cut (off) כרת

D

daughter בַּת (Irr)

David דָּוִד

day יוֹם (Irr)

death מָוֶת

deed מַעֲשֶׂה

delight רָצוֹן

delightful לְרָצוֹן

delight in חפץ; רצה, Q2,4

   (with בְּ)

deliver מלט, Pi. ; ישׁע, Hi1

   (Pass., Ni.)

deliverance יְשׁוּעָה

desert עֲרָבָה

dispossess ירשׁ, Hi1

distressed, be צרר, Q2

do עשׂה, Q1

draw near—see come near

dwell ישׁב, Q1; שׁכן (A)

dwelling place מִשְׁכָּן

E

early, rise שׁכם, Hi.

earth אֶרֶץ (f; 44)

Egypt מִצְרַיִם

enemy אֹיֵב (118)

escape מלט, Ni.

eternity עוֹלָם

evening עֶרֶב

evil רַע ; רָשָׁע (5)

eye עַיִן (f)

F

face פָּנִים (137)

faithful, be אמן, Ni1

faithfulness אֱמוּנָה

family מִשְׁפָּחָה (2)

far as, as עַד

father אָב (Irr)

favor חֵן (5)

fear ירא, Q2 (192, 248)

feast חָג (5)

field שָׂדֶה

fight לחם, Ni.

first-born בְּכוֹר

flee נוּס; ברח

flock צֹאן

food אֹכֶל, אָכְלָה

foot רֶגֶל (f)

for כִּי ;לְ

forget שכח

friend רֵעַ

from מִן

front of, in לִפְנֵי (137)

G

garment בֶּגֶד (i); שִׂמְלָה (2)

gate שַׁעַר

gift קָרְבָּן ;בְּרָכָה

give נתן (256)

glad, make שׂמח, Pi.

glory כָּבוֹד

go הלך (248)

go out יצא (248)

God אֱלֹהִים (50, 56)

gold זָהָב

good טוֹב

goodwill חֶסֶד

governor פֶּחָה (Irr)

grace חֵן (5)

gracious to, be חנן ;רצה, Q¹

great גָּדוֹל

guard שׁמר

H

hand יָד (f; 99)

hard קָשָׁה ;כָּבֵד

head רֹאשׁ (Irr)

hear שׁמע

hearken שׁמע לְ

heart לֵב (5), לֵבָב (Irr)

heed (take) שׁמר, Ni.

help עזר, Q¹

here פֹּה

hero גִּבּוֹר

hide סתר, Hi.

high גָּבֹהַּ, רָם

hill גִּבְעָה (2)

hither הֵנָּה

holy קָדוֹשׁ

holy, keep קדשׁ, Pi. (159)

home בַּיְתָה

horn קֶרֶן (f)

horse סוּס

horseman פָּרָשׁ (‑ fixed)

house בַּיִת (Irr)

how? אֵיךְ

how! מַה (54)

husband אִישׁ (Irr)

I

if אִם

in בְּ

inhabit יֹשֵׁב, Qꜞ

inhabitant יֹשֵׁב

inheritance נַחֲלָה

iniquity אָוֶן; עָוֹן

inquire—*see* search

Israel יִשְׂרָאֵל

J

Jehovah יְהֹוָה (30, 50)

Jerusalem יְרוּשָׁלֵַם

journey דֶּרֶךְ

judge שֹׁפֵט

judgment מִשְׁפָּט

just צַדִּיק

justify צדק, Hi.

K

kindness חֶסֶד

king מֶלֶךְ

king, be מלךְ; make, Hi.

kingdom מַמְלָכָה (2)

knowledge דַּעַת (f)

L

land אֶרֶץ (f; 44)

large גָּדוֹל

law תּוֹרָה

learn למד (A)

leave שׁאר, Hi; יתר, Hiꞟ

length אֹרֶךְ

lest פֶּן (148)

lie שֶׁקֶר (i)

lift up רוּם, Hi.; נשא (257)

like כְּ

look ראה; נבט, Hi.

M

maiden, maid-servant נַעֲרָה (2); אָמָה (Irr)

man אִישׁ (Irr)

manservant עֶבֶד

many רַב (5)

master בַּעַל; אָדוֹן

measure מִדָּה

meeting מוֹעֵד

mention of, make זכר, Hi.

messenger מַלְאָךְ

midst קֶרֶב (i); תָּוֶךְ

miracle מוֹפֵת

misery עֳנִי

month חֹדֶשׁ

morning בֹּקֶר

mother אֵם (5)

mountain הַר (5; 44)

much רַב (5)

N

name שֵׁם (Irr)

nation גּוֹי

near עַל

need עֳנִי

new moon חֹדֶשׁ

night לַיְלָה (Irr; 95)

not לֹא; אַל (168); אֵין (135, 199); בִּלְתִּי (192)

now עַתָּה (and see note 2, p. 164)

number מִסְפָּר

O

offer קרב, Hi.

oil שֶׁמֶן

old man זָקֵן

on בְּ

only אַךְ; רַק

other אַחֵר (Irr)

outer חִיצוֹן

over עַל

overseer, make פָּקַד, Hi.

P

palace הֵיכָל

pass, come to הָיָה (174, 239)

path דֶּרֶךְ

peace שָׁלוֹם

peace, make שָׁלֵם, Hi.

people עַם (5; 44)

perceive בִּין

pitch תָּקַע

place מָקוֹם (Irr)

poverty עֳנִי

power זְרוֹעַ (f)

prayer תְּפִלָּה

present בְּרָכָה

priest כֹּהֵן

prince שַׂר ;נָשִׂיא (5)

prophet נָבִיא

province מְדִינָה

provoke כָּעַס, Hi.

punish יכח, Hi¹

pursue רָדַף

put on לָבַשׁ, Q (A) or Hi.

Q

quickly מַהֵר (193)

R

ram אַיִל

rebel מָרַד (against, Acc.)

receive graciously רָצָה

recount סָפַר, Pi.

refuse מֵאֵן ;מָאַס, Pi.

regarded as, be חָשַׁב, Ni²

remain שָׁאַר, Ni.; יָתַר, Ni.

remember זכר

remnant יֶתֶר (i)

remove רָחַק, Hi.; סוּר, Hi.

reproach חֶרְפָּה (2)

rest, give שָׁבַת, Hi.; נוּחַ, Hi.

(267)

return שׁוּב

righteous צַדִּיק

rise early שׁכם, Hi.

river נָהָר ;יְאֹר

road דֶּרֶךְ

rock צוּר

rod מַטֶּה ;שֵׁבֶט

rule מלךְ (over, עַל);מָשַׁל
(over, בְּ)

S

sabbath שַׁבָּת (5)

sacred קָדֹשׁ

safety יְשׁוּעָה

sanctify קדשׁ, Pi. (159)

sanctuary מִקְדָּשׁ

say אמר, Q⁶

search דרשׁ;בקשׁ, Pi. (158)

see חזה ;ראה, Q³

seed זֶרַע

seize אחז ;תפשׂ, Q⁶

select בדל, Hi.

sell מכר

send שׁלח

servant עֶבֶד

serve עבד, Q¹

servitude עֲבוֹדָה

shepherd רֹעֶה

shield מָגֵן (5; בָ — fixed)

shut up סגר

silver כֶּסֶף

sin חַטָּאת (f; Plu. חַטָּאוֹת)

sit ישׁב, Q¹

son בֵּן (Irr)

so that וּ ;לְמַעַן (178)

soul נֶפֶשׁ (f)

sound קוֹל (Irr)

sow זרע

speak דבר, Pi. (159)

spirit רוּחַ (f)

spread out פרשׂ

stand עמד, Q¹

statute חֹק (5), חֻקָּה

stead, in his תַּחַת (137)

stone אֶבֶן (f; *Irr.*)

stranger גֵּר

street חוּץ (*Irr*)

strength כֹּחַ, חַיִל

strong חָזָק

sword חֶרֶב (f)

T

table שֻׁלְחָן

take לקח (257)

teach למד, Pi.

temple הֵיכָל

tent אֹהֶל

territory גְּבוּל

that לְמַעַן; הוּא; כִּי

thence מִשָּׁם

there שָׁם

therefore עַל־כֵּן; לָכֵן

thief— *see* גנב

thing דָּבָר

this זֹאת, זֶה (61, 62)

throw שׁלך, Hi.; ירה, Hi[1]

thus כֹּה, כֵּן

to לְ

today הַיּוֹם

tongue לָשׁוֹן

tonight הַלַּיְלָה

top רֹאשׁ (*Irr*)

tower מִגְדָּל

transgression פֶּשַׁע (i)

tree עֵץ

tribe שֵׁבֶט; מַטֶּה

trumpet שׁוֹפָר (*Irr*)

trust בטח; אמן, Hi[1]

truth אֱמֶת (f)

turn aside זוּר; סוּר (267)

U

under תַּחַת (137)

until עַד; עַד־אֲשֶׁר

unto אֶל

upon עַל

V

valley גַּיְא ;עֵמֶק (Irr)

vanity אָוֶן

very מְאֹד

vessel כְּלִי (Irr)

village חָצֵר

vineyard כֶּרֶם

visit פקד

voice קוֹל (Irr)

W

walk הלך ;(248) רגל

wall חוֹמָה

war מִלְחָמָה (2)

warrior אִישׁ מִלְחָמָה; גִּבּוֹר

watch שׁמר; נצר

water מַיִם (Irr)

weapon כְּלִי (Irr)

weep בכה (238)

what? מַה (54)

wheat חִטָּה (Irr)

when כִּי

whether אִם

which אֲשֶׁר

who אֲשֶׁר; מִי

why? לָמָה (54)

wicked רָשָׁע ;(5) רַע

wife אִשָּׁה (Irr)

willing, be אבה, Q⁶

wise חָכָם

wisely, act שׂכל, Hi.

with בְּ ;אֵת, עִם

witness עֵד

woman אִשָּׁה (Irr)

word דָּבָר

work מַעֲשֶׂה

write כתב

Y

year שָׁנָה (Irr)

PJ4567 .C7   c.1
Creager, Harold Luth   100106 000
Beginners' Hebrew grammar, by

3 9310 00021200 9
GOSHEN COLLEGE-GOOD LIBRARY

קָהָל 28, congregation

קוֹל 9, voice; sound (*Irr*)

קוּם arise, rise up; Hi., raise up

קָטַל kill

קָטֹן 36, (A) be small; Hi., make small

קָטַר 34, Pi., burn incense

קָלַל Q², be insignificant; Ni., be light; Hi¹, make light

קָנָא jealous

קָנָה get, obtain

קָנֶה reed

קָצֶה end, extremity

קָצִיר harvest

קָצַר 31, reap, harvest

קָרָא befall, happen, meet (230)

קָרָא cry out; call to; name

קָרַב 27, (A) draw near, approach; Hi., bring near, offer

קֶרֶב 15, (i) midst

קָרְבָּן 33, gift

קָרָה Q. *or* Ni., meet

קָרוֹב 10, near

קִרְיָה city, town

קֶרֶן 14, (f) horn

קָרַע 32, rend, tear

קָשֶׁה hard; stubborn

קֶשֶׁת 31, (f) bow

ר

רָאָה 7, see, look; Ni., be seen, appear; Hi., show (238)

רְאוּבֵנִי Reubenites

רָאמֹת Ramoth

רֹאשׁ 10, head, top (*Irr*)

רִאשׁוֹן 10, first

רֵאשִׁית 30, (f) beginning; first-fruits

רֹב abundance, multitude, greatness (5)

רַב great; much, many; enough! (5)

רְבָבָה myriad; ten thousand

רָבָה be, become many, great; increase; Hi., make great, increase; *Inf. Abs.*,

פַּר bullock (5)

פַּרְזִי rustic; עָרֵי פְּרָזִי, country towns

פְּרִי fruit

פָּרַשׂ 30, spread, spread out, scatter

פָּרָשׁ 29, horseman (first— fixed)

פֶּשַׁע 16, (i) transgression, trespass

פֶּתַח (i) door

צ

צֹאן 12, flock

צָבָא 25, host (Irr; 99)

צַדִּיק 10, just, righteous

צָדַק 28, (A) be just, right- eous; Pi. or Hi., make righteous, jus- tify; Hith., justify oneself (158)

צֶדֶק (i) righteousness

צְדָקָה righteousness

צִוָּה Pi., command

צוּר 12, rock

צִידוֹנִים Sidonians

צָלַח prosper, succeed; Hi., give success

צֶלֶם image

צָעַק 32, cry, implore

צָפָה Q. or Pi., look about, watch, observe

צָפוֹן 28, north

צִפּוֹר bird

צַר adversary; distress (5)

צָרַר Q², be pressed, dis- tressed; Hi¹, strait- en, distress

ק

קָבַץ 32, collect, gather, as- semble

קָבַר 34, bury

קָדוֹשׁ 24, holy, sacred

קָדַם 33, Pi., precede

קֶדֶם 28, east

קָדַשׁ 28, (A) be pure, holy; Ni., be sanctified; Pi. or Hi., sanctify, consecrate (159)

קֹדֶשׁ holiness

קָהַל Hi., call together, con- voke

עֵמֶק valley

עָנָה Q[1], answer; speak

עָנָה Q[1], labor, suffer; Pi., oppress, afflict

עֳנִי 9, affliction, misery, poverty

עָנָן cloud

עָפָר 25, dust (*Irr*)

עֵץ tree

עָצוּם mighty, powerful

עֶצֶם (f) bone

עֶרֶב 28, evening

עֲרָבָה 16, desert (Arabah)

עָרַךְ Q[1], prepare, set in array

עֲרֹעֵר Aroer

עֲרָפֶל thick clouds, darkness

עֶרֶשׂ bed, couch

עָשָׂה 14, Q[1], do, make

עֲשָׂרָה, עֶשֶׂר ten

עֵת (f) time (5; *Irr*)

עַתָּה 12, now

פ

פָּדָה set free, ransom

פֹּה 9, here

פֶּה mouth (*Irr*)

פּוּץ Q. *or* Hi., scatter, disperse; Ni., *Pass.*

פֶּחָה governor (*Irr*)

פָּלָא Ni., be wonderful; Part., a wonder; Hi., make great, wonderful

פָּלַל Hith., supplicate, pray, intercede

פֶּן 26, lest (148)

פָּנָה turn

פָּנָה *used only in Plu.*, פָּנִים, face; לִפְנֵי before, in front of (137)

פִּסְגָּה Pisgah

פֶּסֶל carved image

פְּעוֹר Peor

פָּעַל 14, do

פַּעַם 23, (f) time (*Irr*)

פָּקַד 27, visit; charge; look upon; Hi., appoint, set over, make overseer

סֵפֶר book

סָתַר 28, Hi., hide, conceal; Ni. *or* Hith., be hid, hide oneself

ע

עָבַד 13, Q¹, serve; Hi¹, cause to work

עֶבֶד 10, servant; *Abstract Plu.*, bondage

עֲבוֹדָה 14, servitude

עָבַר Q¹, cross over; Hi¹, bring, send over; Hith., be wroth

עֵבֶר 30, region beyond; אֶל־עֵבֶר *or* בְּעֵבֶר, beyond, across

עֵד 12, witness

עַד 9, as far as; until

עַד־אֲשֶׁר 26, until

עַד־מָתַי 26, how long?

עֵדָה congregation; ordinance

עוֹג Og

עוּד Hi., call as witness (בְּ, against)

עוֹד still; yet; again (136, 199)

עוֹלָה 16, burnt-offering

עוֹלָם 25, eternity

עָוֹן iniquity (*Irr*)

עוֹף fly

עוּר awake; be awake; Hi., waken

עִוֵּר blind (118)

עָזַב Q¹, forsake

עָזַר Q¹, help

עַיִן (f) eye

עִיר 16, (f) city (*Irr*)

עַל 7, upon; by, near; concerning; against (77)

עַל־כֵּן 26, therefore

עָלָה Q¹, go up; Hi¹, bring, send up

עַם 8, people (5; 44)

עִם 7, with (76)

עָמַד 14, Q¹, stand; Hi¹, make stand, set, establish

עִמָּד with

עַמּוּד 24, column, pillar

עַמּוֹן Ammon

Rose looked into Marc's eyes when he pulled back from her and thought, *I want to have this man's babies.* Immediately, she wondered where the thought had come from. Rose had never been a desperate woman, and she'd sworn off men ever since the last guy she gave her heart to took it and shattered it. Once the pain had faded, she couldn't bear to give her heart to another man ever again. She had to try to pull herself together—but not until the song ended.

Rose rested her head against Marc's shoulder as they continued to sway to the music. When the song was over, she released another sigh and attempted to take a small step backward, but realized he hadn't let her go just yet.

"Wait," Marc said, holding her for another moment before he stepped back so he could hold her at arm's length.

Confusion swarmed through Marc's mind. Rose Hart disturbed his calm. He'd just met her a little over an hour ago, and she already had him in knots. He was usually attracted to model-thin women, but this beautiful brown honey with her lush curves had changed all that in a matter of minutes. She was an exquisite female, but it wasn't the mere fact that she was beautiful. He'd known gorgeous women all his adult life and had even fallen in love with one, but there was something different about Rose....

He hadn't figured out what exactly, but now he had to decide whether he wanted to take a chance and find out.